MCDONNELL DOUGLAS
F/A-18 HORNET
AND SUPER HORNET
1978 onwards (all marks)

COVER IMAGE: McDonnell Douglas F/A-18E Super Hornet.
(Mike Badrocke)

© Steve Davies 2017

First published in February 2017
Reprinted May and December 2022

A catalogue record for this book is available from the British Library.

ISBN 978 1 78521 054 9

Library of Congress control no. 2016937308

Published by J. H. Haynes & Co. Ltd.,
Sparkford, Yeovil,
Somerset BA22 7JJ, UK.
Tel: 01963 440635
Int. tel: +44 1963 440635
Website: www.haynes.com

Haynes North America Inc.,
2801 Townsgate Road, Suite 340, Thousand Oaks, CA 91361, USA.

Printed in India.

Commissioning editor: Jonathan Falconer
Copy editor: Michelle Tilling
Proof reader: Penny Housden
Indexer: Peter Nicholson
Page design: James Robertson

Acknowledgements

The author would like to thank the following for their assistance in the creation of this book: Cdr Jason 'Tike' Gustin, US Navy; 'ShWRECK', US Navy; Sgt Daniel Paré, CF-18 Crew Chief, RCAF.

MCDONNELL DOUGLAS
F/A-18 HORNET

AND SUPER HORNET
1978 onwards (all marks)

Owners' Workshop Manual

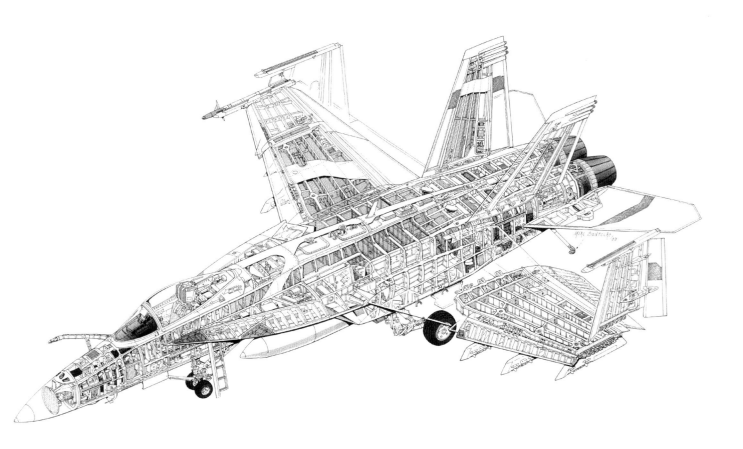

An insight into the design, construction and operation of the
US Navy's supersonic, all-weather multi-role combat jet

Steve Davies

Contents

BELOW Hangar bay sailors prepare to move an F/A-18A+ Hornet assigned to the 'Silver Eagles' from Marine Strike Fighter Squadron (VMFA) 115 into the hangar bay after descending from the flight deck aboard USS Harry S. Truman (CVN 75) in the Persian Gulf. *(US Navy/Phot Mate Airman Jay C. Pugh)*

Introduction

My fascination with the F/A-18 started in a dusty garage at our family home in the 1980s – it came in the form a 1/72nd-scale model kit of the first full-scale development McDonnell Douglas F/A-18A. I rushed to build that plastic kit, soaking up its incredible lines and admiring a resplendent gloss white paint job accented with gold and blue trim.

I knew that the Hornet was sexy long before I knew what that phrase actually meant. I loved its canted tails. The cobra-like leading edge route extensions were unlike anything I had seen before. The twin afterburner nozzles that sat above a heavy-duty arrestor hook spoke to me of raw power, and of acceleration and deceleration forces beyond anything I would ever know. In fact, there was no angle from which I could look at that model and find it wanting.

Of course, I never thought I'd be writing about the Hornet all these years later. And I certainly never thought I'd fly one (or even two!). But here I am, having done just that.

My first Hornet flight was in 2004 with the wonderfully generous Swiss Air Force. I'd 'sandbagged' a variety of backseat rides by that time – the F-15B/D/E and F-16B/D being the obvious ones – but there was something about the Hornet that made it stand out, even to this amateur observer. Hanging upside down at 35,000ft above the Alps was certainly remarkable, as was flying an approach in the weather into Meiringen air base (down a valley

RIGHT Swiss Air Force F/A-18 over the Alps.

between two mountainsides with what felt like not even enough room to swing a cat), but it was the demonstration of the Hornet's flight control laws that really stood out. First, my pilot let me fling the Hornet around for a while, demonstrating vividly that without question he trusted the jet to stay in control while the goon in the back did his best Tom Cruise impression. But then things got serious and he showed me the 'pirouette logic' – we accelerated, pitched into the vertical and climbed until we streamed contrails that pointed straight down at the snow-capped mountains below us. Naturally, we ran out of airspeed, stalled, entered a tail slide and slid backwards into the misty contrails we'd just created. My pilot, 'Elvis', planted the stick in his lap, then fed in boots-full of rudder; first left, then right. The Hornet gracefully pirouetted down towards the mountains below – yawing left and then right, as Elvis commanded. The jet sank, tail-first and nose-high, buffeting, shaking, vibrating . . . but never faltering and never departing controlled flight. Elvis then 'stirred' the stick, manhandling – *mis*handling – the jet, but it batted not an eyelid. It was a visceral demonstration of the F/A-18's legendary high angle-of-attack handling and its phenomenal flight control computers.

Later, in 2009, I'd fly in the back of the Super Hornet with the great folks at VFA-211 'Fighting Checkmates'. My ride was an F/A-18F with the missionised cockpit, meaning that it looked and felt like I was flying in a battle commander's seat. Where flying with the Swiss had shown me how the Hornet lets the pilot just get on with the business of killing the enemy (without the need to worry about that minor detail of flying), the Super Hornet ride gave me an unclassified glimpse of just how far the US Navy had taken the F/A-18 series in terms of avionics development, true multi-role lethality, sensor fusion and battlespace management.

Though backseat rides are fun, I derive just as much satisfaction from the privilege of writing books for like-minded enthusiasts. It has been an honour to write this book about the Hornet and Super Hornet, and I hope that you get as much enjoyment from the pages that follow as I did researching this incredible aircraft.

Your feedback and interaction are always welcome, and you can find me on Facebook at: www.facebook.com/AviationPhotography

Steve Davies
Cambridgeshire, 2016

ABOVE Back-seat ride in an F/A-18F Super Hornet with the great folks at VFA-211 'Fighting Checkmates'.

Chapter One

The Hornet story

In 2016, the F/A-18 Hornet and Super Hornet was in operational service with seven countries around the world. In US service alone, it has been enforcing foreign policy since 1986, has been in combat in the Middle East almost continuously since 1991 and was a key component in enforcing United Nations and NATO policy in the Balkans region in the 1990s.

OPPOSITE The Hornet and the Super Hornet (pictured here), come from humble stock. The product of a failed entry to the USAF's Light Weight Fighter competition, they are today the tactical airpower mainstay of the world's mightiest navy. *(Steve Davies/FJ Photography)*

The F/A-18 is, without doubt, a phenomenal success, and yet it comes from beginnings so humble that it could just as easily have been but a dot on the timeline of modern air warfare, a failed programme of yesteryear.

Born out of the YF-17, Northrop's losing entrant to the US Air Force's Light Weight Fighter (LWF) competition, the Hornet was bested by the diminutive General Dynamics YF-16 and left seemingly without any future. But a partnership with McDonnell Douglas, which had extensive experience designing carrier-borne fighters, saved it from being consigned to history. Together 'McAir' – as the aerospace giant was called – and Northrop redesigned the YF-17 so well that it would go on to become the US Navy's next multi-role fighter.

BELOW Two F/A-18C Hornets assigned to the 'Blue Diamonds' of Strike Fighter Squadron One Four Six (VFA-146), and two F/A-18F Super Hornets assigned to the 'Black Knights' of Strike Fighter Squadron One Five Four (VFA-154), perform a fly-by over USS *Carl Vinson* (CVN 70) to mark the completion of the final combat missions flown over Iraq for Carrier Air Wing Nine (CWW-9). *(US Navy)*

At the time of writing (2016), the F/A-18 had been produced in seven major variants, was operated by both domestic US and international customers and had been in operational service for 33 years. It is also noteworthy for being the first aircraft to have carbon fibre wings, and for being the first tactical jet fighter to use digital fly-by-wire flight controls.

The LWF competition

In the years following the air war over North Vietnam in the 1960s and 1970s, a fighter pilot revolution took place. US Air Force, US Navy and US Marine Corps pilots had learned the hard way that predictions of technology triumphing over numerical supremacy had proven ill-founded.

There was a myriad of reasons for this, but it can be categorised into two main issues: 1) technology had a habit of just not working, which was doubly bad because training and tactics were being devised on the basis that they did work; and 2) politicians, not generals,

were running wars – dictating the rules of engagement and undermining the strengths offered by air power.

The fighter pilots returning from war recognised that the large, complex and heavy fighters the USA had procured were outclassed by small, light, simple and highly manoeuvrable Russian-designed MiGs. Moreover, America's long-range AIM-7 Sparrow and short-range AIM-9 Sidewinder and AIM-4D Falcon missiles either didn't work well enough or could not be employed as designed. This meant that, at a time when its newest fighter – the McDonnell F-4 Phantom II – was being shipped without a gun, America needed gun-toting dogfighters as much as it ever had.

America's air-to-air missiles had been designed to down unmanoeuvrable bombers or unaware fighters. They were no match for an agile, aware or manoeuvring foe. In any case, the Sparrow's long-range capability was worthless if the pilot could not confidently identify the target as a 'bandit'. Typically, that required an 'eyes on' range of just a couple of miles, and at that point – at the so-called 'merge' – long-range missiles were of no use and the short-range, IR-guided ones offered a very low probability of kill (pK).

Unlike the US Air Force, the US Navy at least had a culture of training as they meant to fight, which was one reason why their F-4 crews did comparatively well against North Vietnamese MiGs. Even so, their lack of a gun meant that even they were outgunned by MiGs on many an occasion.

ABOVE LEFT AND ABOVE Northrop's P-530 Cobra design formed the basis for its entry into the Light Weight Fighter competition. The design shared similarities with the Lockheed F-104 Starfighter, most notably its long, pointed fuselage, small wings with an anhedral or wing droop and circular intakes with a spiked inlet ramp. *(Northrop)*

BELOW In formation during the Light Weight Fighter competition are the winning entry, YF-16 (nearest camera), and the losing YF-17. *(Northrop)*

Out of the 'fighter pilot mafia' returning from Vietnam came a range of studies, analyses and attendant proposals. The US Air Force and Navy were brutal in their own debrief of the conflict – a fact that is unsurprising given the loss of life that had been sustained – and resolved to ensure that the mistakes of the past would not be repeated.

Among those who took it upon their shoulders to rectify past failure was Col John Boyd, a Korean War fighter pilot who had always courted controversy, but who, in 1969, had sought the assistance of mathematician Thomas Christie to make one of the single most important contributions to modern air warfare: the 'Energy–Maneuverability theory' (EM).

The EM graph provides a method of expressing an aircraft's performance as a total of kinetic and potential manoeuvrability, meaning that it shows turn rate plotted against Mach

number, allowing a pilot to visualise the optimum manoeuvring performance of his aircraft. When overlaid on to the EM graph of an adversary's aircraft, it graphically illustrates where the strengths and weaknesses lie for each.

EM gave the US Air Force and Navy a quantitative basis from which to lay out a requirement for their new fighter programmes – they could literally plot the performance of known and predicted threats, then define a performance envelope for the design being developed to take them on.

It was against the backdrop of such ground-breaking developments that the US Air Force conducted theoretical studies for a new fighter in the early 1970s. Then, in January 1972, it sent out an RFP (request for proposal) to formally invite a range of defence contractors to submit designs for a new, lightweight fighter – the LWF.

ABOVE AND ABOVE RIGHT Where the YF-16 had blended leading edge root extensions (LERXs) to create powerful vortices that would in turn increase manoeuvrability, the YF-17's LERXs were much more pronounced. Most of the gaps between the fuselage and the extensions seen in these YF-17 photographs would eventually be filled in. *(Northrop)*

BELOW Early YF-17 testing saw the LERXs applied with a liberal pattern of 'tufts'. These were photographed during flight to provide engineers with a way of analysing airflow patterns. *(Northrop)*

The LWF competition sought a 20,000lb fighter with excellent turn rate and acceleration, to be delivered at a flyaway cost of $3 million. It would need to be optimised for manoeuvring at speeds between Mach 0.6 and 1.6 at altitudes of 30,000–40,000ft, since it was in this portion of the flight envelope that most future air combat was expected to occur.

Five companies responded to the RFP, but the two design proposals chosen for the LWF

competition were General Dynamics' (GD) Model 401 and Northrop's P-600. GD received $38 million to manufacture its Model 401 design (designated YF-16 by the US Air Force), while Northrop received $40 million to build its P-600 (designated the YF-17 Cobra). Prototypes were prepared for maiden flights in early 1974, and Northrop's two YF-17s flew for the first time in June and August respectively.

The LWF flight test programme eventually revealed that the YF-16 was more manoeuvrable than the YF-17, particularly at supersonic speeds. In addition, the YF-16 out-accelerated the YF-17, offered lower operating costs and had better range. It therefore came as little surprise when, on 13 January 1975, the Secretary of the Air Force announced that the YF-16 would be the force's new lightweight fighter. The YF-16 would eventually become the F-16 Fighting Falcon.

Navy Air Combat Fighter (NACF)

While the US Air Force continued to grapple with its own internal divisions through the late 1960s and early 1970s – there were those who supported the LWF philosophy, and there were those who extolled the benefits of the bigger, heavier FX fighter competition (which would eventually become the F-15 Eagle) – the Navy had its own internal battles to fight.

By the time the first YF-17 had been assembled in late 1974, the new Grumman F-14 Tomcat had already declared initial

operating capability and was in service as a potent fleet defender (in fact, it flew escort and combat air patrol missions during America's hasty exit from South Vietnam).

The Tomcat's success freed the Navy to pursue its next acquisition programme: the Naval Fighter-Attack (NFAX[1]) competition. NFAX was intended to replace its fleet of ageing fighter-attack aircraft – the Douglas A-4 Skyhawk, the Grumman A-6E Intruder, the LTV A-7 Corsair II and the McDonnell Douglas F-4 Phantom II – and to complement the Tomcat.

However, the NFAX programme was not without its detractors. To make matters worse, in 1973 Congress had instructed the Navy to seek a lower-cost alternative to the Tomcat, meaning that almost everyone was looking at the so-called 'bottom dollar'. While Grumman tabled a stripped-down Tomcat as one option, and McDonnell Douglas offered a navalised F-15 as another, neither offered the kinds of cost savings that the Navy's civilian leaders deemed acceptable. Accordingly, Secretary of Defense James Schlesinger ordered the Navy to look at the two entrants to the US Air Force's LWF competition.

Schlesinger's order was not completely unexpected. After all, Congress was interested in driving down costs and had previously directed that the Air Force and Navy should work together on joint acquisition and development of both

1   Popular wisdom holds that the X stands for 'experimental', but the author understands that the X actually stands for 'unknown'.

airframes and engines. Perhaps more tellingly, with the NFAX programme ready to die a death in early 1974, Congress had also approved the reallocation of funds from it to the new Navy Air Combat Fighter (NACF) programme. This was done with the intention of enabling the Navy to leverage the LWF designs.

Naturally, the Navy looked first to the eventual winner of the LWF competition, but immediately noted that the YF-16's single-engine fighter and narrow track undercarriage were not shoo-ins for carrier aviation. Single-engine fighters flying over expansive tracts of water were not ideal, and spindly undercarriages didn't cope well with the brutal 'controlled crash' that is an arrested carrier landing. Critically, neither of these deficiencies would be cheap to remedy.

ABOVE More tufts adorn the rear fuselage. Note the dorsal airbrake and the narrow spine running from the cockpit to engine nacelles. While the former was retained, the latter was flattened out as the YF-17 metamorphosed into the F/A-18. (Northrop)

LEFT The YF-17 with captive-carry AIM-9 Sidewinder and AIM-7 Sparrow missiles. The Sparrow was heavy, so it is interesting to see it mounted on the wingtip pylon. In operational service, the Sparrow was only ever carried on the semi-recessed intake pylons. (Northrop)

With this in mind, the Navy announced in May 1975 that it had asked Northrop and McDonnell Douglas to redevelop the LWF YF-17 into a design that would meet the requirements of the NACF specification.

NACF sought a fighter that truly was the 'jack of all trades' (which would later give rise to the inevitable accusation that it was 'master of none'). It had to be able to replace the Corsair II in the light attack role, while also taking over from the Phantom II in both air defence and ground attack roles. Above all, it had to be capable of fulfilling all of these roles while operating from an aircraft carrier or from an austere forward airstrip, the latter of which was an expectation of the US Marine Corps (USMC).

BELOW With the appointment of the LWF contract to the YF-16, the sun set on the YF-17. But Northrop was lucky, and their design would live to see another day. *(Northrop)*

Redevelopment: YF-17 Cobra becomes the Hornet

Northrop and McAir planned two redevelopments of the YF-17, which would in 1977 formally become known as the F-18 Hornet. There would be a navalised F-18A version (with three variants) – of which the Navy planned to acquire 780 examples – and there was to be a land-based version designated F-18L, which would be offered to international users as a competitor to the F-16. Eventually, a second land version, the F/A-18L, would be added to the mix.

Though both companies would collaborate on the initial F-18A design, McAir would develop and sell the F-18A domestically, while

LEFT When the Navy looked for its own next-generation fighter, it initially considered the YF-16/F-16, on account of having won the LWF competition. As seen here, the YF-16 (left) was smaller than the YF-17, but it was single-engine and had a narrow track undercarriage, both considerations that would rule it out of contention. *(Northrop)*

RIGHT With McDonnell Douglas's help, Northrop developed the F-18L and marketed it extensively.
(Northrop)

Northrop would be the prime contractor for F-18L sales internationally.

Both aircraft would be powered by the General Electric GE404 afterburning engine, which offered a 400% reliability improvement over the GE J79 turbojet that powered the F-4 and F-104 Starfighter (among others), was 25% shorter, had 7,700 fewer parts and delivered a 240% maintenance improvement.

The F-18A received the McAir internal designation Model 267. The three planned variants were an F-18A fighter variant; an A-18A ground attack variant that would differ only in terms of avionics suite and weapons load; and a TF-18 two-seat trainer variant that would have a marginally reduced fuel load to allow the space for the second occupant.

Ultimately, developments in the fields of computing and electronics meant that it was possible for the fighter F-18A and strike A-18A variants to be combined into a single multi-role Hornet, and so only one variant was ever produced. By 1980, it had become unofficially known by the combined designation F/A-18A, but this was formalised by the US Navy in 1984. The TF-18A two-seat variant would be renamed the F/A-18B at around the same time.

The F/A-18 boasted airframe, undercarriage and tailhook improvements that made it better suited to carrier operations. In addition, a wingfold mechanism was introduced, as were catapult attachments (launch bar and holdback bar). An enlarged dorsal spine allowed the carriage of an additional 4,460lb of fuel, which, when combined with external fuel tanks, allowed the Hornet to meet the Navy's range and fuel reserve requirements.

To improve the aerodynamics of the carrier-based variant, a sawtooth was added to the leading edges of both the wings and to the horizontal stabilators (inhibiting an undesirable aerodynamic effect called aeroelastic flutter), and both wings and stabs were enlarged to lower the wing loading.[2]

2   The ratio of lifting surface area to weight.

NORTHROP **F/A-18L MULTIROLE TACTICAL FIGHTER**

These aerodynamic improvements were made in tandem with the introduction of the first quadruple-redundant fly-by-wire (FBW) control system to be installed in a production jet fighter. The FBW computer would have complete and sole authority over all of the Hornet's control surfaces, to include the leading edge flaps, flaperons on the inboard and outboard trailing edge of the wing, horizontal stabilators (called 'rolling tails' in Northrop's marketing material from the time) and rudders.

To allow the Hughes APG-65 radar's 27in antenna to fit on to the point end of the fighter, the Hornet's nose was also widened. The APG-65 would give the Hornet the ability to reach out and detect air and surface targets, acting as the

ABOVE This mock-up of the F/A-18L, a land-based variant of McAir's F/A-18, depicts the aircraft carrying 18 Mk 20 Rockeye cluster bombs, two fuel tanks, a target pod, two AIM-9s and three AIM-7 Sparrows. An impressive theoretical loadout for the time.
(Northrop)

key sensor in the Hornet's multi-role capability. It offered a myriad air-to-air modes – including the ability to track multiple targets while scanning for other new contacts – but also delivered an impressive set of air-to-ground modes, to include ground moving target track, real beam ground mapping and sea moving target. A podded forward-looking infrared sensor (FLIR), carried on one of the Hornet's two semi-recessed fuselage stations, would complement the radar in detection and tracking of sea, air and land targets.

To round off the extensive changes to the original YF-17 design, the engine inlets were canted outwards, recessed weapons stations were added to the intake and the rear fuselage was extended by a comparatively tiny 4in. In all, McAir had added 10,000lb to the Hornet's weight, bringing it to around 37,000lb gross weight. For the purposes of comparison, that is only around 2,000lb less than the basic operating weight of an F-15A Eagle, which at the time was viewed with derision by some as being far too big and heavy to be a viable fighter – at least, if the lessons of Vietnam were anything to go by.

Northrop's F-18L was closer to that original dream of a 'lightweight' fighter. Very similar to the F/A-18A, it benefited from some – but not all – of the same aerodynamic improvements (it lacked the sawtooth edges, for example). But it forewent the strengthening required for

TOP AND ABOVE The Hornet, and subsequently the Super Hornet, have always come under scrutiny for their comparatively short 'legs', or combat range. Air refuelling was a must, therefore. The YF-17 featured a refuelling receptacle (the 'Air Force way'), but in order to compete for the Navy's NFAX and NACF trade, the aircraft was installed with a retractable probe to allow probe-and-drogue refuelling (the 'Navy way'). *(Northrop)*

RIGHT AND BELOW Getting the Hornet ready for Navy use necessitated replacing the very spindle-like undercarriage (left) of the YF-17 with a solid, carrier-capable undercarriage (right) that could withstand the brutal impact of an arrested landing. *(Northrop)*

carrier operations: it had thinner gauge skin, keels and bulkheads, and did not feature the same beefed-up landing gear, carrier tailhook or space-saving wingfold. Further weight savings were made by removing the internal fuel cells from the wings.

While retaining 90% commonality with the F/A-18 in terms of key systems, Northrop had kept the weight down and delivered an aircraft 30% lighter than the seagoing Hornet – around 7,700lb – and was in the same league as the F-16 in terms of thrust-to-weight ratio.

There followed a second land-based version, the F/A-18L, which Northrop produced by taking the 'heavy' McAir F/A-18A and lightening it by around 3,000lb. This was achieved despite adding a third underwing pylon (giving the F/A-18L 11 weapons stations versus the F/A-18A's 9), installing strengthened wingtip pylons that could carry the Sparrow (or Skyflash, a British-developed derivative of the AIM-7), thereby increasing stores weight from 13,700lb to 20,000lb.

Thus, prospective customers could choose from one of two L-models: one offering the same fuel load as the carrier Hornet, but with an increased weapons load out and carriage capability, 9g performance (versus the F/A-18A's 7.5g limit), and an overall reduction in weight; and another offering much-reduced weight and performance (turn rate, acceleration and range) over the F/A-18A.

TOP, ABOVE AND BELOW While McAir was concentrating on securing domestic trade for the new Hornet designs, Northrop sought to get international buyers for its land-based Hornets. Painting the Hornet in the colours of potential customers – such as Canada (top), Greece (above) and Spain (below) – was a nice idea to help potential customers visualise what their purchase might look like, but despite real interest from Canada and Australia, Northrop came away empty-handed. *(Northrop)*

The F-18L offered a degree of parity with the F-16 in some areas of the EM envelope. In fact, the Hornet would prove to be the better low-speed fighter, given that it can point its nose with greater ease than the F-16. Its superior high angle of attack (AoA) performance is thanks to both a lack of AoA limiter (the F-16 is limited to 25 degrees AoA), which in turn is made possible by the FBW control system, and to superior aerodynamic qualities in this part of the performance envelope. Specifically, the Hornet's very distinctive leading edge root extensions (LERXs) are key to enabling it to remain in controlled flight even at high AoA (50 degrees), with excellent pitch, roll and yaw authority from 25 degrees to the lift limit of 35 degrees. Other aerodynamic facets that contribute to the Hornet's excellent high AoA performance are the outward-canted vertical stabilisers (positioned in the clean airflow coming off the LERXs), rudders that 'toe inwards' in order to generate nose authority, and oversized flaperons.

To cap it all off, with these impressive

ABOVE The A-6E Intruder, seen here dropping cluster bombs on Iranian targets in 1988, was one of several types of aircraft that the Hornet would eventually be expected to succeed. *(US Navy)*

BELOW An A-7E, another of the types that the Hornet would replace, cruises over the ocean carrying a tactical air-launched decoy. *(US Navy)*

designs from both contractors, the Hornet family was marketed as requiring comparatively little maintenance effort to keep it flying: 16.7 total maintenance man hours per flight hour, and an overall record of 2.9 mean flight hours between failures.

The first F/A-18A rolled off the production line on 13 September 1978. Nine full-scale development F/A-18s were to be built, complemented by two FSD TF-18As.

The Hornet had arrived, but for Northrop grey clouds bubbled on the horizon.

Entry to service

The land-based F-18L Hornet was, as Northrop's promotional material chimed, the 'logical choice for the land-based air force'. But the company was struggling to make this case to any international buyers.

While McAir and Northrop shared equally in the manufacture and production of the Hornet family (with final assembly conducted by McAir), it was McDonnell Douglas (now Boeing) that would ultimately enjoy the success that the Hornet had to offer.

The US Navy purchased 379[3] F/A-18As and 42 F/A-18Bs between 1978 and 1979, but the F-18L had been losing customer interest. Smelling a rat, Northrop began legal action against McAir in 1979, arguing that technology developed specifically for the F-18L was being used in the F/A-18A and the two-seat TF-18A. Northrop had also formed the view that McAir planned to pitch the F/A-18A against the F-18L. Things started to become ugly.

The acrimonious relationship between the two sides would come to an end in 1985, when McAir effectively bought the rights to the Hornet from Northrop in an out-of-court settlement that made no admission of the offences of which it had been accused. It was, of course, a shrewd move: the settlement paved the way for McAir to enjoy future foreign sales without fear of legal reprisals (for more detail, see Chapter 3).

Away from the machinations of the corporate world, flight testing of the FSD F/A-18As and TF-18As had run through November 1978

ABOVE McAir and Northrop's partnership was celebrated in the tail flash of the repainted YF-17 demonstrator, but the two companies would eventually part company acrimoniously. *(Northrop)*

onwards. It was clear that the US Navy was very close indeed to having the fighter it wanted. As a result of the testing, small longitudinal gaps between the LERX and the forward fuselage were found to be generating a lot of drag, so around 80% were filled in, leaving just a small gap. No significant changes were required, however.

The first production standard F/A-18A flew on 12 April 1980. Operational testing and carrier suitability trials followed, conducted by VX-4 and VX-5 at NAS Patuxent River, where the vast majority of the Navy's F/A-18 testing took place.

From 1982, the Hornet began arriving at the Fleet Replacement Squadrons that would teach new pilots how to fly the jet and convert seasoned pilots to the type. VFA-125, VFA-106 and VFMAT-101 all took delivery of the new fighter, expressing positive views about it in general, but reserving criticism for its low roll rate and excessive wing flexing when heavy stores were carried on the wing stations.

While F/A-18A and TF-18A had been arriving at Marine Corps and Navy FRSs since 1982, the type formally entered *operational* service with the Marine Corps first – replacing the F-4Ss of VMFA-314 at El Toro Marine Corps Air Station in January 1983. The US Navy's first operational squadron was VFA-25, which said

3   Data sources on this figure do not agree. Figures from credible public domain sources include: 379, 371 and 380. Official figures from the US Navy or Boeing were unavailable at the time of writing.

goodbye to its A-7Es in March that same year.

Keeping an eye on structural loads and stresses, fatigue cracks were soon identified in the outward-canted vertical stabilisers. It is likely that, while the clean air was coming off the LERXs and washing over the stabs at high AoA during air combat training, a turbulent component was also passing over the tails and generating severe lateral loads. As a result

of this, within the first year of operations, the Hornet fleet was temporarily grounded while a strengthening programme was completed. This modification treated the symptom, but it did not address the cause. That came later, in May 1988, when a stubby 'wing fence' was added to the upper side of the LERXs to flatten out the vortices coming off the LERX and to deflect the turbulent air away from the tails.

In September 1987, production of the F/A-18A and F/A-18B (formerly the TF-18A) ceased and the production of the F/A-18C and F/A-18D single- and two-seat variants began.

The Navy would gift seven of its F/A-18As to NASA between 1984 and 1989, and the Navy's Blue Angels flight demonstration team moved from the much-loved A-4 Skyhawk to the Hornet in 1986. While the 'Scooter' could turn tightly, the team's adoption of the Hornet can only be described as a significant upgrade!

As production of the early variants halted, the Hornet had already enjoyed the international success that had eluded the F/A-18L and F-18L. Canada, which would become the biggest international customer for the Hornet, had eyed-up Northrop's offerings, but eventually selected McAir's product. It received its first examples in October 1982 (often referred to as the CF-18A and CF-18B Hornet, but officially designated the CF-188A and CF-188B by the Royal Canadian Air Force). The Royal Australian Air Force had selected the Hornet in 1980, ordered 57 F/A-18As and 18 F/A-18Bs, and began to receive deliveries

in October 1984. Meanwhile, the tiny Gulf state of Kuwait was on the cusp of ordering the jet in 1988, but they would arrive too late to help the nation ward off Saddam Hussein's invasion in August 1990. In the years to come, Switzerland, Spain, Malaysia and Finland would all also buy the Hornet.

By the time the more advanced F/A-18C and F/A-18D were about to enter production, the Hornet had already seen combat in the hands of the US Navy – suppressing Libyan air defences in the dead of an April night in 1986 for Operation Prairie Fire and Operation El Dorado Canyon. Much more combat would come in the decades that followed, proving beyond doubt just how good the Hornet was (see Chapter 4).

Improved stingers

McDonnell Douglas had always excelled at 'smelling what sells', and it had a long history of predicting and cultivating demand for modern tactical fighters. Unsurprisingly, the company had continued to develop advanced

BELOW An F/A-18A Hornet of VMFA-232 'Red Devils' is catapulted down Cat 2 of the USS *Nimitz* (CVN 68). The Hornet's flight control computers automatically pitch the aircraft's nose up to the desired attitude during the cat shot. *(US Navy)*

versions of the F/A-18, culminating in the Hornet 2000 proposal of 1987. Hornet 2000 was split into phases, the first of which – Design I – had more powerful engines and would eventually become the F/A-18C/D.

The C- and D-model Hornets were produced in 1987, with 733 being built in total (549 F/A-18Cs and 184 F/A-18Ds) for the US Navy, Marine Corps and various international customers. An additional 40 airframes were manufactured in a dedicated production run in 1991 for Kuwait.

The new variants ushered in a range of incremental capability improvements that included, among other things, game-changing avionics and weapons improvements. The C- and D-model Hornets enjoyed the introduction of the more capable Hughes APG-73 radar, compatibility with the IR-guided AGM-65D

Maverick air-to-ground missile and integration with the AIM-120 AMRAAM (advanced medium-range air-to-air missile), which superseded the AIM-7 Sparrow. For the existing F/A-18A/B, retrofitting the new APG-73 resulted in the modified designation F/A-18A/B+.

The F/A-18D was slightly more noteworthy in that it was optimised for the Marine Corps' night-attack mission. In addition, 48 examples were built with the nose-mounted M61A1 Vulcan Gatling gun replaced by a pallet containing reconnaissance equipment. These aircraft received the designation F/A-18D(RC).

By this time, it was obvious that the Hornet was a capable performer in all of its roles. Reliable by the standards of those aircraft it replaced, it was also delivering on the promise that Northrop had originally made about its maintainability. Objectively put, it

represented good value for money for an aircraft that was, after all, a jack of all trades but master of none.

But it was not without its critics, and this remains true today. To carry bombs over the same range as the A-7E Corsair II or the A-6E Intruder that it replaced, the F/A-18 must carry large amounts of external fuel, limiting the total payload and hardpoints available for offensive and defensive stores. Some argue that compromise means that it offers less utility than a Corsair or Intruder. The counter argument is that the carrier battlegroup today operates closer to threat nation coastlines, and that in a threat-dense environment, the Hornet has a much better chance of getting bombs on target than its predecessors.

Super Hornet

The F/A-18A/B established itself as very good beyond-visual-range fighter that could dominate in the close-in fight. The F/A-18C/D took these attributes and built on them, bringing true multi-role capability to the mix. But McAir was not finished: a new generation of Hornet was about to emerge – the F/A-18E/F Super Hornet.

McAir had continued its phased Hornet 2000 programme following the success of Design I (which resulted in the F/A-18C/D). Design II

BELOW The Super Hornet would eventually replace the F-14D Tomcat, but the move was contentious to say the least. Here, an outgoing F-14D of VF-2 'Bounty Hunters' flies formation off an incoming F/A-18F Super Hornet.
(US Navy)

added more fuel in a dorsal hump, while Design III represented an altogether larger aircraft with a correspondingly enlarged version of the F404 engine. Design III showed considerable promise since its longer fuselage offered a major increase in fuel capacity without any aerodynamic penalties.

On 12 May 1992 McDonnell Douglas received an 'intent to procure', followed by a $4.88 billion contract to develop the next-generation Hornet. The engineering, manufacturing and development (EMD) award covered the construction of seven flying prototypes (five single-seaters and a pair of two-seaters), plus three ground test airframes for static testing, drop tests and fatigue tests. Some of the contract money went to General Electric to develop the F414 engine.

Under the original Design III, the Super Hornet was to be a scaled-up Hornet, but Navy requirements dictated more wide-ranging developments. The wing was made thicker to support an extra weapons pylon on each side (taking it from 9 to 11 hardpoints in total), and the taper and sweepback of the wings was increased to maintain performance. Finally, a sawtooth was added to the leading edge.

Despite the promise that Design III had to offer, the US Navy's plan to replace the ageing F-14 Tomcat (eventually retired in 2006) immediately attracted criticism, much of it from proponents of a longer-range strike aircraft based on the F-14.

This was a decidedly difficult period in the history of US Navy airpower development and acquisition. The Navy had championed the stealthy McDonnell Douglas A-12 Avenger II, which had started development in 1988, and which should have replaced the A-6 and A-7 in the 1990s. But, following a succession of cost overruns and delays, that programme was cancelled in January 1991 by the then Secretary of Defence, Dick Cheney, on the basis of breach of contract (the resultant lawsuit would run on until 2014, when Boeing and General Dynamic each agreed to pay the US Navy $200 million in damages).

The Navy now had a huge capability gap to fill – the Avenger II had been slated to equip 14 aircraft carriers. Always commercially astute and despite the ongoing litigation of the Avenger II debacle, McDonnell Douglas seized the moment and, refining the Design III Hornet

2000, proposed what it called the 'Hornet II'. The Navy pursued the idea, recognising that such a development could come online far more quickly than a completely new naval strike fighter; acknowlcdging that an upgraded Hornet would exceed the capabilities of both Corsair and Intruder in the air-to-ground role; and wary of the fact that its fleet defender, the revered F-14 Tomcat, was ageing rapidly.

As an interim measure, the F-14 received upgrades – radar, avionics and weapons – that brought it up to date and allowed it to operate as a muti-role fighter (indeed, its new-found air-to-ground capability was utilised to great effect in operations over Afghanistan and Iraq). Meanwhile, the Navy considered a navalised version of the Boeing F-22 Raptor, but the Hornet II appeared the safer option for a stop-gap until the arrival of the fifth-generation Joint Strike Fighter. Hornet II got the go-ahead, and the single-seat F/A-18E and two-seat F/A-18F Super Hornet came to life.

Initial production of the F/A-18E/F began in 1995, with flight testing taking place in 1996. There were some early technical difficulties with the aircraft's new F414 engines – even though these were derived from the F404 engine that powered the Hornet – and wind tunnel tests prompted a minor redesign of the LERXs, while further minor modifications cured handling issues raised in early flight testing.

Next came sea trials, then the completion of developmental test certifications and entry to service in 1999. In total, 3,100 test flights, covering 4,600 flight hours, were flown. Full production began in 1997, and three years later the Super Hornet had passed US Navy operational tests and evaluations and was ready for operational service.

The Pacific Fleet was the first to receive the Super Hornet Block I when, in January 1999, VFA-122 'Flying Eagles' at Naval Air Station (NAS) Lemoore, became the first Super Hornet squadron and was tasked with training the first operational Super Hornet pilots using seven F/A-18E/Fs. Graduating pilots reported to the first front-line unit, VFA-115 at NAS Lemoore, which transitioned to the F/A-18E in December 2000. The squadron declared Initial Operational Capability in September 2001, having received their 'safe for flight' certification in June that year.

ABOVE This 'Bounty Hunters' F/A-18F of VFA-2 is configured as an air-to-air tanker. *(US Navy)*

The Super Hornet – referred to reverentially as the 'Rhino' by its crews – is instantly distinguishable from its older stablemates. It is bigger and has a greater degree of angularity. Its wings and stabilators are enlarged by 25%, it has received an overall size increase of 20% and it is 15,000lb heavier than the 'Legacy' Hornet. The sense of angularity comes from its redesigned engine intakes, which are elongated and rectangular in shape, as opposed to the small circular intakes of the F/A-18A/B/C/D. The aircraft has some stealthy features to reduce its radar signature and boasts a massively improved avionics and weapons package that now includes the APG-79 AESA radar. To power it along, it has F414-GE-400 turbofans (developed for the Avenger II), each producing 22,000lb of thrust in afterburner.

While the Super Hornet replaced the F-14 Tomcat in the fleet defence role, and the A-6 Intruder's long-range strike, strategic (nuclear) strike and interdiction roles, it has also assumed responsibility for the air refuelling role once performed by the S-3 Viking and KA-6D Intruder.

The final role the F/A-18 series would pick up would be the electronic warfare role, but for that a dedicated version would be required. …

Growler

The most recent member of the Hornet family is the EA-18G 'Growler', a dedicated electronic warfare (EW) version of the two-seat F/A-18F Super Hornet.

The Growler is based on the two-seat F/A-18F Block II, and includes the APG-79 AESA radar and advanced rear crew station. Costing $7–9 million more than the nominal Super Hornet unit price of $50 million, the Growler retains its combat capabilities and can be reverted back to the F/A-18F specification with relative ease. This ensures that the US Navy can operate the type as efficiently and flexibly as threat conditions dictate.

In January 2000, the Department of Defense commissioned the 'Joint Airborne Electronic Attack Analysis of Alternatives' study to suggest replacement options for the EA-6B Prowler. Calling on then-recent experience in the Balkans, the study was concluded in late 2000. It looked at a range of options, but the most attractive to the Navy was a dedicated EW version of the Super Hornet, then designated F/A-18G.

EW is a key component in the toolbox of military commanders, with tactical aircraft tasked to provide electronic attack (EA: electronic countermeasures – jamming); electronic protection (EP: counter-countermeasures and passive targeting against jamming sources); and suppression of enemy air defences (SEAD). Executed well, a good EW plan will allow friendly forces to engage and destroy enemy forces with maximum surprise and minimal exposure to surface and airborne threats.

Boeing had already started the engineering design phase on this, the fourth variant of the Hornet, in 1993 – well before the Joint Airborne Electronic Attack Analysis of Alternatives study took place. It took the Super Hornet design and modified it to form what is now officially known as the EA-18G Growler. The Growler is based on the two-seat F/A-18F, with Boeing using the basic airframe and combining it with Northrop Grumman's ICAP-III Airborne Electronic Attack (AEA) system. This approach creates an aircraft that retains 99% commonality with the Super Hornet, meaning that operational costs are minimised and logistical support is simplified for both land- and carrier-based operations.

The first Growler flew in August 2006; however, this aircraft (and the second example, too) are in fact F-model Super Hornets repurposed to act as Growlers for test and evaluation purposes (the US Navy refers to these two examples as NEA-18Gs).

Maturity issues surrounding the actual electronic warfare equipment on the Growler drew questions in a 2006 report by the US Government Accountability Office, but by 2011 these had been suitably answered and the Growler was considered ready for the task at hand by the Navy. In fact, although it had originally (in 2008) planned to buy 85 EA-18Gs to equip 11 squadrons, by 2011 that figure had risen to 114.

The Growler is equipped with the ALQ-218 wideband receiver and ALQ-99 Tactical Jamming System to defeat any radar-guided surface-to-air threat. Combined, these systems allow the jet to undertake SEAD missions using both reactive and pre-emptive jamming techniques; Stand-off and Escort Jamming; Non-Traditional Electronic Attack in coordination with ground forces, using the crew's enhanced situational awareness and uninterrupted communications to help troops on the ground counter hostile forces; and Self-protection and Time-Critical Strike Support, taking full advantage of its AESA radar, digital data links, AIM-120 AMRAAM, AGM-154 JSOW, ASQ-228 ATFLIR, and SHARP recce pod (see Chapter 7), the Growler is able to protect itself and aid strikers in finding, identifying and prosecuting time-sensitive targets.

Impressively, a Precision Airborne Electronic Attack option enables the EA-18G to rapidly sense and locate threats with a significantly higher degree of accuracy than was previously possible. In turn, this so-called 'selective-reactive' technology enables the crew to concentrate jamming energy against threats in a much more effective manner.

Finally, an Advanced Communication Countermeasures set, in the form of the modular ALQ-227, allows it to counter a wide range of communication systems. This interfaces with an Interference Cancellation System (INCANS) that allows the crew to continue communication with other agencies, even while the ALQ-227 is jamming.

In June 2009, the US Navy declared that the EA-18G had reached Initial Operating Capability with VAQ-132 'Scorpions' at NAS Whidbey Island, Washington. It made its first operational deployment in 2011, at which time 48 had been delivered to the Navy.

The venerable EA-6B Prowler was finally retired in March 2015, leaving the Growler as the only manned tactical jamming platform available to the US military.

BELOW An EA-18G Growler assigned to the 'Cougars' of EA Squadron VAQ-139 launches from the aircraft carrier USS *Carl Vinson* (CVN 70). The Growler is now the third major variant to have been derived from McAir's F/A-18 design. *(US Navy)*

Chapter Two

F/A-18 Hornet and F/A-18 Super Hornet variants

The Hornet has been incrementally improved since its 1983 entry to service by means of both hardware and software upgrades. So, while its aerodynamics have remained unchanged since its introduction to service, its capabilities have been updated and improved to keep the Hornet relevant to the combat theatres of today.

OPPOSITE The F/A-18A Hornet proved to offer solid air-to-air capabilities in addition to an austere set of air-to-ground capabilities. This A-model belongs to VFA-97 'Warhawks'. *(US Navy)*

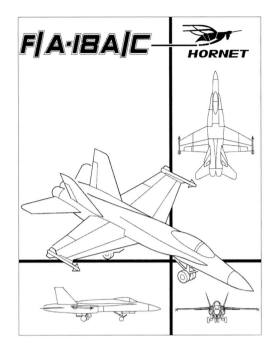

Major incremental developments in the Hornet's design have arrived courtesy of formal programmes that combine hardware and software changes together. The Hornet and Super Hornet are built using a system of 'Lots' (also called 'Blocks' – see Appendix for Block/Lot numbers), so some were upgraded at the time of factory floor assembly, while earlier Lots that had already been delivered to the user have been retrofitted. For example, the APX-111 combined IFF (which features the very visible 'bird slicer' antenna ahead of the forward

canopy and behind the radome) was factory-installed on US Navy and Marine Corps Hornets from Lot 19 onwards, while the system was retrofitted on Hornet Lots 12 to 18.

The Hornet was designed for an approach speed of 125 knots, but development problems raised this to 134 knots – fast for a carrier-based aircraft. This increased approach speed naturally places a hard limit on the Hornet's maximum landing weight that, in turn, has created a barrier for major airframe modifications without sacrificing the number of weapons carried or reducing the already limited range of its operations. In fact, the only significant external modification to the Hornet has been the installation of strakes above the leading edge root extensions (LERXs, installed from Lot 18 onwards) to break up vortices at angles of attack above 45 degrees. Despite this, the F/A-18 family has remained in service longer than many had expected, and with fatigue life indexes being consumed at a rate greater than planned, the aircraft has had its service life extended through a range of structural upgrades.

In some cases, the Hornet's software, hardware and structural modifications have been implemented across the board for all Hornet and Super Hornet operators, but in other instances they are unique to a given operator. Generally, however, the various upgrade programmes result in very similar enhancements. Australia's Hornet UpGrade (HUG) programme, for example, creates an upgraded Hornet that has parity with Canada's Incremental Modernization Program (IMP).

With this in mind, full details of each and every variant, upgrade and modification are beyond the scope of this chapter; instead, what follows should be viewed as a thorough introduction to Hornet variants and upgrades.

F/A-18A/B Hornet

The Hornet family started with the single-seat F/A-18A and the two-seat F/A-18B (originally TF/A-18). This early variant entered service in 1983 and remained in production until 1987. Some 410 examples were built in Lots 0 to 9.

The A/B model is equipped with the F404-GE-400 turbofan engine, the AAS-38A Nite

HAWK FLIR pod and the Hughes APG-65 multimode radar.

The F/A-18A/B has been exported under a range of alternative designations: (A)F/A-18A/B for the Royal Australian Air Force; formerly CF/A-188A/B and now CF-18A/B for the Royal Canadian Air Force; and the EF-18A/B for the Spanish Air Force, designated the C.15 and CE.15 in Spain, and later upgraded to EF-18A+ and EF-18M standard. Canadian Hornets are equipped with a night identification light on the left side of the forward fuselage, approximately aligned with the leading edge of the front canopy. See Chapter 3 for more about international Hornet operators.

A/B model upgrade programmes

F/A-18A/B+ – The US Navy and Marine Corps ran this 1992 upgrade to replace the original APG-65 radar with the new, more capable, APG-73.

Incremental Modernization Program (IMP) – The Royal Canadian Air Force (RCAF) began the two-phase IMP in 2001 to improve both the air-to-air and air-to-ground capabilities of its 80 CF-18s (62 A models and 18 B models), and to extend their service life to 2020. IMP consisted of structural, hardware and software modifications.

The major changes in the first phase included the installation of the more capable APG-73 radar in place of the APG-65; the installation of the APX-111 combined IFF system; new radios; a new mission computer in the form of the AYK-14 XN-8; embedded GPS/INS; and a new stores management

RIGHT **The F/A-18A+, one of which belonging to the 'Silver Eagles' of VMFA-115, brought the earliest Hornet variants up to a standard comparable with the C-model through the installation of the newer APG-73 radar. Here, the two F404 engines go into reheat in preparation for a cat shot off the bow of 'the boat'.** *(US Navy)*

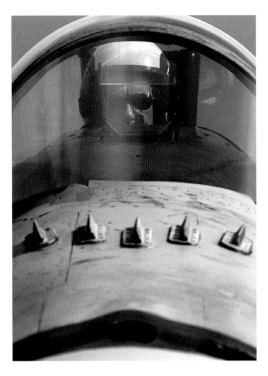

system that adds the MIL-STD-1760 interface and allows the aircraft to employ the AIM-120 AMRAAM and modern GPS-guided weapons. In addition, treatments were applied to the landing gear to slow the effects of corrosion.

Major changes in the second phase, which began in 2005 and concluded in March 2010, included the addition of a Link 16 data link; integration of the Joint Helmet Mounted Cueing System (JHMCS) and improvements to the aircraft's electronic warfare suite. In addition, 40 aircraft also received the CBR structural modification (see CBR+ below).

Hornet UpGrade (HUG) – The Royal Australian Air Force (RAAF) has incrementally upgraded its Hornets under the phased HUG programme since 1999. The upgrade is intended to allow Australia to operate the Legacy Hornet until 2018.

Phase 1 involved the design, development, testing and evaluation of a range of equipment; the installation of upgraded mission computer; jam-resistant radios; embedded GPS/INS; APX-111 combined IFF; Operational Flight Program 13C; and the AIM-120 AMRAAM. HUG Phase 2.2 modifications, completed in 2006, added JHMCS and Link 16 data link, and introduced new colour LCDs in the cockpit. HUG 2.3 and 2.4 added the ALR-67(V)3 and AAQ-28 Litening

target pod integration respectively. Eleven airframes received the CBR structural modification (see below) under HUG Phases 3.1 and 3.2.

EF-18+ and EF-18M – The Spanish Air Force (Ejército del Aire) has upgraded its A/B-model Hornets through two programmes.

The first, the EF-18+ programme, was announced in 1993 and resulted in the fleet being brought to approximately the same capability as the C/D-model Hornet. This predominantly consisted of the installation of the AYK-14 XN-8 mission computer and associated software, and resulted in an improved flight envelope (thanks to the latest flight control computer software) and the integration of the AIM-120 AMRAAM.

Whereas the modification work of the 'Plus' programme was shared by Spain's CASA and McDonnell Douglas, the subsequent EF-18M programme was the sole enterprise of CASA (now EADS CASA). The modification was applied to 67 of Spain's 91 Hornets, and upgraded aircraft are identifiable by the small GPS antennae on the spine between the tails.

The EF-18M upgrade was far-reaching, but the highlights include the installation of a new tactical mission computer; MIL-STD-1553 wiring to the wing pylons; a new heads-up display and new colour, high-definition multifunction screens (bringing the total number of displays to four in the EF-18M cockpit); embedded GPS/INS; MIDS Link 16 data link; integration of IRIS-T and Meteor air-to-air missiles; ARC-210 Have Quick II radios; INDRA ALR-400 radar warning receiver and ALQ-500 jammer; integration of the Paveway III, BPG-2000 and Taurus air-to-ground weapons; and integration with the AAQ-28 Litening target pod and Reccelite tactical reconnaissance pod. The upgrade ran through 2008 and was completed in October 2009.

F/A-18C/D Hornet

While offering superb close-in dogfighting manoeuvrability and a solid beyond-visual-range capability, continued developments in engineering, weapons systems and computing all paved the way for improvements to be made to the Hornet's air- and ground-attack capabilities. What resulted was the

F/A-18C/D Hornet, deliveries of which began in September 1987 and ended in 1999, running from Lots 10 to 21.

Designed to accommodate new avionics equipment and weapons, the F/A-18C/D looks almost identical to the earlier variants on the outside but is, of course, quite different from the A/B-model Hornet. C/D-model Hornets lack the solid-looking 'cleats' on the inside of the vertical tails, but are most easily distinguished from earlier Hornets by the presence of the ALQ-126 airborne self-protection jammer's (ASPJ) antennae. C/D models feature six forward-fuselage blisters: two just behind the canopy on the left and right side of the dorsal spine, two on the underside of the forward fuselage and two on the sides of the forward fuselage just above and behind the smaller blisters of the radar warning receiver (RWR). They also feature two ALQ-126 antennae on the trailing edge of both vertical tails (it's easiest to just count the tailing edge 'bumps' that run parallel with and upwards from the red strobe located on the outboard surface of each tail: three for the C/D, two for the A/B).

At the heart of the C/D Hornet is the AN/AYK-14 XN-8 mission computer. Superseded by the XN-8+ system in US and USMC models in the early 2000s, this central computer represented a significant leap in capability in terms of processing power and speed. Put simply, it could crunch more numbers and do it faster, making it possible to get more out of the Hornet's radar, stores management system, electronic warfare components and flight computers.

The C/D Hornet is also the beneficiary of developments in radar-absorbent material, applied to the Hornet under the 'Glass Hornet' programme, and contributing to a reduced radar cross-section (RCS). Glass Hornet F/A-18C/Ds feature canopies coated with a thin layer of indium tin oxide (ITO) that reflects radar signals away from the transmitter and RAM (radiation-absorbent material) paint on the engine inlets that helps to absorb radar energy. These additional coatings come at the cost of a 250lb weight gain, further reducing the Hornet's bring-back load.

The addition of a multi-sensor integration (MSI) system was also new to the C/D variants. The MSI computer takes the processed data from the radar, electronic warfare equipment and other weapons sensors such as the AGM-88 HARM anti-radiation missile, correlates the data, and then presents it to the pilot as a synthetic picture of the battlespace – tactical symbols (aircraft, emitters, threats and other categories of object) overlaid on to the aircraft's moving map display. This fusion of sensor data allows the pilot quickly to assess the

ABOVE An F/A-18D of Marine Fighter Attack Training Squadron 101 (VMFAT-101) is cleaned during operations aboard the USS _Nimitz_ (CVN 68). _(US Navy)_

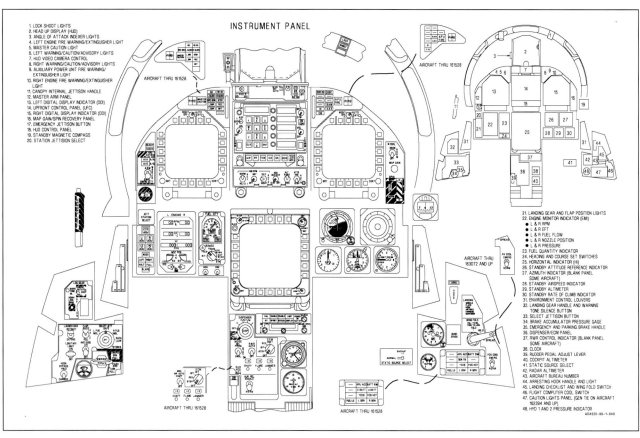

INSTRUMENT PANEL

1. LOCK SHOOT LIGHTS
2. HEAD UP DISPLAY (HUD)
3. ANGLE OF ATTACK INDEXER LIGHTS
4. LEFT ENGINE FIRE WARNING/EXTINGUISHER LIGHT
5. MASTER CAUTION LIGHT
6. LEFT WARNING/CAUTION/ADVISORY LIGHTS
7. HUD VIDEO CAMERA CONTROL
8. RIGHT WARNING/CAUTION/ADVISORY LIGHTS
9. AUXILIARY POWER UNIT FIRE WARNING/
   EXTINGUISHER LIGHT
10. RIGHT ENGINE FIRE WARNING/EXTINGUISHER
    LIGHT
11. CANOPY INTERNAL JETTISON HANDLE
12. MASTER ARM PANEL
13. LEFT DIGITAL DISPLAY INDICATOR (DDI)
14. UPFRONT CONTROL PANEL (UFC)
15. RIGHT DIGITAL DISPLAY INDICATOR (DDI)
16. MAP GAIN/SPIN RECOVERY PANEL
17. EMERGENCY JETTISON BUTTON
18. HUD CONTROL PANEL
19. STANDBY MAGNETIC COMPASS
20. STATION JETTISON SELECT

21. LANDING GEAR AND FLAP POSITION LIGHTS
22. ENGINE MONITOR INDICATOR (EMI)
   ● L & R RPM
   ● L & R FIT
   ● L & R FUEL FLOW
   ● L & R NOZZLE POSITION
   ● L & R PRESSURE
23. FUEL QUANTITY INDICATOR
24. HEADING AND COURSE SET SWITCHES
25. HORIZONTAL INDICATOR (HI)
26. STANDBY ATTITUDE REFERENCE INDICATOR
27. AZIMUTH INDICATOR (BLANK PANEL
    SOME AIRCRAFT)
28. STANDBY AIRSPEED INDICATOR
29. STANDBY ALTIMETER
30. STANDBY RATE OF CLIMB INDICATOR
31. ENVIRONMENT CONTROL LOUVERS
32. LANDING GEAR HANDLE AND WARNING
    TONE SILENCE BUTTON
33. SELECT JETTISON BUTTON
34. BRAKE ACCUMULATOR PRESSURE GAGE
35. EMERGENCY AND PARKING BRAKE HANDLE
36. DISPENSER/ECM PANEL
37. RWR CONTROL INDICATOR (BLANK PANEL
    SOME AIRCRAFT)
38. CLOCK
39. RUDDER PEDAL ADJUST LEVER
40. COCKPIT ALTIMETER
41. STATIC SOURCE SELECT
42. RADAR ALTIMETER
43. AIRCRAFT BUREAU NUMBER
44. ARRESTING HOOK HANDLE AND LIGHT
45. LANDING CHECKLIST AND WING FOLD SWITCH
46. FLIGHT COMPUTER COOL SWITCH
47. CAUTION LIGHTS PANEL (GEN TIE ON AIRCRAFT
    162394 AND UP)
48. HYD 1 AND 2 PRESSURE INDICATOR

ADA520-88-1-043

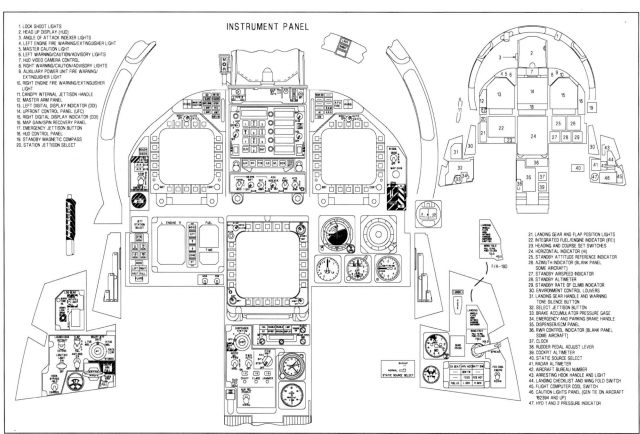

INSTRUMENT PANEL

1. LOCK SHOOT LIGHTS
2. HEAD UP DISPLAY (HUD)
3. ANGLE OF ATTACK INDEXER LIGHTS
4. LEFT ENGINE FIRE WARNING/EXTINGUISHER LIGHT
5. MASTER CAUTION LIGHT
6. LEFT WARNING/CAUTION/ADVISORY LIGHTS
7. HUD VIDEO CAMERA CONTROL
8. RIGHT WARNING/CAUTION/ADVISORY LIGHTS
9. AUXILIARY POWER UNIT FIRE WARNING/
   EXTINGUISHER LIGHT
10. RIGHT ENGINE FIRE WARNING/EXTINGUISHER LIGHT
11. CANOPY INTERNAL JETTISON HANDLE
12. MASTER ARM PANEL
13. LEFT DIGITAL DISPLAY INDICATOR (DDI)
14. UPFRONT CONTROL PANEL (UFC)
15. RIGHT DIGITAL DISPLAY INDICATOR (DDI)
16. MAP GAIN/SPIN RECOVERY PANEL
17. EMERGENCY JETTISON BUTTON
18. HUD CONTROL PANEL
19. STANDBY MAGNETIC COMPASS
20. STATION JETTISON SELECT

21. LANDING GEAR AND FLAP POSITION LIGHTS
22. INTEGRATED FUEL/ENGINE INDICATOR (IFE)
23. HEADING AND COURSE SET SWITCHES
24. HORIZONTAL INDICATOR (HI)
25. STANDBY ATTITUDE REFERENCE INDICATOR
26. AZIMUTH INDICATOR (BLANK PANEL
    SOME AIRCRAFT)
27. STANDBY AIRSPEED INDICATOR
28. STANDBY ALTIMETER
29. STANDBY RATE OF CLIMB INDICATOR
30. ENVIRONMENT CONTROL LOUVERS
31. LANDING GEAR HANDLE AND WARNING
    TONE SILENCE BUTTON
32. SELECT JETTISON BUTTON
33. BRAKE ACCUMULATOR PRESSURE GAGE
34. EMERGENCY AND PARKING BRAKE HANDLE
35. DISPENSER/ECM PANEL
36. RWR CONTROL INDICATOR (BLANK PANEL
    SOME AIRCRAFT)
37. CLOCK
38. RUDDER PEDAL ADJUST LEVER
39. COCKPIT ALTIMETER
40. STATIC SOURCE SELECT
41. RADAR ALTIMETER
42. AIRCRAFT BUREAU NUMBER
43. ARRESTING HOOK HANDLE AND LIGHT
44. LANDING CHECKLIST AND WING FOLD SWITCH
45. FLIGHT COMPUTER COOL SWITCH
46. CAUTION LIGHTS PANEL (GEN TIE ON AIRCRAFT
    162394 AND UP)
47. HYD 1 AND 2 PRESSURE INDICATOR

battlespace and is particularly useful in SEAD/ DEAD (suppression/destruction of enemy air defences) missions.

By 1994, all US C/D Hornets had been retrofitted with the APG-73 radar, which increased air-to-air detection ranges in the order of 7–20%, and offered higher-resolution ground mapping. The APG-73 makes use of the same antenna and travelling-wave tube transmitter as the APG-65, but boasts what was (in the 1990s) the latest generation of hardware in all other respects. For example, it features a more sophisticated receiver–exciter, which offers better long-range resolution by accelerating the analogue-to-digital conversion, thus allowing the radar to cut the incoming signal into smaller fragments.

Representing a massive leap forward in air-to-air capability over the AIM-7 Sparrow, the AIM-120 AMRAAM was also integrated into the C/D. For the air-to-ground mission, the AGM-65D IR Maverick ground-attack missile was added, as was the AAS-38B Nite HAWK with its combined FLIR, laser rangefinder and designator and laser spot tracker.

The C/D model has been sold internationally (see Chapter 3) under a range of designations, including the KAF-18C/D for the Kuwaiti Air Force, and F-18C/D for the Finnish Air Force. Swiss Hornets, which are sometimes referred to as SF/A-18s, feature a night identification light on the left side of the forward fuselage, approximately aligned with the leading edge of the front canopy.

C/D model upgrade programmes

The F/A-18C/D has received a small number of upgrades, some of which have been implemented under the auspices of a formal upgrade programme. For example, when the Kuwaiti Air Force ordered its Hornets, it specified a more reliable IFF system. When the integration of this new IFF was complete (the cost being borne by Kuwait), the US Navy and Marine Corps retrofitted it to their aircraft, but

not as part of an overarching modernisation or upgrade programme. The list below is therefore illustrative, not exhaustive.

F/A-18C(N) Night Attack, F/A-18D and F/A-18D(RC) Attack Deltas – The US Marine Corps uses modified C-model and D-model Hornets in the night-attack role, with the emphasis on night-attack expertise being placed on squadrons equipped predominantly with the two-seat variant.

The single-seat F/A-18C(N) is distinguished by the carriage of a Hughes AN/AAR-50 thermal imaging pod in addition to the AAS-38 Nite HAWK.

ABOVE **The Hornet cockpit is considered well designed, spacious and comfortable, especially by the standards of contemporary fighters.** *(US Marine Corps)*

BELOW **A Marine All-Weather Fighter Attack Squadron 533 (VMFA(AW)-533) F/A-18D Hornet prepares for a sortie at Osan Air Base, Republic of Korea. The Marine D models are used extensively in the forward air control and night-attack missions.** *(US Marine Corps)*

ATARS is controlled by a dedicated reconnaissance management system and uses its two digital recorders to capture imagery from the EO sensor and to record synthetic aperture radar imagery from the APG-73 radar. A digital data link pod mounted on the centreline pylon allows the crew to transmit their 'take' to battlefield commanders in near-real time.

F/A-18D and F/A-18C(N) aircraft can have the ATARS module removed, allowing them to be restored to standard combat configuration. However, 60 D models were built with the ATARS module as a permanent fit, resulting in the designation F/A-18D(RC).

Upgrade 21 and Upgrade 25 – The Swiss Air Force (Schweizer Luftwaffe) commenced Upgrade 21 to add Link 16 MIDS data link, JHMCS and AIM-9X to the fleet. It followed with Upgrade 25 in 2007 to further extend the useful life of its 33 C/D-model Hornets. Upgrade 25 brought about similar improvements to the Canadian and Australian A/B-model upgrade programmes, and included ASQ-228 Advanced Tactical Forward-Looking Infrared (ATFLIR) target pods, ALR-67(V)3 electronic warfare countermeasures sets, APX-111 IFF, embedded

ABOVE The Marine Corps purchased F/A-18D(RC) 'Attack Delta' Hornets, featuring the ATARS module in the nose. This Attack Delta, photographed at MCAS Iwakuni, Japan, belongs to VMFA(AW)-224, the 'Fighting Bengals'.
(US Marine Corps)

BELOW Spain has extensively upgraded its fleet of F-18 fighters in order to maintain their relevance in today's increasingly complex threat environments.
(Spanish Air Force)

The Marine Corps received its first F/A-18D Night Attack Hornet in November 1989, and a total of 98 were ordered. The Night Attack Hornet boasts the removable installation of the Advanced Tactical Air Reconnaissance System (ATARS) module in the nose (replacing the M61 Vulcan cannon), which incorporates a low- and medium-altitude EO (electro-optical) sensor and an infrared linescan imager. In addition, the AN/UPD-8 side-looking radar can also be carried.

GPS/INS, improved cockpit displays and integration with the AAQ-28 Litening target pod.

Mid-Life Update (MLU) – The Finnish Air Force (Suomen Ilmavoimat) has embarked on a multi-phase MLU programme that is expected to keep its Hornets in operation until 2025. The final MLU 1-configured aircraft was rolled out in late 2010, completing a phase that focused on improving air-to-air capabilities by adding the JHMCS helmet-mounted sighting system and the AIM-9X Sidewinder IR guided missile. The APX-111 IFF was also fitted, and a tactical moving map was added.

The second phase, MLU 2, is ongoing at the time of writing and will give the Hornet an improved surface attack capability thanks to the AAQ-28 Litening pod and expanded stores compatibility, improved AIM-120C-7 AMRAAM, an updated communication and navigation system and a MIDS Link-16 data link for interoperability with NATO air forces. In addition, the original cathode ray tube cockpit displays will be replaced by LCD units, and the radar and electronic countermeasures suite will be updated. MLU Phase 2 is expected to be completed in 2016.

Kuwaiti GPS upgrade – The Kuwaiti Air Force (al-Quwwat al-Jawwiya al-Kuwaitiya) upgraded its 39 F/A-18C/Ds in 2010, adding a Miniature Airborne Global Positioning Receiver 2000

McDONNELL DOUGLAS F/A-18 HORNET MANUAL

with selective availability anti-spoofing module (SAASM), a new tactical moving map display and a cockpit pressurisation warning system.

F/A-18E/F Super Hornet

The first Super Hornet was built in Lot 18, but most have been built in Lots 22 to 28. It is manufactured in single-seat F/A-18E and two-seat F/A-18F configurations, and remains in production in 2016 with more than 500 examples built to date.

For the US Navy, the Super Hornet is helping to meet the 'near-term (2018–20) strike fighter inventory capacity challenge, and longer-term (2020–35) strike fighter model balance' in

seagoing squadrons – more simply, it is helping to offset the delayed entry to service of the F-35B Lightning II, and to reduce dependency on the rapidly ageing Legacy Hornet fleet.

Despite similarities in appearance, airframe commonality between the first-generation F/A-18A and the F/A-18E sits at only around 10%. The aircraft has an enhanced FBW flight control system that offers levels of confidence that have allowed the mechanical backup of the Legacy Hornet to be removed. The Super Hornet is also noteworthy for an improved cockpit. F/A-18Fs delivered from Lot 26 onwards all feature a missionised rear cockpit, which includes removal of dual controls, the addition of twin hand controllers and the installation of an 8×10in LCD display in place of the aft multi-purpose colour display (MPCD). These aircraft can be returned to 'twin stick' configuration, if required.

To cope with the additional data processing requirements of the Super Hornet, some aircraft have had their AYK-14 mission computers replaced with the Advanced Mission Computer and Display (AMCD) modification. For the F/A-18Fs with the missionised cockpits, the even more powerful AMCD II computers are required. The AMCD II computer provides digital video colour capability to the 8×10 display via a Fiber

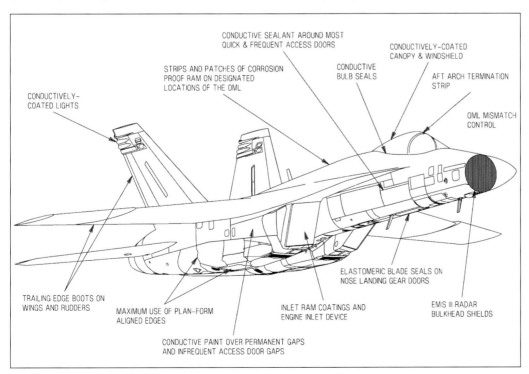

CONDUCTIVE SEALANT AROUND MOST QUICK & FREQUENT ACCESS DOORS

CONDUCTIVELY-COATED CANOPY & WINDSHIELD

STRIPS AND PATCHES OF CORROSION PROOF RAM ON DESIGNATED LOCATIONS OF THE OML

CONDUCTIVE BULB SEALS

AFT ARCH TERMINATION STRIP

CONDUCTIVELY-COATED LIGHTS

OML MISMATCH CONTROL

ELASTOMERIC BLADE SEALS ON NOSE LANDING GEAR DOORS

TRAILING EDGE BOOTS ON WINGS AND RUDDERS

MAXIMUM USE OF PLAN-FORM ALIGNED EDGES

INLET RAM COATINGS AND ENGINE INLET DEVICE

EMIS III RADAR BULKHEAD SHIELDS

CONDUCTIVE PAINT OVER PERMANENT GAPS AND INFREQUENT ACCESS DOOR GAPS

LEFT A wide range of small modifications have been made to the Super Hornet that collectively help to reduce its overall radar cross-section. *(US Navy)*

LEFT This F/A-18F image dramatically illustrates the growth of the Super Hornet's leading edge root extensions (LERXs). The dark grey patch on the forward part of the port (left) LERX is an anti-slip coating that prevents the crew and maintainers from slipping while accessing the cockpit. *(US Navy)*

BELOW An F/A-18F Super Hornet of the 'Flying Eagles', VFA-122, flies over the USS *George Washington* (CVN 73). VFA-122 is the Fleet Replacement Squadron for the F/A-18E/F Super Hornet. *(US Navy)*

Channel Network Switch (FCNS) and High-Speed Video Network (HSVN).

The F/A-18E/F is 25% larger than the Legacy variants, with large rectangular-section, stealthy raked intakes, a sawtooth wing leading edge, bigger LERXs and larger control surfaces and stabilators (vertical and horizontal). A lengthened fuselage delivers a roughly 30% boost in internal fuel capacity. Most impressive of all, thanks to clever use of advanced materials and reliance on modern manufacturing techniques, the Super Hornet's growth has come not only without any major weight penalty, but also with a 42% reduction in parts count.

While parts commonality with the Hornet is superficial at best, avionics commonality remains high. That results in a low unit cost for the customer (within 15% of the cost of the F/A-18C) and also simplifies aircrew transition from one variant to another.

Although bigger in size, the Super Hornet enjoys lower levels of drag and benefits from a reduced approach speed despite its higher maximum landing weight. This translates into a much-improved 'bringback' capability – allowing the aircraft to land with unused ordnance that the original Hornet would have had to jettison before landing. Full-span slotted flaps bring carrier approach speeds to around 135 knots, some 10 knots slower than the F/A-18C.

RCS reduction is a significant feature of the Super Hornet, and this is achieved through numerous airframe design features, including planform alignment of as many surface edges as feasible, a smooth outer mould line and a conductive surface that reduces radar scattering. To complement these design features, treatments have been applied to various airframe components, including metalising the navigation lights, canopy and windscreen.

In line with dedicated stealth aircraft, permanent joints and gaps around infrequently opened panels are filled with a form-in-place (FIP) sealant, which is then blended flush and conductively painted. Gaps around frequently opened panels are filled with a conductive FIP (CFIP) sealant, while conductive tape is applied to gaps where there is no substructure to support FIP, such as along LEX edges.

Frequently opened panels have a corrosion-proof radar absorbing material (RAM) applied in

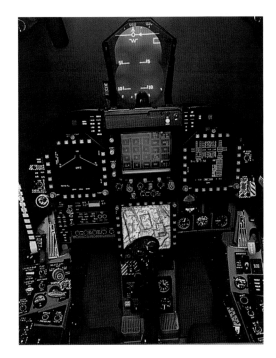

their gaps, and the same material is also found on the inlet lip and duct, the diamond-shaped patches around drain holes, and around pitot tubes, vertical tail openings, vents and screens, flap hinges and fairings and portions of the pylons and external tanks. A multi-layer RAM is used in a few locations, such as around AOA probes and on the upper front surface of the pylons.

Super Hornet upgrades and blocks

The Super Hornet has been released to service in two major blocks to date, each of which represents a significant capability improvement.

Given that the US Navy plans to have the Super Hornet operating alongside the F-35 Lightning II until 2030, there currently exists a range of proposals to develop a third block that will increase the aircraft's lethality and combat range, as well as reduce its radar signature.

Block I (all aircraft up to Lot 24) – this was the launch configuration for the Super Hornet, as described above and in Chapter 1.

Block II (Lot 25 and upwards) – with deliveries commencing in April 2005, the Lot II Super Hornet is equipped with the APG-79 Active Electronically Scanned Array (AESA) radar, the Advanced Crew Station and with advanced mission computers and displays. The Block II

BELOW A VX-31 F/A-18F ascends towards the heavens. The Super Hornet's performance remains stellar despite its physical growth. *(US Navy)*

configuration, which can be retrofitted to Block I aircraft, also provides enhanced interconnectivity among the aircraft's mission systems.

Block III Advanced Super Hornet – flight testing of the Block III aircraft commenced in 2014 and has so far yielded positive feedback from the US Navy, but no commitment to

buy. It adds conformal fuel tanks (3,500lb fuel capacity) and a stealthy external weapons pod, and according to Boeing delivers a 50% overall signature reduction. Boeing has also proposed that an upgraded radar, 11×9in cockpit display, an IR search and track (IRST) system and improved engines be incorporated into the Block III developments.

IRST21 – the US Navy approved low-rate initial production of Lockheed Marin's IRST21 IR search and track system in early 2015, with deliveries expected in 2017. The sensor is derived from that installed on the F-14D and international variants of the F-15E and will be installed in the nose section of the Super Hornet's centreline FPU-13 fuel tank.

EA-18G Growler

The EA-18G Growler is a carrier-based electronic attack aircraft. It features an Airborne Electronic Attack (AEA) system, the purpose of which is to provide electronic surveillance and electronic attack capabilities.

The AEA system incorporates the Electronic Attack Unit (EAU) as the AEA system controller, the ALQ-218(V)2 receiver system, the ALQ-227B Communications Countermeasures Set (CCS), the Multimission Advanced Tactical Terminal Block 3 (MATT) and ALQ-99 jamming pods.

The EA-18G employs EW tactics to offensively jam threat radar and communications. It is therefore equipped with a digital memory device (DMD) and an Interference Cancellation Unit (INCANS) that allow it to operate without jamming its own sensors.

The purpose of the Growler is the suppression of hostile search, acquisition, tracking and guidance radar systems, as well as RF (radio frequency) communications that might be employed against friendly aircraft. This mission encompasses the protection of friendly aircraft as they enter and depart a battlefield region, as well as during friendly aircraft missions in the battlespace. The Growler accomplishes the mission through means of EA and by employing weapons against the threat.

ABOVE A yellow-shirt passes an EA-18G Growler from the 'Cougars' of EA Squadron VAQ-139 on the flight deck of the USS *Carl Vinson* (CVN 70). *(US Navy)*

BELOW A VAQ-139 Growler launches off the waist catapult. The wingtip-mounted ALQ-218 pods make it easy to identify the EA-18G from the rest of the Hornet family. *(US Navy)*

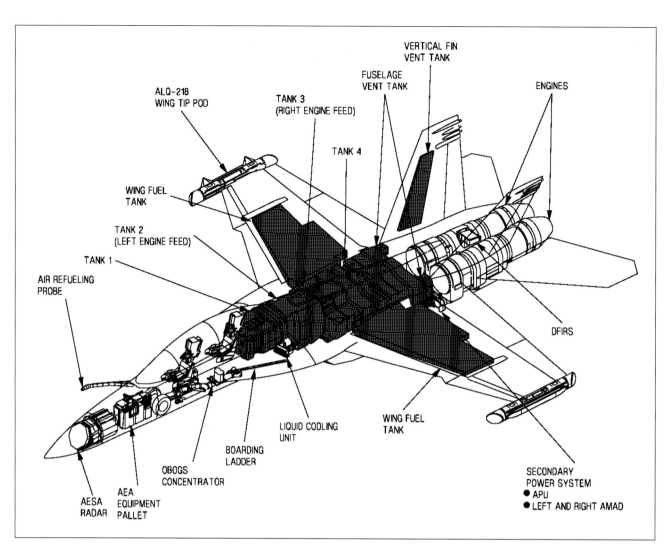

VERTICAL FIN
VENT TANK

FUSELAGE
VENT TANK

ENGINES

ALQ-218
WING TIP POD

TANK 3
(RIGHT ENGINE FEED)

TANK 4

WING FUEL
TANK

TANK 2
(LEFT ENGINE FEED)

TANK 1

AIR REFUELING
PROBE

DFIRS

LIQUID COOLING
UNIT

WING FUEL
TANK

BOARDING
LADDER

OBOGS
CONCENTRATOR

AESA
RADAR

AEA
EQUIPMENT
PALLET

SECONDARY
POWER SYSTEM
● APU
● LEFT AND RIGHT AMAD

ABOVE The EA-18G basic specification. Note the wingtip pods and forward fuselage-mounted EAE equipment pallet.
(US Navy)

The EA portion of this mission is accomplished via the crew vehicle interface (CVI) with the AEA subsystem functionality controlled through the mission computers (MCs). This interface includes both display of threat Situational Awareness (SA) provided by AEA subsystem, threat detection trackfile information processed in the MCs and a command and control interface of the AEA subsystem. The crew can choose from a number of display formats, and interface with the MCs by means of the cockpit hand controls and HOTAS (hands on throttle and stick) switches.

F/A-18 structural upgrades

Delays in the introduction to service of the F-35 have meant that some nations – the USA and Australia in particular – have felt the pinch of their ageing Legacy Hornet fleets more than others. The US Chief of Naval Operations, Adm Jonathan Greenert, stated in March 2015 that he had a shortfall of three Super Hornet squadrons due to his Hornets eating through their fatigue life faster than anticipated. Navy planners had predicted the need to extend the service life of the Hornet, initiating structural upgrades as early as 2001. Moreover, delays to the F-35 programme now mean that the Super Hornet fleet will also have to be scheduled for a service life extension programme.

Keeping them flying – CBR+ and SLEP

The US Navy's Hornet fleet is now growing long in the tooth, and with the delayed entry to service of the Lockheed F-35C Lightning II that is intended to replace the Legacy Hornet (the

F-35B will replace the Hornet for the Marine Corps), there are now questions over how to make sure that the Super Hornet does not run out of airframe hours. Given that the Navy's objective is to see a mixed force of Super Hornets and Lightnings operating together as far into the future as 2024, that is a real concern.

The US Navy had a fleet of around 300 *serviceable* C-model Hornets in service in March 2015. Intended originally to have only a 20-year service life (100 carrier landings per year and 6,000 total flight hours), the operational tempo of decades' worth of combat (to include returning to the ship heavy with unexpended ordnance) has accelerated that ageing process.

While the Hornet has been the beneficiary of numerous software and hardware avionics and weapons upgrades, it is the aircraft's structural integrity that it the most difficult challenge to overcome. The US Navy and Marine Corps Hornet has fulfilled the conventional and nuclear strike workload that was once shared by the A-7E and A-6E. It has also been extensively engaged in conflicts and global policing roles in the Balkans and, most particularly, the Middle East, that have steadily consumed fatigue life hours, further exacerbating the problem.

The same problems plague a number of international customers who had purchased the F/A-18A/B; they too must meet the demand to keep the aircraft in service longer than originally anticipated, but are also limited by how many flying hours remain on their fleets.

Efforts to extend fatigue life have come courtesy of the Centre Barrel Replacement Plus (CBR+) programme, which replaced the centre part of the Hornet's fuselage (supporting the wings and undercarriage) with new structures. Thus, the CBR programme has enabled (and is continuing to enable) the American, Canadian and Australian Hornet fleets to remain operational until either replaced by Super Hornets or superseded by the troubled F-35 Lightning II. CBR prototyping began in December 2000 and finished in 2001. By November 2014, 200 US Navy Hornets had received the treatment (at an average cost of $2 million per aircraft).

To complement CBR+, the Navy is also embarked on a service life extension programme (SLEP) to take 150 handpicked Hornets to 10,000 flight hours. For the Super Hornet fleet, the Navy must now get around 563 E and F models to the 9,000-hour mark, and that will also require a SLEP programme.

F/A-18 software upgrades

The Hornet and Super Hornet have had their capabilities increased incrementally by means of Operational Flight Programmes (OFP), while Software Configuration Sets (SCS) are used to deliver major combat capability improvements. OFP and SCS are software changes that are installed on to the F/A-18's mission computers at either local- or depot-level maintenance facilities. They add new functionality, remove old functionality or modify the behaviour of existing functionality across the aircraft – from radar, stores management and sensors to flight control laws.

According to the US Navy, all EA-18Gs and Block 2 F/A-18E/Fs (production Lot 25 and beyond) use high-order language, or 'H-series' software, while F/A-18E/Fs prior to Lot 25 and all legacy F/A-18 A/B/C/D aircraft use 'X-series' software. This means that there are parallel software versions in development at any one time, each of which is identified with either an H or an X suffix, depending upon which Hornet variant they are destined for. By way of illustration, in 2014, the US Navy released H8E and continued testing on 25X.

Software testing is completed in phases, so Phase 1 testing for H8E ran from June 2012 to May 2013, totalling 1,296 flight hours. Phase II focused on improvements to the APG-79 radar, and consumed 1,884 hours of flight testing between October 2013 and June 2014.

SCS and OFP software can be used to add and integrate new hardware. For example, H4E software brought in the JHMCS and the APG-79 AESA radar for the Super Hornet. The next iteration, H5E, added (among other things) the Link 16 MIDS joint tactical radio system, the AGM-154 Joint Stand-Off Weapon and the AGM-84H/K Stand-off Land Attack Missile Expanded Response (SLAM-ER). H8E delivered improved AESA radar performance.

Chapter Three

F/A-18 and EA-18G operators – US and international

In addition to becoming the mainstay of US Navy and Marine tactical airpower, the F/A-18 has also seen moderate success internationally. From the freezing terrain of Finland to the barren deserts of Kuwait, the Hornet is in operation with a number of wealthy and/or advanced world air arms.

OPPOSITE The number of early A- and B-model Hornets in US service has shrunk dramatically. This F/A-18A Hornet is assigned to the 'Red Devils' of Marine Fighter Attack Squadron **VMFA-232.** *(US Navy)*

49

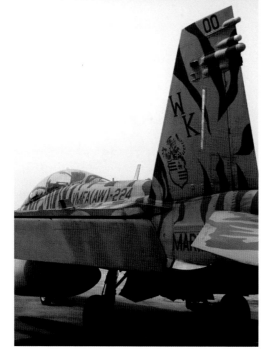

United States Navy (USN) and US Marine Corps (USMC)

The US Navy purchased 379 F/A-18As and 42 F/A-18Bs between 1978 and 1979. Operational test squadrons VX-4 and VX-5 conducted carrier suitability trials from NAS Patuxent River. With the Hornet given the green light by the VX community, Fleet Replacement Squadrons VFA-125 and VFA-106 and Marine squadron VFMAT-101 began receiving aircraft from 1982. The F/A-18A and TF/A-18A entered frontline operational service the following year, arriving first with the Marine Corps and then with the Navy.

In September 1987, production of the F/A-18A and F/A-18B (formerly the TF-18A) ceased and the production of the F/A-18C and F/A-18D single- and two-seat variants began. By 1995, the US Navy had retired most of its A/B models from carrier-based service.

Despite the removal of the A/B Hornet to mostly shore-based operations, the F/A-18+ update (see Chapter 2) allowed the variant to remain relevant to the training and operational requirements of the Marine Corps, the Navy's Adversary training squadrons and to the Navy and Marine Corps' reserve squadrons.

The US Navy at one time had 20 squadrons of Hornets at sea, but the Super Hornet is now the dominant variant. As of early 2016, the US Navy had only seven so-called Legacy Hornet (F/A-18A/B/C/D) squadrons earmarked for cruises. By 2014, Boeing had delivered 487 of a planned purchase of 563 Super Hornets to the US Navy.

A typical Legacy Hornet squadron is made up of between 10 and 12 aircraft, whereas each Super Hornet squadron consists of between 12 and 14 aircraft, depending on whether the squadron comprises the single-seat F/A-18E or the two-seat F/A-18F. An air wing can mix the two types of Super Hornet in order to achieve an overall balance, meaning that they can take advantage of the two-seat jet's suitability to ground-attack roles if that is their mission focus, or they can increase the number of single-seat aircraft if their focus is purely on air-to-air.

The Navy organises its front-line Hornet and Super Hornet units into West or East Coast fleets. US Navy Carrier Air Wings are divided between these fleets, and each Strike Fighter Squadron is assigned to a Carrier Air Wing, which is in turn attached to an aircraft carrier. The squadrons are shore-based when not deployed. For example, the West Coast Fleet commands Carrier Air Wing Nine (CVW-9), which (as of January 2016) is equipped by four Super Hornet squadrons (VFA-14, VFA-41, VFA-97 and VFA-157), a Growler squadron (VAQ-133), and squadrons of E-2C Hawkeye, MH-60 Seahawk and C-2A Greyhound aircraft. CVW-9 is attached to the USS *John C. Stennis* (CVN-74), and, when not deployed, is based at NAS Lemoore, California.

The East Coast's operational F/A-18 squadrons are based at NAS Oceana, Virginia, which is

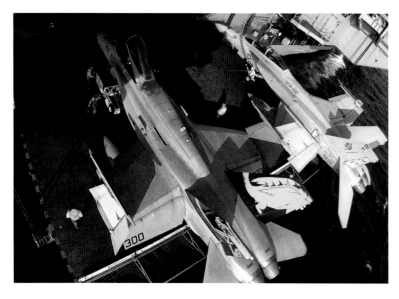

designated a Master Jet Base. VFA-106 is the East Coast fleet replenishment squadron (FRS), training new aircrew and those returning to the jet following a ground tour. Most of the West Coast's F/A-18s are based at NAS Lemoore, California, where VFA-125 'Rough Raiders' is the FRS.

Two squadrons are based abroad: VFA-115 'Eagles' and VFA-195 'Dambusters' are located at Naval Air Facility Atsugi, Japan, and both are attached to CVW-5, USS *Ronald Reagan* (CVN-76).

The USMC operates its Hornets in two distinct types of squadron: Marine Fighter Attack Squadrons (VMFAs) and Marine Fighter Attack Squadrons (All Weather) (VMFA(AW)). The squadrons are organised into Marine Aircraft Groups (MAGs) and Marine Air Wings (MAWs), and typically a wing will have a mix of VFMA and VFMA(AW) squadrons. Marine Fighter Attack Training Squadron VMFAT-101 'Sharpshooters', MAG-11, 3rd MAW, trains new naval aviators to fly the F/A-18, and is based at MCAS Miramar near San Diego in California.

The USMC's VMFA(AW) units operate the F/A-18D, which is a dedicated night-strike platform that replaced the service's A-6E Intruders. In November 1989 VMFA(AW)-121 became the first USMC unit equipped with the D model, and by 2009, six VMFA squadrons were divided into three units at Beaufort, South Carolina, and three at Miramar, each tasked with the roles of FAC(A) (forward air controller (airborne)), TAC(A) (tactical air controller (airborne)) and close air support (CAS). The

squadrons share from a pool of 18 two-seat Hornets equipped with the Advanced Tactical Airborne Reconnaissance System.

Legacy Hornet units

US Navy Atlantic Fleet

- VFA-15 'Valions' (marked for disestablishment in 2017)
- VFA-34 'Blue Blasters'
- VFA-37 'Ragin' Bulls'
- VFA-83 'Rampagers'
- VFA-87 'Golden Warriors'
- VFA-131 'Wildcats'

US Navy Pacific Fleet

- VFA-113 'Stingers'

ABOVE The US Navy Test Pilot school is one of a number of non-combat units that operate the Hornet. In this case, a USNTPS F/A-18B Hornet takes off from NAS Patuxent River. *(US Navy)*

BELOW An F/A-18C Hornet of the 'Thunderbolts', VMFA-251, launches from the waist catapult of USS *Theodore Roosevelt* (CVN 71). *(US Navy)*

ABOVE An F/A-18D(RC) Hornet at Al Asad Air Base, Iraq. The aircraft is armed with AGM-65 Maverick missiles, and is assigned to VMFA(AW)-332. *(US Navy)*

US Marine Corps
MAW-1, MAG-12, MCAS Iwakuni, Japan
■ VMFA(AW)-242 'Batman' F/A-18D

MAW-2, MAG-31, MCAS Beaufort
■ VMFA-115 'Silver Eagles' F/A-18A+
■ VMFA-122 'Crusaders' F/A-18A+/C
■ VMFA-251 'Thunderbolts' F/A-18A+/C
■ VMFA-312 'Checkerboards' F/A-18A+/C
■ VMFA(AW)-224 'Bengals' F/A-18D
■ VMFA(AW)-533 'Hawks' F/A-18D

MAW-3, MAG-11, MCAS Miramar
■ VMFA-232 'Red Devils' F/A-18C
■ VMFA-323 'Death Rattlers' F/A-18C
■ VMFA(AW)-225 'Vikings' F/A-18D(R)
■ VMFA(AW)-242 'Bats' F/A-18D
■ VMFAT-101 'Shooters' F/A-18C/D

US Marine Corps Reserve
MAW-4 (Reserve)
■ VMFA-112 'Cowboys' F/A-18A+
Fort Worth

US Navy Test
■ SN Test Pilot School, F/A-18A/B+ (NAWC Patuxent River)
■ NWTS 'Dust Devils, F/A-18A+/C/D (NAWC China Lake)
■ VX-9 'Vampires', F/A-18C/D (NAWC China Lake)

US Navy Air Reserve Force
■ VFA-204 'River Rattlers', F/A-18A+ (NAS New Orleans)
■ VFC-12 'Fighting Omars', F/A-18A+ (NAS Oceana)

BELOW AA tail codes help identify this Super Hornet as an F/A-18F belonging to the 'Red Rippers', VFA-11. The aircraft is seen catching an arresting wire with its tailhook aboard the Nimitz-class aircraft carrier USS *Dwight D. Eisenhower* (CVN 69). *(US Navy)*

Super Hornet units
US Navy Atlantic Fleet
■ VFA-11 'Red Rippers'
■ VFA-31 'Tomcatters'
■ VFA-32 'Swordsmen'
■ VFA-34 'Blue Blasters'
■ VFA-81 'Sunliners'
■ VFA-103 'Jolly Rogers'
■ VFA-105 'Gunslingers'
■ VFA-106 'Gladiators', East Coast Fleet Replacement Squadron
■ VFA-136 'Knighthawks'
■ VFA-143 'Pukin' Dogs'
■ VFA-211 'Fighting Checkmates'
■ VFA-213 'Black Lions'

US Navy Pacific Fleet
■ VFA-2 'Bounty Hunters'
■ VFA-14 'Tophatters'
■ VFA-22 'Fighting Redcocks'
■ VFA-25 'Fist of the Fleet'
■ VFA-27 'Royal Maces'
■ VFA-41 'Black Aces'
■ VFA-86 'Sidewinders'
■ VFA-94 'Mighty Shrikes'
■ VFA-97 'Warhawks'

RIGHT A plane captain signals to the pilot of an F/A-18F Super Hornet from the 'Diamondbacks' of Strike Fighter Squadron One Zero Two (VFA-102) that the aircraft is ready to fly, prior to a scheduled training mission aboard USS *John C. Stennis* (CVN 74). *(US Navy)*

BELOW A 'Fist of the Fleet', VFA-25, F/A-18E Super Hornet streaks past the USS *Harry S. Truman* (CVN 75) during a deployment to the Gulf of Oman. *(US Navy)*

BOTTOM An F/A-18E outfitted for aerial refuelling trails the hose from the A/A 42R-1 pod. The aircraft belongs to VFA-97 – the 'Warhawks'. *(US Navy)*

ABOVE Bright red markings on this F/A-18F celebrate 50 years of squadron operations for VFA-102, the 'Diamondbacks'. *(US Navy)*

BELOW An EA-18G Growler assigned to the 'Gauntlets' of VAQ-136 awaits its next sortie aboard the USS *Ronald Reagan* (CVN 76). *(US Navy)*

BELOW An F/A-18F Super Hornet assigned to Air Test and Evaluation Squadron Nine (VX-9) conducts an operational test mission over Owens Lake, Eastern High Sierra and Mojave test ranges. At the time of the photograph, the squadron was testing the APG-79 Active Electronically Scanned Array (AESA) radar. *(US Navy)*

- VFA-102 'Diamondbacks'
- VFA-115 'Eagles'
- VFA-122 'Flying Eagles', West Coast Fleet Replacement Squadron
- VFA-137 'Kestrels'
- VFA-146 'Blue Diamonds'
- VFA-147 'Argonauts'
- VFA-151 'Vigilantes'
- VFA-154 'Black Knights'
- VFA-192 'Golden Dragons'
- VFA-195 'Dambusters'

US Navy Test and Evaluation Units

- VX-9 'Vampires', Air Test and Evaluation Squadron
- VX-23 'Salty Dogs', Air Test and Evaluation Squadron
- VX-31 'Dust Devils', Air Test and Evaluation Squadron
- NSAWC (Naval Strike and Air Warfare Center)

Growler units (NAS Whidbey Island, unless otherwise stated)

- VAQ-129 Fleet Replacement Squadron
- VAQ-130 'Zappers'
- VAQ-132 'Scorpions'
- VAQ-133 'Wizards'
- VAQ-134 'Garudas' (set to become a land-based expeditionary unit in 2017)
- VAQ-135 'Thunder', expeditionary unit
- VAQ-136 'The Gauntlets' (NAS Atsugi, Japan)
- VAQ-137 'Rooks'
- VAQ-138 'Yellow Jackets', expeditionary unit
- VAQ-139 'Cougars'
- VAQ-141 'Shadowhawks' (NAS Atsugi, Japan)
- VX-9 'Vampires', Air Test and Evaluation Squadron (Naval Air Weapons Station, China Lake)
- Naval Strike and Air Warfare Center (NAS Fallon)

US Air Force (aircrew training)
Mountain Home Air Force Base, Idaho
- 390th Electronic Combat Squadron, 366th Wing

US Navy Reserve
- VAQ-209 'Star Warriors', NAS Whidbey Island.

Royal Australian Air Force (RAAF)

The Royal Australian Air Force purchased 57 F/A-18As and 18 F/A-18Bs in October 1981 to replace its fleet of Dassault Mirage IIIOs. Selection of the Hornet followed Australia's comparative assessment of the F-15A Eagle, the F-16 Falcon and the F/A-18. The F-16's single engine and the F-15's limited air-to-ground capability were to be the undoing of those two contenders, leaving the F/A-18A/B as the obvious choice.

Australia's Government Aircraft Factories assembled all but the first two of the RAAF's Hornets, with deliveries commencing in late October 1984 and continuing through to May 1990. The Mirage was finally retired in 1988, leaving the Hornet to take on the mantle of air interception, air combat, close air support of ground troops and interdiction of enemy supply lines, including anti-shipping.

Australia initially removed the Hornet's nosewheel tow bar – the strut used to lock into the deck-mounted shuttle for catapult launches – but this resulted in nosewheel shimmy during high-speed taxiing, so a mass balancer (effectively a dummy tow bar) was later fitted. Additional antipodean modifications came in the form of an ILS/VOR (Instrument Landing System/Very High-Frequency Omnidirectional Range) navigation system (replacing the carrier landing system), an HF radio, an indigenously produced fatigue data analysis system and an upgraded video and voice cockpit recording system used for mission debriefing.

According to the RAAF, of the initial purchase of 75 aircraft, 71 Hornets remained in service in January 2016. The aircraft have been put through the iterative Hornet UpGrade (HUG) programme

ABOVE **Two Royal Australian Air Force F/A-18s prepare for air refuelling from a US Air Force KC-135 (out of shot).** (US Air Force)

since 1999, enabling them to remain operationally effective until 2018,[1] at which time (in theory, at least) the Legacy Hornet will be replaced by 72[2] fifth-generation F-35A Lightning IIs.

F/A-18A/B units:

RAAF Base Williamtown

- 3 Squadron
- 77 Squadron
- 2 Operational Conversion Unit

RAAF Base Tindal

- 75 Squadron

In addition to the F/A-18A/B, Australia has purchased 24 F/A-18F Block II Super Hornets for air interception, air combat, close air support of ground troops and interdiction. The Super Hornet was purchased as a stop-gap measure until the arrival of the F-35A.

Deliveries began in 2009, and operational capability was declared in December 2012. Among the Lot Australia purchased are 12 aircraft that have received additional wiring to allow them to be reconfigured as EA-18Gs (see below).

F/A-18F units:

RAAF Base Amberley

- 1 Squadron
- 6 Squadron (operating both Super Hornet and Growler)

In late July 2015, the RAAF received the first of 12 EA-18Gs due for delivery through 2017. In doing so, Australia became the first Growler export customer. The country had been granted export approval for the EA-18G in 2008 as part of its Super Hornet order, but it ordered its first dedicated new-build Growlers in May 2013. Australia's Growlers carry the ASQ-228 ATFLIR and the AIM-9X.

EA-18G units:

RAAF Base Amberley

- 6 Squadron (operating both Super Hornet and Growler).

1   It should be noted that the dates and quantities cited here for the F-35 are those given by the RAAF (January 2016). However, public sources cite 2020 as the revised delivery date for the F-35 and 'up to 100' as the number of F-35s that will be acquired.
2   See previous footnote.

Royal Canadian Air Force (RCAF)

Canada was the first export customer for the Hornet, ordering 98 CF-188A/CF-18As (F/A-18As) and 40 CF-188B/CF-18Bs (F/A-18Bs) in 1980, with deliveries commencing in 1982 and ending in 1988. The colloquial designation for Canada's Hornets is CF-18, but the designation CF-188 is often seen in formal documentation.

The CF-18, which was selected following Canada's New Fighter Aircraft programme, would eventually replace the Lockheed/Canadair CF-104 Starfighter in the air reconnaissance and strike role and the McDonnell CF-101 Voodoo in the air interception role. It also supplemented the Northrop/Canadair CF-116/CF-5A Freedom Fighter in the ground-attack role. Reflecting the need for the Hornet to get up close and personal with the target during an air interception, Canada's Hornets feature a night identification light embedded flush with the fuselage on the left side. This huge lamp is located below and slightly ahead of the pilot and allows him to visually identify the target aircraft in low light and night-time conditions.

Canada had originally eyed the F-18L as its new fighter, but with Northrop's offering existing only on paper at that point, and with Northrop's future hanging in the balance of future contracts (specifically, it needed to sell the F-18L in greater volumes than a solitary order from Canada would provide) the RCAF's Air Command looked elsewhere. Initially it seemed likely that Canada would buy F-14s from Iran, which was under US embargo and might soon find itself unable to operate the type through lack of spares. Eventually, however, the more affordable Hornet won the day.

Once the RCAF's 410 Operational Training Unit (OTU) had enough of the type on strength, the first deliveries to operational squadrons began. These front-line aircraft arrived at Baden–Soellingen Air Base, West Germany, to equip 409, 439 and 421 Squadrons.

No fewer than 62 CF-18As and 18 CF-18Bs were recipients of the Incremental Modernization Project, completed in two

phases between 2001 and 2010. IMP was spawned by Canada's combat experiences in the Balkans in the 1990s and was intended to improve the CF-18 fleet's air-to-air and air-to-ground combat capabilities through software and hardware upgrades. It gives these 'old' Canuck Hornets parity with the newer C/D models used by other nations.

ABOVE A Royal Canadian Air Force F/A-18B 'plugs in the blower' and climbs skywards. Canada has two wings operating the Hornet. *(Royal Canadian Air Force)*

BELOW Two Royal Canadian Air Force CF-188 Hornet fighter aircraft approach a Colombian Air Force Boeing KC-767 tanker (out of shot) during Exercise Maple Flag in 2013. Note the false canopy painted beneath the forward fuselage. *(Royal Canadian Air Force)*

Canada had originally planned to replace its Hornets with 65 F-35 Lightning IIs. However, the 2015 election of a Liberal Party government may result in the cancellation of the F-35 purchase and perhaps a temporary reprieve for the CF-18.

Units:
3rd Wing, Canadian Forces Base (CFB) Bagotville
■ 425th Tactical Fighter Squadron
■ 433rd Tactical Fighter Squadron

4th Wing, CFB Cold Lake
■ 401st Tactical Fighter Squadron
■ 409th Tactical Fighter Squadron
■ 410th Tactical Fighter Operational Training Squadron.

Finnish Air Force (Suomen Ilmavoimat)

The Finnish Air Force's F-18C and F-18D Hornets are the Scandinavian country's primary tactical fighters. The small nation, which has seen an increasing number of airspace violations by a more belligerent Russia in recent years, operates the type in the air policing and defensive counter air (DCA) roles.

In 1992, the Finns ordered 64 F-18C/Ds, comprising 57 C models and 7 D models, for delivery from June 1995 onwards. The Hornet replaced the MiG-21bis and Saab 35 Draken. Finland's F-18Ds were built by McDonnell Douglas, while its F-18Cs were assembled at the Patria Finavitec plant in Finland.

Finnish Hornets are equipped with the ALQ-165 Airborne Self-Protection Jammer (ASPJ). The fleet has been upgraded by means of a multi-phase MLU programme, over half of which had been through Phase II by the summer of 2015.

The FAF deletes the 'A' prefix from the Hornet designation as a reflection of the fact that the aircraft are dedicated to air defence duties. However, the MLU has delivered a significant air-to-ground capability – with a focus on precision weapons integration – and in 2015 the Hornet became the first Finnish aircraft to drop live bombs in 70 years. Finland has also purchased the AGM-158 Joint Air-to-

Surface Stand-off Missile (JASSM). FAF Hornets carry the AAQ-28 Litening target pod on the centreline station.

The FAF claimed to have 55 C-model and 7 D-model Hornets on strength in February 2015, spread across three squadrons (each with two flights).

Units:
Lapland Air Command, Rovaniemi AB
■ Fighter Squadron 11 (Hävittäjälentolaivue 11)

Satakunta Air Command, Tampere-Pirkkala AB
■ Fighter Squadron 21 (Hävittäjälentolaivue 21)

Karelia Air Command, Kuopio-Rissala AB
■ Fighter Squadron 31 (Hävittäjälentolaivue 31)

Kuwaiti Air Force (al-Quwwat al-Jawwiya al-Kuwaitiya)

Kuwait purchased 32 KAF-18C and eight KAF-18D Hornets in 1988. The first Hornets, which would eventually replace a fleet of well-worn A-4KU Skyhawks, were delivered in October 1991 – about one year too late for the small Gulf state to use to protect itself from the dramatic aggression of neighbouring Iraq.

Kuwait's Hornets have received GPS navigation and cockpit pressurisation updates, and 27 single-seat Hornets remained in operation through 2015 (the number of two-seaters in operation is unknown).

Kuwait announced plans to purchase 28 Super Hornets, with an option for 12 more, in mid-2015. Despite this, the US export approvals process has dragged on. In February 2016, the Italian government announced that it had brokered a sale to Kuwait of the Eurofighter Typhoon, but given the fickle nature in which some nations acquire defence equipment, the deal may yet fall through.

Units:
Ahmed al Jaber Air Base
■ 9th Squadron
■ 25th Squadron.

Royal Malaysian Air Force (Tentera Udara Diraja Malaysia)

The Royal Malaysian Air Force (TUDM) operates an unusual mix of US, British and Russian hardware. The eight F/A-18Ds it purchased in 1997 operate in coordination with Sukhoi Su-30MKI Super Flankers, BAe Hawk 208s, Northrop F-5E/F Tiger IIs and Mikoyan-Gurevich MiG-29N Fulcrums.

With Malaysia currently running its Multi-Role Combat Aircraft programme to acquire a 4.5 Gen fighter to replace the MiG-29N, media reports in mid-2015 indicated that not only is Boeing actively marketing the Super Hornet to Malaysia, but that it is also offering to upgrade the country's D-model Hornets with an AESA radar.

Malaysia is expected to make a decision about which airframe it will choose in 2016. The contenders are the Eurofighter Typhoon, SAAB Gripen, Dassault Rafale and Super Hornet.

Units:
1st Division, Butterworth AFB
■ 18 Squadron.

Spanish Air Force (Ejército del Aire)

Spain acquired the Hornet following its Future Fighter Attack Aircraft programme (FACA) of the late 1970s. FACA was intended to find a replacement for Spain's Mirage III, F-5A/B and the F-4C Phantom II aircraft. It saw the evaluation of a range of options, including the F-5E/F, F-15, F-14, F-16, Panavia Tornado and Mirage 2000.

Like Canada, Spain saw potential in the F-18L, but it too was wary of placing an order for an aircraft that might never be built. Instead, Spain selected McAir's F/A-18A, originally intending to purchase 144 examples, but actually placing a reduced order for 72 examples in May 1983. The order comprised 60 EF-18A/C.15 and 12 EF-18B/CE.15 Hornets, with deliveries running from November 1985 to July 1990.

Spain's Hornets are operated as all-weather interceptors, but each of the SAF's four Hornet squadrons has a responsibility for being experts in a secondary role, whether that be maritime operations, air combat or suppression of enemy air defences.

In 1990, the fleet was upgraded to EF-18A+ and EF-18B+ standard. Spain then purchased

BELOW A Spanish Air Force F/A-18A of Ala 15, based at Zaragoza Air Base, takes off on a sortie. The difference in colour of the inside sections of the exhaust petals – one a cream colour, the other a dark grey – indicate that the port (left) engine has recently been replaced and has yet to be blackened with soot. *(Spanish Air Force)*

ABOVE With streamers condensing off the wingtips and afterburners fully engaged, this C.15 takes to the skies carrying a single Enhanced Laser-Guided Training Round. *(US Navy)*

an additional 24 ex-US Navy F/A-18As upgraded to the + configuration prior to delivery, receiving the aircraft over a four-year period from December 1995 to December 1999.

More recently, Spain has completed the far-reaching EF-18M upgrade through military contractor EADS CASA. It has also integrated the IRIS-T short-range IR missile as an alternative to the AIM-9X or AIM-132 ASRAAM used by other European and world air forces.

Units:
Madrid-Torrejon AB, 12th Wing (Ala 12), 12th Group (Groupo 12)
- 121 Squadron (121 Escuadron)
- 122 Squadron (122 Escuadron)

Zaragoza AB, 15th Wing (Ala 15)
- 151 Squadron (151 Escuadron)
- 152 Squadron (152 Escuadron)
- 153 Squadron (153 Escuadron)

Las Palmas – Grando Air Base, 46th Wing (Ala 46)
- 462 Squadron (462 Escuadron).

Swiss Air Force (Schweizer Luftwaffe/ Forces Aériennes Suisses)

With the imminent retirement of a stalwart fleet of Mirage IIIS fighter-bombers in the late 1990s, Switzerland found herself in need of a suitable air defence replacement to see her well into the 21st century.

The procurement process began in 1985 when the requirements and definition for a new fighter were created. The aircraft's role was limited to that of air defence, and the government considered the Dassault Mirage 2000 and Rafale, the Israel Aircraft Industries Lavi, Northrop F-20 and F/A-18, General Dynamics F-16 and the SAAB JAS-39 Gripen.

Switzerland settled on two finalists in May 1988: the F-16 and the F/A-18. A fly-off

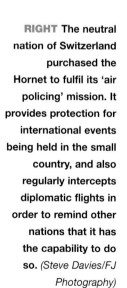

RIGHT The neutral nation of Switzerland purchased the Hornet to fulfil its 'air policing' mission. It provides protection for international events being held in the small country, and also regularly intercepts diplomatic flights in order to remind other nations that it has the capability to do so. *(Steve Davies/FJ Photography)*

competition ensued, and in October 1988 the Hornet was announced the winner. The competition was reopened in 1991 so that the Mikoyan MiG-29 and the Dassault Mirage 2000-5 could be considered, but it was to no avail and the original plan to buy 26 F/A-18Cs and 8 F/A-18Ds remained firm.

Despite plans to sign the contract with Boeing in 1992, the purchase (or, more specifically, the cost of the purchase – 3,495 million Swiss Francs) was seen by many to exceed the requirements of a neutral nation. A popular referendum was held accordingly on 6 June 1993, the outcome of which narrowly approved the purchase.

The Hornet was attractive for a number of reasons, foremost among which was the ability of the aircraft to operate from short landing strips; its excellent acceleration and climb rate capabilities, which are key statistics for interception duties; and the aircraft's excellent dual-role war fighting abilities, which would give the Swiss Air Force flexibility despite its early insistence that the Hornet would be employed strictly as an air defence fighter.

A number of changes were made to the standard F/A-18C/D to make the aircraft even better suited to its needs: the improved APG-73 radar was installed, as it promised better look-down performance; titanium reinforcement was carried out to the aircraft's dorsal spine, providing a 30-year service life (up to 5,000 hours from a fatigue life of 3,000 hours) and making the Swiss Hornet the first 9g-capable F/A-18; and an embedded GPS/Inertial Navigation System (EGI) was installed. Finally, to satisfy the need to operate the jet from wartime caverns dug into the rock of Switzerland's many mountains, a second internal battery was installed. In common with Canada, the Swiss purchased the night visual identification light.

The primary focus of the Swiss Hornet is air defence and interception, and although the aircraft retains its air-to-ground software, the Swiss Air Force does not focus on ground attack. Having opted for the F404-GE-402 Improved Performance Engines to increase interception capabilities, the Swiss also commissioned the design of low-drag AIM-120 pylons to replace the bulky ones supplied.

Specially developed to accommodate one AMRAAM or one AIM-9P-5 Sidewinder, in a typical intercept mission profile the time to climb to an altitude of 49,000ft at Mach 1.4 from release of the brakes is reduced by 25%.

Some 26 single-seat F/A-18Cs and 8 dual-seat F/A-18Ds were duly purchased from Boeing, all but two of which were shipped to Switzerland in kit form to be assembled domestically by Schweizer Flugzeuge and System AG at Emmen.[3] This pseudo-offset agreement was of little monetary value to Switzerland, but conferred a greater level of experience in working with the Hornet to a domestic aviation manufacturer.

The first F/A-18D for the Swiss Air Force (J-5231) took to the skies from St Louis, Missouri, on 20 January 1996. The first F/A-18C (J-5001) followed suit a few months later (8 April). The first Swiss-built Hornet, F/A-18D J-5232, was formally handed over to the Schweizer Luftwaffe on 23 January 1997.

No 17 Fliegerstaffel (Squadron) at Payerne became the first to acquire the Hornet in September 1997, followed soon after by fellow Payerne resident, Fliegerstaffel 18, in 1998. The final squadron to re-equip with the Hornet was 11 Squadron at Dübendorf, which relinquished its F-5E/F Tigers IIs for Hornets in November 1999. No 11 Squadron has since moved to the 'secret' mountain air base at Meiringen. In December 1999, the final F/A-18C (J-5026) was delivered.

The Swiss Air Force has completed both Upgrade 21 and Upgrade 25 programmes to extend the life of its Hornet fleet; 26 F/A-18Cs and 5 F/A-18Ds remain in service as of October 2015.

Units:
Meiringen AB
■ Fliegerstaffel 11, Air Wing 13

Payerne AB
■ Fliegerstaffel 17, Air Wing 11
■ Fliegerstaffel 18, Air Wing 14.

---

3   Public source figures on the number of Hornets purchased by Switzerland, and on the number remaining in operation vary. The acquisition figures used here are those supplied to the author by the Swiss Air Force when he visited 11 and 18 Squadrons in 2005; the current operational figures are those published by Flight Global in 2015.

Chapter Four

F/A-18 at war

The Hornet's baptism of fire came in April 1986, when pilots of VFA-132, VMFA-314 and VMFA-323 launched off the USS *Coral Sea* and flew suppression of enemy air defence sorties during America's one-off strikes against Libya. Code named Operation El Dorado Canyon (USAF) and Operation Prairie Fire (USN and USMC), the strikes were ordered by President Ronald Reagan in response to Libyan acts of terror against American civilian and military targets.

OPPOSITE The F/A-18 was designed to operate in all weathers, day or night. It is fitting then that its first combat exploits occurred in the dead of night off the coast of Libya in April 1986. In the years that have followed, the Hornet has been optimised still further for all-weather operations, day or night. *(US Navy)*

With its stinger bloodied over Libya, the Hornet would go on to establish itself as the most versatile and capable tactical naval strike fighter of all time. Since 1986, it has proceeded to fly self-escorted strike missions in the 1991 Gulf War in the hands of US Navy and RCAF pilots, has operated with distinction over the former Yugoslavia during the 1990s in yet another display of US-led multinational F/A-18 operations and has contributed to NATO- and UN-sanctioned operations over Iraq, Syria, Afghanistan and Libya once more.

Iraq, 1991

The first Gulf War – Operation Desert Storm (ODS) – commenced on 17 January 1991. The Hornet was in the thick of it from the start, with two Navy Hornet pilots scoring MiG kills while carrying out strike missions, thereby validating the multi-role capabilities of the aircraft beyond any doubt. While the conflict lasted only a few months, US Navy, US Marine Corps and Royal Canadian Air Force Hornets would fly 4,551 sorties for the loss of only two US Navy Hornets and pilots.

The US Navy deployed nine carrier-borne squadrons of Hornets (VFA-15, -81, -82, -83, -86, -87, -151, -192 and -195) to Desert Storm, and four more squadrons also participated in the defensive operation (Operation Desert Shield) that preceded the shooting war. In total, the Navy and Marine Corps deployed 190 Hornets between them (106 F/A-18A/Cs and 84 F/A-18A/C/Ds respectively). In fact, of eight aircraft carriers deployed during the conflict, only the USS *Ranger* and USS *John F. Kennedy* had air wings that did not include at least two squadrons of F/A-18s. The USS *Midway* actually embarked three squadrons.

In addition to the Hornets deployed to sea, six USMC squadrons operated from shore, flying out of Sheikh Isa, Bahrain, and committing their numerous D-model Hornets predominantly to the 'fast FAC' role. Such was the demand for forward air controllers and close air support, the Marine Corps' Hornets would go on to fly more ground-attack sorties than any other air arm involved in the war.

The RCAF, the only other operator of the Hornet to participate in ODS, deployed 24[1] CF-18s to Doha, Qatar, as part of Canada's own contribution, code named Operation Friction. CF-18s were tasked with combat air patrol (CAP) and escort missions in the early weeks of the conflict, but as Coalition ground forces

---

1   24 is the number given by the RCAF's official history. Public sources cite 26 aircraft.

advanced north in February, they were re-rolled to strike artillery and to interdict supplies and marshalling points. In all, Canada's Hornets flew 2,700 CAP missions and accumulated more than 5,700 hours of combat time.

Balkans, 1990s

For the duration of the 1990s, the United States and her allies were embroiled in a range of offensive and defensive operations over the Balkans region of central Europe. With relatively advanced threats (to include mobile SA-6 and SA-8 surface-to-air missiles and MiG-29 Fulcrums), and with poor weather and a very rugged topography, the Balkans theatre would test to the limit the Hornet's day and night, multi-role and precision-attack capability.

These operations, starting in 1993 and ending in 1999, demonstrated to the US, Canada and Spain the pressing need to modernise their Hornets. In fact, it was this set of operations that led the US to develop a broad range of GPS-guided munitions – weapons that could be employed regardless of the weather over the target.

In the summer of 1992, Hornets were among the first NATO aircraft to be deployed to the Balkans when US and allied naval forces were tasked to enforce a UN arms embargo against former elements of the Federal Socialist Republic of Yugoslavia.

By April 1993, USMC F/A-18s based at Aviano Air Base, Italy, were also involved in the enforcement of the No-Fly Zone. From June that year, Navy and Marine Corps Hornets also provided CAS for United Nations 'peacekeeping' forces on the ground, and SEAD for other NATO aircraft.

On 21 November 1994, US F/A-18s were the central protagonists in a large airstrike on Udbina airfield in Croatia, putting the military facility out of action so that Serbian aircraft could no longer stage attacks from it against Bosnian positions.

As political attempts to bring 'peace' to the region came to nothing, Operation Deliberate Force (ODF) commenced on 30 August 1995. ODF delivered a punishing series of airstrikes against Serbian military targets, starting with the belligerent nation's Integrated Air Defence System (IADS) around Sarajevo. F-14s and

ABOVE A yellow-shirt marshals an F/A-18A over the shuttle of the deck catapult. The Navy's ability to sail to a conflict zone and launch swarms of Hornets has allowed successive US administrations to enforce foreign policy the world over. *(US Navy)*

F/A-18s (VFA-15, VFA-87 and VMFA-312) from the USS *Theodore Roosevelt* attacked targets with AGM-88 HARM missiles, AGM-84 Stand-off Land-Attack Missiles and Paveway LGBs (laser-guided bombs). USS *America*'s three Hornet units – VFA-82, VFA-86 and VMFA-251 – soon replaced the *Roosevelt*. Meanwhile, shore-based F/A-18Ds of VFMA(AW)-533 (replaced by VFMA-224 from 15 September) and the Spanish Air Force's EF-18 Hornets of 12/15 Ala flew CAP, SEAD and strike missions out of Aviano Air Base, Italy.

BELOW A Royal Canadian Air Force Hornet carries GBU-12 laser-guided bombs. Canada's Hornets first stung during the Balkan conflicts of the 1990s and have regularly seen action since then. *(Royal Canadian Air Force)*

The Marine Corps' F/A-18Ds were equipped with the APG-73 radar, F404-GE-402 engines, laser designators and (from summer 1995) ALQ-165 ASPJ EW systems, making them the most advanced Hornets in theatre. Typical weapons loads included two AIM-9s, one AIM-7 or AIM-120, two GBU-12 500lb LGBs, a Mk 82 Low-Drag General-Purpose 500lb unguided bomb and a FLIR/LTD-R pod. For SEAD missions, the GBU-16 1,000lb LGB was the weapon of choice.

Marine Corps weapons systems operators (WSOs) also carried digital cameras with zoom lenses to capture images of targets, bomb damage, helicopter landing sites and other subjects of interest. Marine F/A-18Ds flew more than 100 strike missions during Operation Deliberate Force.

The Dayton Peace Accords were signed in November 1995, but the multinational contingent of Hornets joined other NATO aircraft in continuing to fly regular sorties over the Balkans to monitor Serbian compliance with the Dayton Accords. Canada's Hornets joined the monitoring effort during the months of August to November 1997 under the Canadian code name Operation Mirador.

To round off a decade of troubles in the region, the Hornet was once more called upon, delivering a pivotal contribution to Operation Allied Force (OAF) in March 1999. OAF was NATO's response to Serbian president Milošević's refusal to withdraw his ground forces from Kosovo. USMC F/A-18D units had already been rotating in and out of Aviano, maintaining a constant presence in the region, and yet more

F/A-18Ds of VMFAs-332 and 533 had deployed to Taszar Air Base, Hungary, to join the fray. Further Hornets came in the form of the F/A-18Cs that formed the backbone of the Sixth Fleet carrier air wings deployed to the Adriatic. From an international user perspective, Spain's 8 EF-18s had continued to operate from an increasingly crowded ramp at Aviano, having been joined in late June 1998 by 18 Canadian CF-18s (code named Operation Echo).

Combat operations commenced on 24 March, resulting in the Hungary-based Marine Deltas flying a total of 597 strike missions, dropping more than 303,500lb of ordnance in the process and using the ATARS recce suite in combat for the first time. Some Deltas carried unguided phosphorus rockets to execute FAC(A) and target-marking for other strikers, while others engaged hostile radar sites with AGM-88 HARMs. Meanwhile, CF-18 sorties would account for 10% of the total NATO count: 120 defensive counter air escort and 558 strike sorties, totalling 678 sorties and 2,577 combat hours. CF-18s dropped a total of 397 precision munitions and 171 unguided munitions.

Iraq No-Fly Zone operations, 1991–2003

While Saddam Hussein's forces had been roundly defeated in the 1991 Gulf War, the United Nations approved the establishment of a No-Fly Zone (NFZ) first in the northern latitudes, and later in the southern latitudes, of Iraq.

The northern NFZ was enforced initially through Operations Provide Comfort (OPC)

BELOW Two F/A-18D Hornets, assigned to the 'Knighthawks' of Marine Fighter Attack Squadron Five Three Three (VMFA-533) taxi on the flightline at Al Asad Air Base, Iraq. VMFA-533 is deployed with 1st Marine Expeditionary Force (FWD) (IMEF) in support of the global war on terrorism.
(US Navy)

and Provide Comfort II, which protected the Kurds from Iraqi aggression in the immediate aftermath of the Gulf War. Of course, OPC did nothing to stop the Turkish government from bombing the Kurds, much to the disgust of many Coalition aircrew.

In 1992, OPC was replaced by Operation Northern Watch (ONW), while the southern NFZ was enforced under Operation Southern Watch (OSW). America's commitment to ONW and OSW would last more than a decade, and the two operations would be responsible for consuming vast quantities of fatigue life among US tactical strike fighters, including the F-16, F-15E and F/A-18. Enforcement of the NFZs involved the Hornets of a number of nations, including those of Kuwait (which participated in at least one OSW deployment).

Hornets had been patrolling the NFZ of Iraq's southern border for six years when, in December 1998, they took part in Operation Desert Fox (ODF). This operation followed years of combat operations that had for the most part been limited to punitive 'response options' (ROs).

ROs were typically pre-planned and simple in nature, and they were intended to punish the Iraqi leadership's transgressions in short, sharp doses. However, when Saddam Hussein pushed the United States particularly hard, much bigger responses could follow. Thus, ODF would be a major bombing campaign that spanned a four-day period and delivered massive destruction of Iraqi military targets and the Iraqi leadership. Politically driven and designed to curb Iraq's ability to create weapons of mass destruction, it was a direct response to Saddam Hussein's refusal to cooperate with UN weapons inspectors.

Carrier Air Wing 3's (CWW-3) USS *Enterprise* (CVN-65) and Carrier Air Wing 11's (CWW-11) USS *Carl Vinson* (CVN-70) each carried two squadrons of Hornets. These aircraft would contribute to ODF by striking more than 25 air defence targets without loss.

OFD was deemed a success, but it irritated an intransigent Hussein, making him even more belligerent in the assignation of his air defence and interceptor forces to challenge the NFZs in the years to come. Following the period spanning November 2000 and January 2001, in which Coalition aircraft had been fired upon 60 times in 60 days, the America's leaders tasked CWW-3 aboard the USS *Harry S. Truman* (CVN-75) to launch a large-scale RO that involved both Hornets and Tomcats. Between them, they struck five Command, Control and Communications sites inside Iraq in February, once again without sustaining losses.

By September 2002, CWW-17 aboard the USS *George Washington* (CVN-73) had been tasked to use its three F/A-18C squadrons (VFA-34 'Blue Blasters', VFA-81 'Sunliners' and VFA-83 'Rampagers') to strike Ar-Rutbah South Air Base in Iraq, as part of another expanded RO.

At this point in time, the Navy's Super Hornets had already arrived in theatre aboard the USS *Abraham Lincoln* (CVN 72) battle group as part of Carrier Air Wing 14. They had flown the F/A-18E/F's first combat sorties in the summer, but they had to wait until 6 November actually to engage the enemy. On that date, two F/A-18Es conducted an RO strike,

ABOVE A B-52 Stratofortress flies past the USS *Nimitz* as two US Navy F/A-18 Hornets intercept. The B-52 is from the 96th Expeditionary Bomb Squadron deployed to Andersen Air Force Base, Guam. *(US Navy)*

ABOVE VMFA-121 F/A-18Ds armed with AGM-65 Mavericks could attack targets autonomously, but were widely used over Iraq as FAC(A)s, controlling other tactical strikers and orchestrating the destruction of enemy targets of opportunity. *(US Navy)*

BELOW An F/A-18D of VMFA(AW)-332 takes off on another Operation Iraqi Freedom (OIF) counter-insurgency sortie. The GBU-12 LGB was useful for striking targets in urban areas, but at 500lb it still had the potential to cause significant collateral damage. *(US Navy)*

delivering 2,000lb GBU-31 JDAMs against two SAM launchers at Al Kut, and an air defence command and control bunker at Tallil Air Base.

In all, VFA-115 made its presence felt throughout the OSW deployment, expending twice the ordnance compared to other squadrons deployed aboard the *Abraham Lincoln*, recording a hit rate of 100% (22 JDAM on 14 targets in Iraq), and exceeding all mission readiness requirements for the duration. This latter requirement is particularly crucial in combat, and thankfully the Super Hornet requires 75% fewer labour hours per flight hour than the Tomcat it replaced.

By this time, the United States was involved in operations in Afghanistan as part of its global war on terror (see the following section), and the Navy's new Super Hornet squadron was in high demand, particularly in the FAC(A) role. The Navy responded by accelerating its conversion of Hornet squadrons to what by now had been christened the 'Rhino'. The first deployment of Super Hornets in two squadrons took place in March 2003, when VFA-14 'Top Hatters' and VFA-41 'Black Aces' deployed aboard USS *Nimitz* (CVN 68). A handful of the new F/A-18Fs were mixed with their trusted F-14D Tomcats in the air refuelling and FAC(A) missions.

With the commencement of Operation Iraqi Freedom in March 2003 came the end of OSW and ONW.

Middle East, 'global war on terror', 2001 to present

While CVW-17 was attacking the Ar-Rutbah South Air Base in southern Iraq, America was leading a Coalition force in a war against Afghanistan's Taliban government. Falling under the umbrella 'global war on terror', but with the efforts in Afghanistan being referred to as Operation Enduring Freedom (OEF), US President George W. Bush had ordered his forces to neutralise the Taliban government and to shut down the Al-Qaeda network. Hornets of the Fifth Fleet were tasked to participate in this objective, and its carriers sailed east into the Arabian Sea and the Indian Ocean. Meanwhile, Australia contributed four Hornets to the tiny island of Diego Garcia for air defence – a token gesture of commitment to the cause.

Flying missions that typically lasted up to eight hours, American F/A-18 pilots initially flew combat air patrols over Pakistan, but when combat operations in Afghanistan commenced on 7 October 2001, VFA-15 'Valions' became the first Hornets to strike the Taliban. With no air threat and no air defence threat to speak of, the F/A-18s struck fixed targets associated with the Taliban's command and control apparatus, pursuing the retreating forces as they sought refuge in the mountains.

For these missions, the AAS-38 NITE Hawk pod was instrumental in locating and tracking fleeting targets under cover of darkness,

permitting the employment with pinpoint accuracy of 500lb GBU-12 laser-guided bombs. By spring 2002 the Taliban had been ousted from power and the air war was increasingly oriented around supporting ground operations by Coalition infantry, principally in the form of CAS.

Insistent that terrorism and supporters of it be rooted out the world over, America's President was soon returning his focus to Iraq and Saddam Hussein. Under the now-infamous excuse that Hussein could mobilise weapons of mass destruction against the West within 45 minutes, America and Britain vowed to remove the dictator from power.

This renewed focus on Iraq would see the Super Hornet flex to a new role – strike coordination attack reconnaissance, or SCAR. Coined in mid-2002, SCAR was closely related to the time-critical targeting work that the Super Hornet had been conducting over Afghanistan and it also related to the hunter-killer tactics that the Legacy Hornet and F-14D 'Bombcat' communities had been flying for many years.

SCAR enables all of the platforms in a given area to efficiently kill the enemy, and places the burden of responsibility on the Super Hornet crew for finding, identifying, evaluating for collateral damage and handing off targets to other strike platforms as they entered the area. It is very similar to the FAC(A) role, although it is flown only when friendly troops are not in physical contact with the enemy. The big difference between SCAR and FAC(A) missions is that SCAR platforms cannot clear other aircraft 'hot' to attack targets: they can only hand over a target and allow the other aircraft to conduct its own target and collateral damage assessments before releasing ordnance.

A number of strike fighters, including the Super Hornet, were assigned geographically defined 'kill boxes' for SCAR patrol during the March 2003 invasion of Iraq. This had the advantage of concentrating the search for targets in a specific area, and of deconflicting the ongoing activities of hundreds of Coalition fighters as they criss-crossed the Iraqi landscape in search of targets. A two-ship of Super Hornets would arrive at their kill box, usually tasked primarily with Kill Box Interdiction (KI) against fixed targets, or CAS to cover the rapid advance of the ground troops northwards. They would then patrol 30×30-mile

grids that defined a kill box. Having completed their primary mission, they would then 're-role' to SCAR against other fixed targets or targets of opportunity.

SCAR tactics can vary depending on a number of conditions, but one option taken by Super Hornet crews over Iraq was to fly at medium altitude searching for targets using the three main sensors at their disposal: ATFLIR, radar and eyeballs. Typically, before handing off targets to other fighters in the area, the crews would expend their own ordnance first. When a target was found, the No 2 aircraft was sometimes the first to release ordnance. The flight lead flew over the target and ensured that it was both hostile and that striking it would not result in civilian casualties; he would then clear No 2 – who was usually flying 3 miles in trail – to drop his laser-guided or GPS-guided weapons. This tactic had the additional advantage of reducing No 2's weapons load, allowing him to save additional fuel. This is important, as wingmen typically burn more fuel than the flight lead because they must manipulate the throttle more often to stay in formation.

Among those Super Hornet squadrons that flew such SCAR missions were the 'Valions'. The squadron had already spent four weeks flying combat missions against the Taliban, and now returned with their Hornets to the Persian Gulf aboard the *Theodore Roosevelt* in time for the 'shooting war' to begin – Operation Iraqi Freedom (OIF), on 19 March 2003.

On the evening of 19 March, VFA-25 'Fists' and VFA-113 'Stingers' aboard the *Abraham Lincoln* were tasked with first-night airstrikes that took them over Baghdad. They were to be part of a campaign that had been sold to

ABOVE A VMFA-332 pilot pre-flights an FA-18D before a combat sortie. Marine aircrew always wear a camouflage-patterned cloth over their flight helmet – while it might offer practical benefits if it survives the windblast of an ejection, the real reasons for this is to remind the Hornet crew that they are there to serve their Marine brethren on the ground. *(US Navy)*

ABOVE Royal Canadian Air Force CF-18 Hornets of 410 Tactical Fighter (Operational Training) Squadron fly alongside a 22nd Air Refuelling Wing KC-135 Stratotanker as the CF-18s each take turns taking on fuel from a multi-point refuelling system pod during exercise Amalgam Dart 15-2 over the Arctic Ocean on 29 May 2015. These pod modifications enhance the efficiency and flexibility of the Air Force's aerial refuelling fleet, enabling KC-135s to refuel NATO and US Navy aircraft. The KC-135 was from McConnell Air Force Base, Kansas, and operated by a 92nd Air Refuelling Wing crew from Fairchild AFB, Washington. *(US Air Force photo/Staff Sgt Benjamin W. Stratton)*

BELOW Photographer's Mates install the data storage unit into the Shared Reconnaissance Pod (SHARP) installed on centreline station of an F/A-18F. SHARP is capable of simultaneous airborne and ground imaging, and was designed to replace the Navy's Tactical Airborne Reconnaissance Pod System (TARPS). *(US Navy)*

the media in advance as one that would deliver shock and awe.

The F/A-18 squadrons certainly played their part in delivering both shock and awe elements. The 'Fists' sustained an average of 20 daily combat sorties, being responsible for attacking targets in Basra, An Nasiriya, Al Kut, Najaf, Al Hillah and ultimately Baghdad. They flew 272 combat sorties in 18 days, neutralising armoured divisions, military airfields, facilities and command and control infrastructures. By 15 April, the 'Valions' had employed more than 245,000lb of ordnance against Iraqi targets.

These F/A-18 squadrons were just three components of a much larger Hornet contribution to OIF, however. VFA-137 and VFA-151 on the USS *Constellation*; VFA-27, VFA-195 and VFA-192 on the USS *Kitty Hawk*; VFA-82 and VFA-86 on the USS *Enterprise*; and VFA-97 and VFA-94 on the USS *Nimitz* were also flying combat sorties in their Legacy Hornets at a frenetic pace. An international dimension came courtesy of the 14 F/A-18A/Bs of the RAAF's 75 Squadron, which operated out of Qatar as part of Australia's Operation Falconer.

With the war in full swing, US forces as a whole made extensive use of the newly arrived GBU-38 500lb Joint Direct Attack Munition – a dumb bomb with a guidance kit and control fins strapped on to it. JDAM was born from the lessons learned in the Balkans, where weather impacted the ability of laser-guided bombs, and where the ability to strike targets with pinpoint accuracy was essential. JDAM also came in the form of the GBU-32 and GBU-31 (1,000lb and 2,000lb respectively), and the Hornet and Super Hornet made use of them all. It also employed GBU-12 LGB and AGM-65 Maverick missiles, relying on these in particular when the F/A-18 community moved from flying interdiction and strike missions to providing close air support and FAC(A) to those on the ground.

The AGM-145 JSOW was also employed in limited numbers – the three Hornet squadrons aboard the *Abraham Lincoln* launched only 65, for example. Even less common was employment of the AGM-84 SLAM-ER, of which Hornets fired only three during the entire war.

Ever reliable, the Attack Delta continued to function as the USMC's workhorse, providing night attack and FAC(A) capabilities, corralling

RIGHT With dorsal speedbrake extended to reveal a star-spangled banner paint job, this F/A-18A+ of the 'Silver Eagles', VMFA-115, prepares to launch from the USS *Harry S. Truman* (CVN 75). *(US Navy)*

CENTRE A red-shirt – a weapons specialist – checks that the wing-mounted GBU-12 and wingtip-mounted AIM-9X are ready for a combat mission. Where there is no appreciable air threat, Hornets and Super Hornets have been operated over Iraq and Afghanistan without air-to-air munitions. *(US Navy)*

USAF, USN and Coalition strikers using the same kill box system as was being used in SCAR. To place them close to the action, Marine Deltas were forward-deployed to captured Iraqi airfields.

Saddam's regime had rapidly capitulated, and the 'shooting war' in Iraq was over by the end of April 2003, barely six weeks after it had started. From this point on, the F/A-18 supported US and Coalition troops as small contacts with enemy insurgents took on an increasingly urban feel.

For the 'Eagles' of VFA-115, it was not enough that they had flown 214 combat missions in support of both Operation Enduring Freedom and OSW – they were once again in the thick of it as part of OIF. On 3 April they flew the first operational flight of the Fast Tactical Imagery (FTI-II) photoreconnaissance pod, but the entire wing was largely tasked with CAS, strike, escort, SEAD and aerial refuelling.

Sharing flight deck space with VFA-115 was the small detachment of Super Hornets from VFA-14 and VFA-41, which had been forward-deployed to the USS *Abraham Lincoln* from the USS *Nimitz*. The two F/A-18Es from VFA-14 flew mostly as buddy tankers, while the two F/A-18Fs from VFA-41 operated in the

RIGHT A KC-135 Stratotanker from the Kansas Air National Guard's 190th Air Refuelling Wing prepares to refuel Navy F/A-18 Hornets over Wake Island during an escort mission from Japan to the United States. *(US Air Force photo/ Staff Sgt Ben Fulton)*

ABOVE A US Navy F-18 Hornet receives fuel from a 908th Expeditionary Air Refuelling Squadron KC-10A Extender over Afghanistan, 2 October 2009. *(USAF)*

BELOW Members of the 451st Expeditionary Logistics Readiness Squadron aerial port flight and 22nd Airlift Squadron prepare to load a US Navy F/A-18 Super Hornet fighter aircraft on to a US Air Force C-5 Galaxy cargo aircraft on Kandahar Airfield, Afghanistan, 18 August 2011. The Hornet experienced malfunctions which caused it to divert and land at Kandahar in March while supporting Operation Enduring Freedom. *(US Air Force photo/Senior Airman David Carajal)*

FAC(A) role. Meanwhile, the remainder of both squadrons waited patiently aboard the *Nimitz* as she sailed quickly to the Persian Gulf. When they arrived on station, neither squadron wasted time in getting a piece of the action.

At the point where major combat operations had been declared complete, the *Abraham Lincoln*'s F/A-18s had dropped 380,000lb of ordnance and used more than 3.5 million pounds of aviation gas in the tanker role. This wartime performance earned the 'Eagles' and the Lincoln Battle Group the Navy Unit Commendation.

As Saddam Hussein's regime crumbled, OIF quickly deteriorated into an urban war in which enemy combatants looked just like Iraqi non-combatants – the enemy was, after all, made up of fractious militia groups.

Coalition fast jets remained heavily tasked in support of troops on the ground, and the Super Hornet – of which more and more squadrons were coming online – and Hornet were no exception. Moreover, the F/A-18 community was still deploying not only to OIF, but to Afghanistan and OEF, too.

For most squadrons, this truly global application of US foreign policy meant

successive deployments to one or both theatres of operation. By way of example, VFA-14 'Top Hatters' deployed to OIF in March/April 2003, then returned in 2005 aboard USS *Ronald Reagan* (CVN-76) and racked up more than 2,100 combat sorties and over 4,300 flight hours. Likewise, VFA-154's Super Hornets (Carrier Air Wing 9, aboard USS *Carl Vinson* (CVN-70)) were engaged in OIF in April 2005 as part of their first Super Hornet cruise, and would later return to fly both OIF and OEF sorties in 2007, this time aboard USS *John C. Stennis* (CVN-74).

Navy and Marine Hornets continued to go to sea in support of OEF and OIF in 2016, although the pace and frequency of operations has slowed dramatically since the first years of both operations. In the case of OIF, that operation has almost completely wound down and, since 2009, there have been months where Coalition strikers have not dropped a single weapon in anger.

War planners need not have feared the prospect of creeping boredom, though. As the West extricated itself from Iraq and Afghanistan, it was getting ready to interfere in the running of yet another sovereign nation.

Libya, 2011

Though operations in Iraq and Afghanistan slowed towards the end of the first decade of the 21st century, in 2011 the West made it their business to support an uprising and topple the Libyan dictator, Col Muammar Gaddafi. The mission – a NATO blockade of the Libyan

government – was given the name Operation Odyssey Dawn (OOD) by the United States, but this changed to Operation Unified Protector when NATO took over responsibility for the operation. Other nations referred to the operation by their own code names (the Canadians called it Operation Mobile, for example).

In addition to an array of European and US strike aircraft, OOD also involved an international contingent of Hornets, courtesy of four Spanish EF-18Ms, seven RCAF CF-18s and US Navy Hornets and Super Hornets. These aircraft participated in imposing the NATO-enforced NFZ. The Canadian Hornets operated from Trapani-Birgi Air Force Base in western Sicily, while Spain's aircraft were stationed at Decimomannu Air Base in Sardinia.

Canada's Hornets came from 425 and 409 TFSs of Cold Lake's 4th Wing, and were named Task Force Libeccio. They flew their first escort sorties in late March 2011, eventually also operating in the interdiction role, and ended the campaign in November with a tally of 946 sorties and 696 munitions dropped, which equated to 10% of NATO strike sorties.

Meanwhile, the Spanish EF-18s of Ala 15 were noted to be flying with the AAQ-28 Litening target pod, enhancing their ability to fulfil the defensive counter air mission and enforce the NFZ. Between 19 March and 17 April, Spanish Hornets flew 45 combat air patrol missions totalling 328 combat hours.

OOD would also mark what the US Navy curiously called the combat debut of EA-18G (curious because the Growler had been

ABOVE Returning to the boat tired following a long combat sortie, it is always good to know that there is a Super Hornet airborne and ready to provide gas. This tanker-configured F/A-18F is from the 'Checkmates' of Strike Fighter Attack Squadron 211. *(US Navy)*

ABOVE An F/A-18F Super Hornet assigned to the 'Black Aces' of VFA-41 conducts a mission over the Persian Gulf. *(US Navy)*

BELOW Trapping aboard the USS *Carl Vinson* (CVN 70) following another combat sortie over Syria, an EA-18G Growler from the 'Cougars', VAQ-139, looks to catch the three-wire. The Growlers provide US and Coalition aircraft with protection from any attempted interference by Syrian air defence systems. *(US Navy)*

deployed to OIF for some time, jamming mobile phone links to IEDs). Over Libya, the G model pinpointed threat emitters and conducted communications jamming, passing off targets via data link to Coalition strikers.

Syria and Iraq, combating Islamic State, June 2014 to present

Operation Inherent Resolve is the name given to US operations against Islamic State (IS) in Iraq and Syria.

Between June 2014 and December 2015, the operation saw more than 7,800 airstrikes against some 5,000 targets in Iraq and 2,700 in Syria. Of these, Super Hornets and Hornets of the US Navy and Marine Corps have made significant contributions over four successive deployments of four carrier strike groups, each equipped with four squadrons of Hornets and Super Hornets. Marine Hornets have also operated from shore, notably VMFA-232 at Isa Air Base, Bahrain.

American Hornets have been joined by CF-18s from Canada and F/A-18As and F/A-18Fs from Australia. Operating under the code name Operation Impact, CF-18s deployed to Kuwait in September 2014 and conducted their first strike on 2 November. They had accounted for 200 strikes by November 2015 (2.5% of total Coalition strikes), and 2,038 sorties as of 17 January 2016. Canada's incoming Liberal government withdrew the CF-18s from Operation Impact on 22 February 2016.

Meanwhile, six RAAF Super Hornets were deployed to Al Minhad Air Base, UAE, under the Australian government's Operation Okra in August 2014. The F/A-18Fs were relieved by six F/A-18As of 75 Squadron in March 2015. Official figures show that between them, the Hornets and Super Hornets had flown 5,000 hours of combat and dropped 400 munitions by June 2015. By November, the F/A-18As had added another 580 sorties and 363 bombs dropped.

North American Air Defence

In the immediate aftermath of the 9/11 attacks, the United States instigated Operation Noble Eagle (ONE) – a joint operation between the US and Canada to secure airports, military facilities, infrastructure, civilian population centres, political centres and other potential targets in North America.

To protect these locations using airpower,

NORAD (North American Aid Defense Command) tasked US and Canadian fighters, including US Navy and Marine Corps F/A-18s and RCAF CF-18s, with air policing and surveillance.

While most of the c3,000 incidents that CF-18s have responded to since 14 September 2001 have been unremarkable, Canada's Hornet fleet is increasingly finding itself intercepting and escorting the more nefarious Tupolev Tu-95 Bear bomber, Ilyushin Il-20 surveillance aircraft, MiG-31 Foxhound and MiG-29 Fulcrum of the Russian Air Force out of Canadian and American airspace.

Borneo, Lahad Datu stand-off, 2013

Malaysia's F/A-18Ds made their combat debut in March 2013, when three TUDM Hornets and five BAe Hawk 208s struck a militant camp, softening it up for a Malaysian Army and Royal Malaysia Police assault. Some 235 members of the Royal Security Forces of the Sultanate of Sulu and North Borneo had occupied the camp near the town of Lahad Datu as part of an unresolved territorial claim of the Philippines over the Sabah region (formerly North Borneo).

BELOW May 2015: an F/A-18E of VFA-136 'Knighthawks' launches from the USS *Theodore Roosevelt* (CVN 71) on a sortie to hit Islamic State targets in Iraq and Syria. It is armed with GBU-38 and AGM-65 munitions. *(US Navy)*

Chapter Five

Anatomy of the F/A-18E/F Super Hornet

Weighing in at 31,000lb, the single-seat F/A-18E is larger and heavier than the 23,000lb F/A-18C. The Super Hornet's size and weight present an indication of just how different it is from its older brother, a fact that becomes even more apparent when you delve below the surface.

OPPOSITE Aviation Structural Mechanics replace tyres on an F/A-18E Super Hornet assigned to the VFA-122 'Flying Eagles' on the flight deck of USS *John C. Stennis* (CVN 74). With the battering that is an arrested landing, tyres don't last long in carrier aviation. *(US Navy)*

RIGHT The Super
Hornet is readily
identifiable from the
Legacy Hornet – just
look for the enlarged
Cobra-like leading
edge root extensions,
angular intake
geometry and enlarged
stabs, wings and flight
control surfaces.
(US Navy)

The F/A-18E/F Super Hornet is a carrier-based strike fighter aircraft. The aircraft weighs approximately 31,500lb for the F/A-18E and 32,000lb for the F/A-18F.

The aircraft is powered by two General Electric F414-GE-400 turbofan engines utilising Full Authority Digital Engine Control (FADEC – see Chapter 6). The pressurised cockpit is enclosed by an electrically operated clamshell canopy. An aircraft-mounted auxiliary power unit (APU) provides self-contained engine-start capability.

BELOW The Super
Hornet's fuselage is
littered with antennae,
blisters, air scoops
and vents. Among
these is the APU
exhaust, located on
the underside of the
fuselage between the
engines. (US Navy)

The Super Hornet features a variable camber mid-wing with leading edge extensions (LEX) mounted on each side of the fuselage. Twin vertical tails are angled outboard 20 degrees from the vertical. It was designed with relaxed static stability to increase manoeuvrability and to reduce approach and landing speed. Accordingly, it is controlled by a digital fly-by-wire flight control system (FCS) through hydraulically actuated flight control surfaces: ailerons, twin rudders, leading edge flaps, trailing edge flaps, LEX spoilers and differential stabilators. The leading edge of the wing incorporates a 'snag' (sometimes also referred to as a 'dogtooth' or 'sawtooth'), which increases outboard wing area and increases roll authority in the approach and landing configuration. Whereas the Legacy Hornet features a dorsal speed brake, the F/A-18E/F has a speed brake 'function' that is provided by differential deflection of the primary flight control surfaces.

The F/A-18F is the two-seat model of the Super Hornet and is configured with tandem cockpits. The rear cockpit can be configured with a stick, throttles and rudder pedals (trainer configuration); or with two hand controllers, a UFCD adapter and foot-operated communication switches (missionised configuration). The rear cockpit controls and displays operate independently of those in the front cockpit.

Secondary power system

The F/A-18E/F secondary power system contains two airframe-mounted accessory drives (AMAD) and a single auxiliary power unit (APU).

During normal operation, each AMAD is mechanically driven by its corresponding engine through a power transmission shaft and is used to drive the following: a fuel boost/motive flow pump, an AC/DC electrical generator, and a 3,000/5,000psi hydraulic pump. Pneumatic pressure is used to rotate an air turbine starter (ATS) on each AMAD for engine crank/start capability.

The APU is a small gas turbine engine used to generate a source of air to power the ATS for normal engine start or to provide an alternate

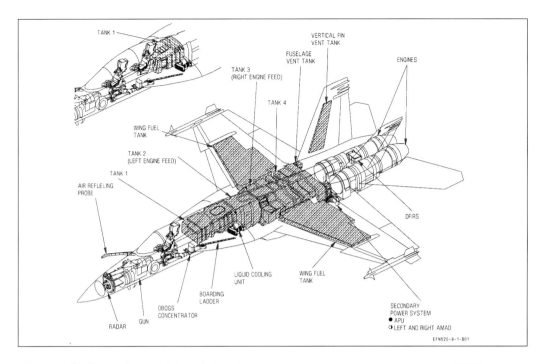

LEFT A schematic shows the Super Hornet's general arrangement, illustrating the fuselage fuel tanks (1-4) and the wing tanks, in addition to a fin tank in the right vertical stab that feeds fuel to the jettison nozzle when the latter is activated. *(US Navy)*.

BELOW An Aviation Electrician's Mate uses a multimeter to check resistance on a generator converter unit for an F/A-18 Super Hornet. *(US Navy)*

air source for the environmental control system (ECS). The APU is located between the engines, with intake and exhaust facing downwards.

A battery provides electrical power for APU ignition and start. A hydraulic motor powered by the APU accumulator is used to start the APU. The APU receives fuel from the left engine feed line upstream of the left engine feed shut-off valve. During normal operation, the APU shaft turns a separate compressor which supplies air for main engine start or alternate ECS operation.

Electrical power supply system

The electrical power supply system consists of two generators, two transformer-rectifiers (TR), one battery with dedicated battery charger and a power distribution (bus) system. The electrical system provides fault protection with generator isolation, bus tie, generator automatic reset and AC bus isolation circuitry.

Each generator provides a primary AC source and three isolated DC sources from a permanent magnet generator (PMG). During normal operation, the left generator powers only the left buses, while the right generator powers only the right buses. If one generator fails, the other generator is capable of carrying the entire electrical load of the aircraft.

Battery power is provided for normal engine start. External electrical power can be applied to power the entire system on the ground. The bus system consists of the left and right 115V AC buses, right 26V AC bus, left and right 28V DC buses, 28V DC essential bus and a 28V DC maintenance bus.

DC electrical power is provided by two TRs (transformer-rectifiers), three DC outputs from each PMG, the battery and the battery charger.

While each TR is powered by its respective 115V AC bus, the output of each TR is connected in parallel, powering both the left and right 28V DC buses and providing primary power for the essential bus. If one TR fails, the other powers the entire DC system.

The PMG in each generator provides three DC sources, two for FCC (flight control computer) channels and one for essential bus backup. The left PMG provides the primary power source for FCC A (channels 1 and 2), while the right PMG provides the primary power source for FCC B (channels 3 and 4). The PMGs come online when the engine reaches approximately 50% N2 rpm (turbine speed) on spool-up.

The primary operational use of the battery is engine start. The battery powers the maintenance bus directly, allowing operation of the canopy, ladder and maintenance monitor in the absence of AC electrical power. In the unlikely event of a total AC/DC failure in flight, the battery provides the last level of essential bus backup capability, providing about 5 to 10 minutes of power for the FCCs, after which aircraft control is lost.

Lighting

Exterior lighting highlights aircraft position and aspect to other aircraft, provides AOA indications to a landing signal officer (LSO), lights the aircraft path for in-flight refuelling, landing or taxi and distinguishes the F/A-18E/F from other F/A-18 models. The following exterior lights are

provided: strobe lights, position lights, formation lights, approach lights, refuelling probe light and landing/taxi light. Strobe lights and formation lights have two operating modes, normal and NVIS (night vision).

Hydraulic power supply system

The hydraulic power supply system is a dual pressure system (3,000 and 5,000psi) used to power and actuate primary flight control surfaces and to run the following utility hydraulic functions: landing gear, wheel brakes and anti-skid, hook, launch bar, refuelling probe, nosewheel steering (NWS), gun and parking brake. Two hydraulic

accumulators provide emergency hydraulic power for critical utility functions.

The system incorporates two independent hydraulic systems – HYD 1 and HYD 2. Each system is divided into two branches, providing four independent hydraulic circuits identified as 1A and 1B for the left system and 2A and 2B for the right system. HYD 1 circuits are dedicated solely to flight controls. HYD 2A powers flight controls as well as most utility hydraulic

ABOVE At night, the dangers of the carrier deck increase. This F/A-18E demonstrates the importance of being seen as it prepares to launch off the USS *Nimitz*. *(US Navy)*

BELOW F/A-18E Super Hornets of VFA-86 'Sidewinders' launch from the flight deck of the aircraft carrier USS *Dwight D. Eisenhower* (CVN 69). While the Super Hornet has lighting visible to the eye, it also has covert NVIS lights that are visible only through night vision devices. *(US Navy)*

RIGHT Maintainers service the hydraulic actuators on this VMFA-251 F/A-18C. The Legacy Hornet's hydraulic pumps supply fluid at 3,000psi, but the Super Hornet's dual-pressure pumps can switch to a 5,000psi mode to drive its much larger flight control surfaces against high air loads. *(US Navy)*

functions. HYD 2B powers the flight controls and arresting hook and pressurises both the APU and emergency brake accumulators.

All flight control surface actuators are powered by one HYD 1 circuit and one HYD 2 circuit, either simultaneously or through hydraulic switching valves.

BELOW The nose landing gear features a launch bar and indexer lights. The former is lowered prior to launch so that the shuttle can engage it; the latter provide the landing signals officers (LSOs) with a visual confirmation of the aircraft's angle of attack during the final phases of landing. *(US Navy)*

The utility system operates at 3,000psi only. Two pressure reducers, one on HYD 2A and one on HYD 2B, reduce utility circuit pressure to 3,000psi when pump output is 5,000psi.

Each system is pressurised by a single, dual-pressure, variable displacement pump mounted on an AMAD. Pump output pressure is commanded by the FCCs based on aircraft flight condition, with 5,000psi utilised during high-speed flight when air loads are high. One pump is capable of powering the entire flight control system in the event of a single-system failure. A hydraulic pressure transducer relays system pressure to a hydraulic pressure gauge in the cockpit. Hydraulic cautions (HYD 1A, HYD 1B, HYD 2A, HYD 2B) are set when individual hydraulic pressure switches detect circuit pressure below 1,400psi.

Hydraulic fluid is supplied to each system by a separate hydraulic reservoir. The HYD 2 reservoir is larger than the HYD 1 reservoir in order to accommodate the utility system.

The utility hydraulic functions are powered by HYD 2 and include landing gear extension and retraction, nosewheel steering, wheel braking and anti-skid, launch bar extension, arresting hook retraction and in-flight refuelling probe extension and retraction. Operation of the in-flight refuelling probe is described in the fuel system section on page 111.

Landing gear system

The landing gear is a tricycle design and includes a nose landing gear with steerable nosewheel and two fixed main landing gear. The nose landing gear retracts forward, while the main landing gear retract aft and inwards. When the landing gear is extended, all landing gear doors remain open.

Each main landing gear assembly incorporates a planing link designed to properly align the mainwheels after landing gear extension. The joint which connects the wheel to the main landing gear lever is designed to rotate off-axis, so that the wheel fits properly into the main landing gear wheelwell. The planing link rotates the main wheel from its stowed orientation, aligns it with the longitudinal axis of the aircraft and locks over-centre.

Normal landing gear extension and retraction is electrically controlled by the LDG GEAR handle and uses hydraulic pressure from HYD 2A. With weight off the nose gear and the launch bar retracted, moving the LDG GEAR handle to the UP position sends an electrical signal to the landing gear selector valves to initiate normal landing gear retraction. Likewise, moving the LDG GEAR handle to the DN position sends an electrical signal to the landing gear selector valves to initiate normal landing gear extension.

If the launch bar does not return to the up and locked position after catapult launch, or the nose gear indicates WOW (weight on wheels), the nose landing gear cannot be retracted. In either case, placing the LDG GEAR handle UP will raise the main landing gear and leave the nose landing gear extended.

Emergency landing gear extension is mechanically controlled by the LDG GEAR handle (front cockpit) or the EMERG LDG GEAR handle (rear cockpit Lots 21 to 25) and uses hydraulic pressure provided by the APU accumulator. Both handles are mechanically connected to the landing gear emergency selector valves by a series of levers and cables.

The NWS system is used to provide directional control and shimmy damping during ground operations. The NWS hydraulic power unit, attached to the nose landing gear strut, is electrically controlled by commands from the FCCs and is hydraulically actuated by pressure from HYD 2A (primary) or HYD 2B/ APU accumulator (backup). In the event of a HYD 2A failure, a pressure-biased shuttle valve routes HYD 2B pressure (if available), or APU accumulator pressure to the NWS unit for

LEFT A maintainer rests his hand against the launch bar attached to the nose landing gear. Dual tyres on the NLG help spread the load of the F/A-18's controlled crash landings aboard the carrier. *(US Navy)*

backup operation. The FCCs accept input from the rudder pedals to provide NWS commands.

The NWS system has two modes: NWS (low) and NWS HI. In the low mode (NWS cue in the HUD), full rudder-pedal deflection commands approximately 22.5 degrees of nosewheel deflection. In the high mode (NWS HI cue in the HUD), full rudder-pedal deflection commands approximately 75 degrees of nosewheel deflection. The NWS system (low gain) incorporates a yaw rate feedback input from the FCCs, which is designed to suppress directional PIO (pilot-induced oscillation) tendencies by increasing directional damping during take-off and landing roll.

The aircraft's wheel brake system provides normal braking, anti-skid, emergency braking, a parking brake and mainwheel anti-spin. Normal braking utilises HYD 2A pressure and is capable of functioning with a separate anti-skid system. The anti-skid system, when enabled, provides maximum braking effectiveness on wet runways or during heavy braking by preventing wheel skid. When selected, emergency braking utilises HYD 2B pressure, if available, or brake and APU accumulator pressure to provide backup braking capability following a HYD 2A failure. The anti-spin function stops main landing gear wheel rotation prior to landing gear retraction.

Each mainwheel brake is controlled by a separate brake pedal, integrated into the rudder/brake pedal mechanism. Pilot-applied force to the top of each brake pedal is transmitted by a series of cables and pulleys directly to the brake control hydraulic

LEFT AND CENTRE The Hornet family's main landing gear retracts inwards and rearwards and, with the aircraft weight off, hangs below the aircraft making it appear very much like the flying insect after which it is named. The rear landing gear doors close when the gear is fully lowered, but as shown in the lower image, can be opened on the ground to allow maintenance access. *(US Navy)*

servovalves, located in the nose wheelwell. The amount of hydraulic pressure applied to the wheel brakes by the servovalves is directly proportional to brake pedal force. Dual brake-pedal action provides symmetric braking, while individual brake pedal action provides differential braking. In the F/A-18F (trainer configuration), a second set of cables are routed to the servovalves from the rear cockpit brake pedals. The servovalves are controlled by the pilot applying the greatest brake pedal force.

The parking brake is used to lock the main landing gear wheels when the aircraft is parked. Backup hydraulic pressure from HYD 2B or the brake and APU accumulators is applied to the wheel brake hydraulic servovalves and routed to the mainwheel brakes through the emergency brake lines.

Arresting hook

The arresting hook is always down-loaded by a nitrogen-charged accumulator (arresting hook snubber) contained in the arresting hook retract actuator. Arresting hook extension is therefore accomplished by mechanically releasing the arresting hook uplatch mechanism (HOOK handle down) and allowing snubber pressure and gravity to extend the hook. The hook should extend in less than 2 seconds. At touchdown, the arresting hook snubber controls hook bounce and provides a hold downforce for arresting cable engagement.

LEFT Bolted to the airframe and designed to stop the Super Hornet during an arrested landing, the tailhook – also known as the arresting hook – is deployed mechanically and takes about 2 seconds to lower fully. *(US Navy)*

Arresting hook retraction is accomplished by raising the HOOK handle. This electrically opens the aft isolation valve and the arresting hook selector valve, routing HYD 2B pressure to the arresting hook retract actuator. HYD 2B pressure overcomes the snubber down-load pressure and raises the hook. The arresting hook uplatch mechanism captures and locks the hook in the up position. The hook should retract in less than 4 seconds. If HYD 2B pressure is lost, the arresting hook cannot be retracted.

Wingfold system

The aircraft's outer wing panels are designed to fold vertically to reduce the amount of deck space occupied by the aircraft in the carrier environment. Each wing contains an independent wingfold mechanism, which consists of two electric motors (one to lock/unlock the wings and one to spread/fold the wings). During normal operation, the wings are spread, locked, unlocked and folded in unison.

Each wingfold mechanism contains a

ABOVE This image showcases both the Super Hornet's wingfold mechanism, above the impressive size of the trailing edge control surfaces to good effect. *(US Navy)*

BELOW An F/A-18E Super Hornet assigned to the 'Pukin' Dogs' of VFA-143 lands on the flight deck of the aircraft carrier USS *Harry S. Truman* (CVN 75). The extended hook must grab one of the four arresting wires without skipping over them. *(US Navy)*

McDonnell Douglas F-18E Super Hornet. *(Mike Badrocke)*

1 Composite radome
2 Radome open position for access
3 Raytheon AN/APG-73 multi-mode radar scanner
4 Radome hinge
5 Scanner tracking mechanism
6 Radar mounting bulkhead
7 Active Electronically-Scanned Array (AESA) radar for future integration
8 AN/ALR low band antenna
9 Radar equipment module
10 Electro-luminescent formation lighting strip
11 Cannon barrels
12 Cannon port and blast-diffuser vents
13 Flight-refuelling probe, extended
14 Probe actuating link
15 Upper combined interrogator IFF antenna
16 M61A2 Vulcan 20mm cannon
17 Cannon ammunition drum, 570 rounds
18 Incidence transmitter
19 Lower VHF/UHF/L-band antenna
20 Pitot head
21 Gun gas vents
22 Cockpit front pressure bulkhead
23 Nosewheel door
24 Ground power socket
25 Avionics ground cooling air fan and ducting
26 Rudder pedals
27 Instrument panel, full-colour multi-function CRT displays
28 Instrument panel shroud
29 Frameless windscreen panel
30 Head-up Display (HUD)
31 Upward-hinging cockpit canopy
32 Martin-Baker NACES zero-zero ejection seat
33 Starboard side console panel
34 Control column, digital fly-by-wire flight control system
35 Port side console with engine throttle levers, full HOTAS controls
36 Sloping seat-mounting bulkhead
37 Boarding step
38 Forward fuselage lateral equipment bays, 3 per side
39 Nosewheel leg pivot mounting
40 Landing light
41 Deck approach signal lights
42 Nosewheel steering unit
43 Catapult strop link
44 Twin nosewheels, forward retracting
45 Torque scissor links incorporating holdback fitting
46 Folding boarding ladder
47 Nosewheel retraction jack
48 AN/ALQ-165 EW transmitting antenna
49 Boarding ladder stowage
50 LEX equipment bay
51 Cockpit rear pressure bulkhead
52 Cockpit avionics equipment bay
53 Canopy rotary actuator
54 Starboard AN/ALQ transmitting antenna
55 Canopy actuating strut
56 Canopy hinge point
57 No 1 fuselage bag-type fuel tank
58 Sloping bulkhead, structural provision for two-seat F-18F
59 EW receiver
60 LEX rib structure

61 Port leading edge extension (LEX) chine member
62 480 US-gal external fuel tank, centreline refuelling store as alternative
63 Port position light
64 Liquid cooling system equipment, reservoir, heat-exchanger and ground running fan
65 Forward slinging point
66 Forward tank bay access panel
67 Starboard position light
68 Starboard LEX avionics equipment bay
69 Spoiler panel
70 LEX vent, operates in conjunction with leading edge flap (initial production aircraft only)
71 Intake boundary layer spill duct
72 GPS antenna
73 No 2 tank bay access panel
74 No 2 bag-type fuel tank
75 Port spoiler
76 Spoiler hydraulic actuator
77 Boundary layer bleed-air ducts
78 Bleed-air spill duct
79 Port LEX vent
80 Perforated intake wall bleed air spill duct
81 Port 'Caret-type' fixed geometry air intake
82 Mainwheel leg door
83 Main undercarriage leg strut
84 Trailing axle suspension
85 Port mainwheel
86 Shock absorber strut
87 Mainwheel door
88 LAU-116 missile carrier/launch unit
89 Mainwheel leg pivot mounting
90 Hydraulic retraction jack
91 Intake duct framing
92 Wing panel attachment joints
93 Machined titanium fuselage main bulkheads
94 No 3 bag-type fuel tank
95 No 4 bag-type fuel tank
96 No 3 tank access panel
97 IFF antenna
98 Dorsal fairing access panels
99 Upper VHF/UHF/L-band antenna
100 Starboard wing panel bolted attachment joints
101 Starboard wing integral fuel tank
102 Leading edge flap hydraulic drive unit and rotary actuator
103 Wing carbon-fibre composite (CFC) skin paneling
104 Starboard stores pylons, wing pylons canted 4deg inboard
105 Leading edge dog-tooth
106 Wing-fold hinge fairing porous panel
107 Outboard leading edge flap rotary actuator
108 Two-segment leading edge flap
109 Outer wing panel dry bay
110 Wingtip position light
111 Formation light fairing
112 Wingtip missile installation
113 Starboard outer wing panel folded position
114 Drooping aileron
115 Aileron hydraulic actuator
116 Wing-fold hydraulic jack
117 Aileron and flap opposed movement as airbrake function
118 Starboard single-slotted trailing edge flap
119 Hinged flap shroud
120 Flap hydraulic actuator
121 Dorsal equipment bay

122 No 4 tank bay access panel
123 Ram-air from intake duct to ECS
124 Rear fuselage slinging points
125 Environment control system (ECS) equipment bay
126 ECS hinged auxiliary intake doors
127 Fuselage fuel vent tanks, port and starboard
128 Primary (starboard) and secondary (port) heat exchangers
129 Heat exchanger exhaust ducts
130 Engine pressure balance vent
131 Starboard fin bolted attachment joints
132 Fin integral vent tank
133 Multi-spar fin structure
134 Leading edge structure, CFC skin with honeycomb core
135 Fin CFC skin paneling
136 CFC fin tip fairing
137 Rear position light
138 Aft AM/ALQ-165 receiving antenna
139 AN/ALR-67 RWR antenna
140 Fuel jettison
141 Starboard rudder, CFC skin with honeycomb core structure
142 Rudder hydraulic actuator
143 Starboard engine bay
144 Rear engine mounting support structure
145 Starboard all-moving tailplane
146 Flight data recorder
147 Fin formation lighting strip
148 Fuel venting ram-air intake
149 Anti-collision beacon
150 AN/ALQ-165 high and low band transmitting antennae
151 Port AN/ALR-67 RWR antenna
152 Fuel jettison
153 Port rudder
154 Rudders move in opposing directions as airbrake function
155 Variable area afterburner exhaust nozzles
156 Nozzle sealing flaps
157 Engine bay vent, above and below
158 Afterburner nozzle 'fueldraulic' actuator (3)
159 Afterburner duct

160 AN/QALE-50 Towed Radar Decoy (TRD), three in ventral stowage, AN/ALE-55 for future integration
161 Port all-moving tailplane
162 CFC tailplane skin panel on aluminium honeycomb substrate
163 Tailplane pivot support structure
164 Pivot mounting
165 Tailplane hinge arm
166 Tailplane hydraulic actuator
167 Fin root attachment joints ,
168 Rear fuselage formation lighting strip
169 General Electric F414-GE-400 afterburning low-bypass turbofan engine
170 Main engine mounting
171 Full Authority Digital Engine Controller (FADEC)
172 Deck arrester hook
173 Engine accessory equipment
174 Engine oil tank
175 Engine bay venting ram air intake
176 Compressor intake
177 Airframe-mounted accessory equipment gearbox, port and starboard, shaft-driven from engine
178 Generator

179 Stationary intake duct-mounted compressor radar-return shielding device
180 Trailing edge flap root fairing
181 Central Auxiliary Power Unit (APU)
182 Port mainwheel, stowed position
183 Wing root attachment fittings
184 Port flap hydraulic actuator
185 Inboard flap hinge
186 Flap CFC rib and skin structure
187 Port hinged flap shroud
188 Wing panel multi-spar structure
189 Port wing integral fuel tank, fire suppressant foam filled
190 Inboard 'wet' pylon hard points
191 Leading edge flap rotary actuator
192 Hydraulic flap drive unit and torque shaft

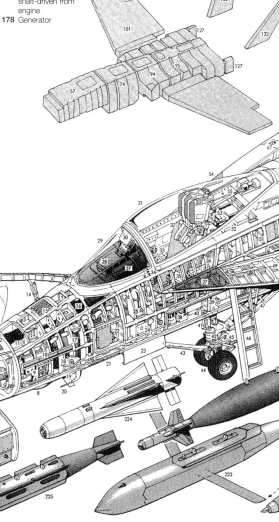

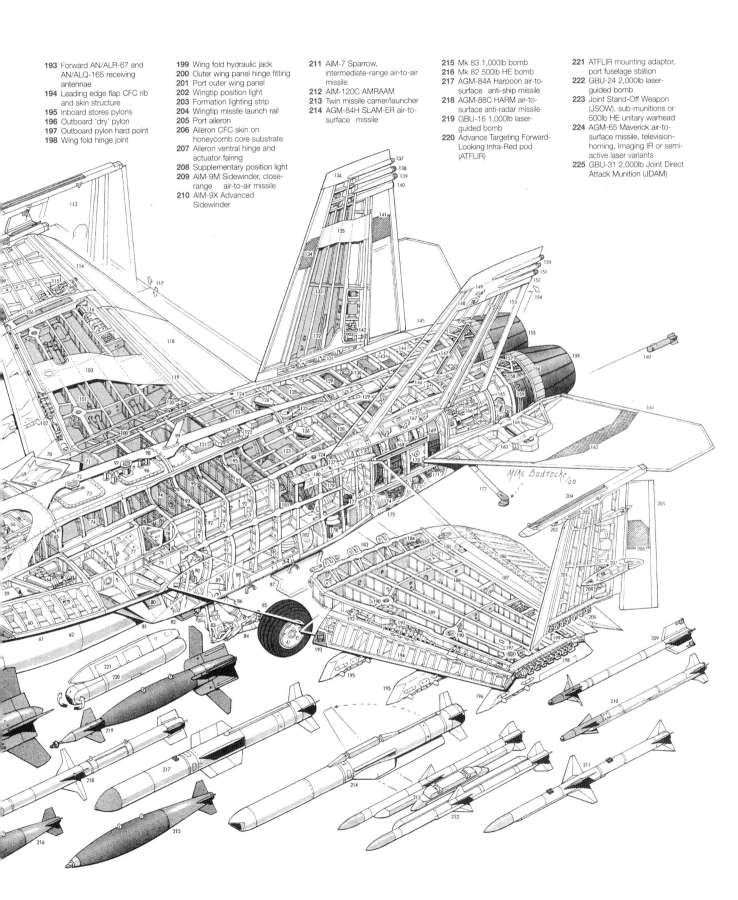

193 Forward AN/ALR-67 and AN/ALQ-165 receiving antennae
194 Leading edge flap CFC rib and skin structure
195 Inboard stores pylons
196 Outboard 'dry' pylon
197 Outboard pylon hard point
198 Wing fold hinge joint

199 Wing fold hydraulic jack
200 Outer wing panel hinge fitting
201 Port outer wing panel
202 Wingtip position light
203 Formation lighting strip
204 Wingtip missile launch rail
205 Port aileron
206 Aileron CFC skin on honeycomb core substrate
207 Aileron ventral hinge and actuator fairing
208 Supplementary position light
209 AIM-9M Sidewinder, close-range   air-to-air missile
210 AIM-9X Advanced Sidewinder

211 AIM-7 Sparrow, intermediate-range air-to-air missile
212 AIM-120C AMRAAM
213 Twin missile carrier/launcher
214 AGM-84H SLAM-ER air-to-surface   missile

215 Mk 83 1,000lb bomb
216 Mk 82 500lb HE bomb
217 AGM-84A Harpoon air-to-surface anti-ship missile
218 AGM-88C HARM air-to-surface anti-radar missile
219 GBU-16 1,000lb laser-guided bomb
220 Advance Targeting Forward-Looking Infra-Red pod (ATFLIR)

221 ATFLIR mounting adaptor, port fuselage station
222 GBU-24 2,000lb laser-guided bomb
223 Joint Stand-Off Weapon (JSOW), sub-munitions or 500lb HE unitary warhead
224 AGM-65 Maverick air-to-surface missile, television-homing, Imaging IR or semi-active laser variants
225 GBU-31 2,000lb Joint Direct Attack Munition (JDAM)

ABOVE AND ABOVE RIGHT The F/A-18 wingfold mechanism features a DC electric motor and an AC electric drive unit that spreads and folds the wings. The system saves valuable deck and hangar space while at sea. *(US Navy)*

BELOW The flight control system functional diagram illustrates the interaction between flight controls, pilot controls and FCC components. *(US Navy)*

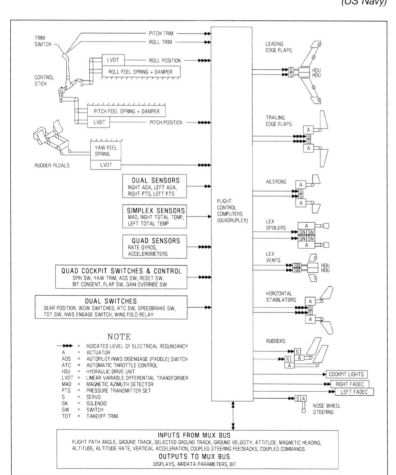

DC electric motor, which locks and unlocks the wings, and an AC electric drive unit, which spreads and folds the wings. When the wings are spread and locked, a locking bolt is electrically driven through the wingfold hinge, holding it in place. When the wings are unlocked, a wing unlock flag (commonly called a 'beer can') protrudes from the upper surface of the wing near the leading edge of the wingfold hinge, indicating that the locking bolt is unstowed. The shaft of each beer can is painted red for easy identification. When the wings are locked, the top of the beer can should be flush or near-flush with the upper surface of the wing, and no red should be showing.

Additionally, when the wings are folded, the ailerons are mechanically locked in the faired position by a hook on the inboard aileron hinge, which engages an aileron locking pin. The aileron locking pin is mechanically extended as the wings fold. The hook and locking pin are designed to prevent the ailerons from blowing inboard over the trailing edge flaps (TEFs) when hydraulic power is not applied. If an aileron locking pin should break, it is possible for the aileron to blow inward over the TEF. If this condition exists during engine start, the TEF will retract into the aileron, damaging both surfaces.

Flight control system

The flight control system (FCS) is a fly-by-wire, full-authority control augmentation system (CAS). The FCS provides four basic functions: aircraft stability, aircraft control, departure resistance and structural loads management.

Because the basic airframe is statically neutral to slightly unstable, a primary function of the FCS is to maintain aircraft stability at all flight conditions. The FCS also provides full authority control of the aircraft by implementing the basic flight control laws which determine aircraft response to pilot inputs. Pilot inputs from the stick and rudder pedals send electrical commands to two quad-redundant, digital flight control computers: FCC A and FCC B.

There is no mechanical linkage between the stick and rudder pedals and the flight control surfaces. FCC software determines what commands are sent to the various flight control surfaces to exercise pitch, roll and yaw control of the aircraft. Additionally, the FCS provides departure resistance by either refusing to accept or by tailoring pilot inputs that would otherwise lead to an aircraft departure. Lastly, the FCS provides structural loads management by limiting g-available to prevent an aircraft overstress or by retracting flight control surfaces at airspeeds that would otherwise exceed the structural limits of the airframe.

The aircraft has 12 primary flight control surfaces, consisting of two sets (one on each side) of leading edge flaps (LEFs), trailing edge flaps (TEFs), ailerons, twin rudders, horizontal stabilators and spoilers. LEFs, TEFs, ailerons and stabilators can be moved either symmetrically or differentially for pitch and roll control.

Pitch control is accomplished with symmetric stabilators and, in some conditions, with rudder toe-in or rudder flare. Roll control is accomplished with combinations of ailerons, differential stabilators, differential LEFs and differential TEFs, dependent on flight condition and CAS operating mode. The twin rudders deflect symmetrically for directional control. There is no dedicated speedbrake surface. Instead, a 'speedbrake function' is provided by partial deflection of several of the primary flight control surfaces.

Hydraulic power to all flight control surface actuators is supplied by HYD 1 and HYD 2. Stabilator and TEF actuators are powered simultaneously by one HYD circuit from each system. All other actuators are powered by a single primary HYD circuit, with backup hydraulic power available through a hydromechanical switching valve. See the section on the hydraulic system, and more

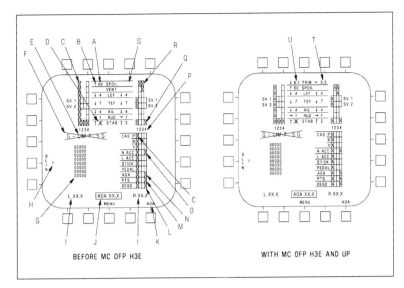

BEFORE MC OFP H3E

WITH MC OFP H3E AND UP

specifically the Hydraulic Flow Diagram, to determine which HYD circuits power each flight control surface actuator.

The spoilers are mounted on top of the fuselage near the aft end of the LEX. The spoilers are controlled by the FCCs and have two fixed positions: 0 degrees (down) or 60 degrees TEU (trailing edge up). The 60-degree TEU position is activated by the speedbrake function or when more than 15 degrees TED (trailing edge down) stabilator is commanded (forward stick) above 22 degrees AOA to aid in recovery from high AOA.

FCC A and FCC B provide the computations which implement the aircraft's flight control laws. A four-channel architecture is used to provide FCS redundancy. Each FCC contains two individual central processing units (CPUs), which each run one channel of the FCS. CH 1 and CH 2 are resident in FCC A, with CH 3 and CH 4 in FCC B.

Most inputs to the FCCs (rate gyros, accelerometers, air data sensors, stick and rudder pedal position sensors) are quad-redundant, with one input for each channel. Each of the four CPUs runs independent and parallel flight control computations. Sensor inputs as well as CPU outputs are continuously monitored by the FCCs for agreement. When there is disagreement, the erroneous signal is discarded, if possible.

Rate and acceleration data are provided by two independent Attitude and Heading Reference Sets (AHRS), one for each FCC. Each AHRS has two sets of ring laser rate gyros and two sets of accelerometers, which provide

ABOVE The FCS fault page is usually called up on the right display during take-off and landing. It provides the pilot with a simple matrix that gives, at a glance, a very tidy indication of how well the F/A-18's AFCS is behaving. (US Navy)

four independent sources of pitch, roll and yaw rate information, and four independent sources of normal and lateral acceleration.

The physical rate and acceleration sensors in each AHRS channel are not aligned with the aircraft's pitch, roll and yaw axis. This raw sensor data is converted to the aircraft's pitch, roll and yaw axis by microprocessors internal to each AHRS. As a result of this architecture, a single-rate gyro failure in one channel results in all three axis rates being unusable in that same channel. Similarly, if any of the accelerometers fail, all acceleration data from that AHRS channel is unusable.

FCC channel outputs are transmitted to the appropriate flight control actuators and to other aircraft systems such as the MCs (mission computers). While FCC computations run in all four channels, all flight control actuators are not commanded in all four channels. The stabilators and TEF actuators do receive command signals from all four FCC channels. However, each aileron, rudder, spoiler and LEF actuator only receives command signals from two FCC channels – one from FCC A and one from FCC B. The two-channel actuators on the left side of the aircraft receive inputs from CH 1 and CH 4, while the two-channel actuators on the right side receive inputs from CH 2 and CH 3.

Hydraulic redundancy is provided by distributing flight control actuators among the four HYD circuits. This arrangement minimises the probability of losing multiple actuators due to catastrophic damage to any single actuator or its hydraulic lines. Following a single HYD system failure, the other HYD system is capable of powering the entire FCS. Loss of HYD 1 or HYD 2 in 'up and away' flight (UA) does not affect aircraft control. However, in the take-off and landing configuration, small but controllable roll and/or yaw excursions may be expected as hydraulic switching valves cycle to their backup circuits.

The primary electrical power source for each FCC channel is a dedicated output from one of the two PMGs. Should a power interruption occur to any single FCC channel, the FCC power supply automatically switches to a 'keep alive' circuit connected directly to the maintenance bus for 7 to 10 seconds. This ensures that the FCCs have uninterrupted power to maintain full operation during all predictable electrical bus switching transients.

For survivability, wiring for one channel from each computer is routed through the upper part of the aircraft with wiring for the other through the lower part of the aircraft. This routing minimises the possibility of loss of any one flight control surface due to system failures or battle damage. If a stabilator actuator fails due to multiple FCS or hydraulic failures, the FCS automatically reconfigures to maintain three-axis control and acceptable handling qualities by using the remaining surfaces. There is no mechanical FCS reversion mode.

Control augmentation system

The control augmentation system (CAS) operates in two basic modes: Powered Approach (PA) and Up-AUTO (UA). Mode selection is controlled by FLAP switch position and airspeed.

With the FLAP switch in HALF or FULL and with airspeed below approximately 240 KCAS, CAS implements flight control laws tailored for the take-off and landing configuration (PA). With the FLAP switch in AUTO, CAS implements flight control laws tailored for 'up and away' flight. If the FLAP switch is left in HALF or FULL, the aircraft automatically transitions from PA to UA when airspeed increases above approximately 240 KCAS. The flight control laws utilised in each mode are tailored to provide maximum manoeuvrability while maintaining predictable handling qualities and departure resistance.

Pitch CAS (P CAS) utilises normal acceleration, pitch rate and AOA feedback, each scheduled based on aircraft flight conditions, to tailor aircraft response to pilot stick inputs and to provide stabilator actuator commands. P CAS operates by comparing aircraft response to the pilot's longitudinal stick input, driving the stabilator actuators symmetrically until the difference is reduced to zero.

In UA, with neutral longitudinal stick, comparing pilot input to aircraft response has the effect of constantly trimming the aircraft to steady-state, hands-off 1g flight, essentially removing the requirement for manual trim. In manoeuvring flight, P CAS modifies aircraft response to stick inputs, creating the effect of changing stick forces to provide pilot cueing, but actual stick forces for a given stick displacement do not change with flight condition. At high airspeeds, P CAS is a g-command system requiring 3.5lb of stick-force-per-g. At medium airspeeds, P CAS acts as a hybrid pitch rate and g-command system. Pitch rate feedback is used to increase apparent stick-force-per-g (heavier stick forces) to cue the pilot that airspeed is decreasing and less g is available. At low airspeed, P CAS is primarily an AOA command system using AOA feedback above 22 degrees AOA to provide increasing stick forces with increasing AOA. With large forward stick inputs, P CAS augments nose-down pitch rates by flaring the rudders and raising the spoilers.

In PA, AOA and pitch rate feedbacks are used to augment inherent airframe pitch damping and stability. P CAS nulls the difference between the commanded AOA and actual AOA. With neutral longitudinal stick, P CAS maintains trim AOA. Unlike UA, pitch trim is required in PA to trim the aircraft on-speed. Rudder toe-in is used to improve longitudinal stability and to aid aircraft rotation during take-off or bolter. Rudder toe-in is a function of AOA. At 0 degrees AOA or with WOW, the rudders are toed-in 40 degrees. Rudder toe-in decreases linearly to 0 degrees of toe at 12 degrees AOA. Additional AOA feedback is provided above 12 degrees AOA which increases stick forces with increasing AOA to provide stall warning. Pitch rate feedback helps maintain tight pitch attitude control during turns.

Roll CAS (R CAS) schedules aileron, differential LEF, differential TEF and differential stabilator commands in response to lateral stick inputs to achieve the desired roll characteristics. Roll rate feedback, scheduled based on aircraft flight conditions, is used to augment inherent airframe roll damping. Differential LEFs and TEFs are only used in UA. The LEFs deflect differentially up to 5 degrees when below 25,000ft and above Mach 0.6. Differential TEFs are not used above 10 degrees AOA or below -5 degrees AOA. At high airspeeds, aileron, differential stabilator and differential TEF travel are reduced to provide consistent roll rate response and to aid in preventing structural load exceedances. At low airspeeds, aileron and differential stabilator travel are reduced with increasing AOA to minimise adverse yaw. Differential stabilator may also be limited due to pitch commands which have priority over lateral commands.

With clean wing or air-to-air (A/A) missile loadings (no wing tanks), maximum roll rate is limited to approximately 225 degrees per second. With A/G store or external fuel tank

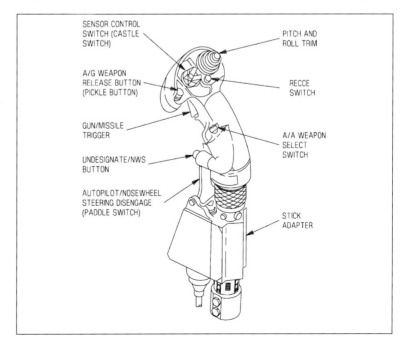

SENSOR CONTROL SWITCH (CASTLE SWITCH)

PITCH AND ROLL TRIM

A/G WEAPON RELEASE BUTTON (PICKLE BUTTON)

RECCE SWITCH

GUN/MISSILE TRIGGER

A/A WEAPON SELECT SWITCH

UNDESIGNATE/NWS BUTTON

AUTOPILOT/NOSEWHEEL STEERING DISENGAGE (PADDLE SWITCH)

STICK ADAPTER

codes set in the armament computer for any wing station and the pylon rack hooks closed for those stations, maximum roll rate is limited to approximately 150 degrees per second to avoid exceeding pylon structural load limits.

R CAS incorporates two features to reduce pitch–roll inertial coupling-induced departures. Based on pitch rate and Mach number, the first feature reduces the roll command when the pilot applies an excessive combined lateral/ longitudinal stick input. The second feature limits the roll command when the aircraft is already rolling and longitudinal stick is moved rapidly. This second feature is removed at low altitude and high speed since available pitch rate does not result in significant pitch–roll inertial coupling.

Yaw CAS (Y CAS) uses yaw rate and lateral acceleration feedback to provide directional axis damping and to augment pilot commands to the twin rudder actuators. A rolling-surface-to-rudder interconnect (RSRI) adjusted by roll-rate-to-rudder cross-feed (scheduled with AOA), and lateral acceleration feedback are used to minimise sideslip for roll coordination. To provide departure resistance and enhanced manoeuvrability at high AOA, directional stability is augmented utilising inertial navigation system (INS) pitch-and-roll attitudes along with the FCS sensors to synthesise sideslip and sideslip rate feedback to the ailerons and differential stabilators. These lateral surfaces are used in this sense as directional controllers by taking advantage of the strong yawing moments they produce at high AOA.

Below 13 degrees AOA, rudder pedal deflections provide yaw by symmetric rudder deflection. At 25 degrees AOA and above, rudder pedal deflections no longer provide yaw control inputs but instead act entirely as a roll controller (identical to lateral stick input) by commanding aileron and differential stabilator with the RSRI commanding the required rudder deflection for roll coordination. Rudder pedal inputs are summed with lateral stick inputs and this combined input is limited to a value equal to a maximum lateral stick input. Therefore, applying pedal opposite to lateral stick cancels lateral stick inputs proportional to the pedal input, i.e., full opposite pedal cancels a full lateral stick command resulting in zero roll rate. Between 13 degrees and 25 degrees AOA, rudder pedal deflection gradually changes

from pure yaw control to pure roll control. This method of control provides enhanced departure resistance at high AOA.

Some traditional directional control capability is returned at low airspeed and high AOA only when the pilot applies lateral stick and rudder in the same direction. This feature starts becoming effective only at airspeeds below approximately 225 KCAS, from 20 degrees to 40 degrees AOA, but is most effective at approximately 170 KCAS and 34 degrees AOA. Enabling this feature outside these conditions would compromise departure resistance. When this feature is enabled, the sum of lateral stick and rudder pedal command is no longer limited to a value equal to a full lateral stick input. The excess roll command is fed to the directional axis to command sideslip. For example, adding full rudder pedal with a full lateral stick input provides a maximum roll and yaw command. Alternatively, adding lateral stick to an existing full rudder pedal input has the same effect. The resulting aircraft motion is a highly controllable nose-high to nose-low reversal.

At high airspeeds, symmetric rudder deflection is reduced and the rudders are toed-in to avoid exceeding vertical tail structural limits.

In PA mode, synthesised sideslip rate feedback augments aerodynamic directional damping and stability.

The aircraft was designed to sustain a limit-g of +7.5g or -3.0g (symmetric) only at or below its fighter design gross weight of 42,097lb. At higher gross weights, design limit-g is reduced to keep from exceeding the structural limitations of the airframe. An 'overstress' is defined as a g-level that exceeds the design limit-g at the aircraft's current gross weight. Above 42,097lb gross weight, design limit-g is reduced by the aircraft's relative gross weight (42,097/GW), such that the positive design limit is +7.5g* (42,097/GW) and the negative design limit is -0.4* (positive limit-g). At the aircraft's maximum gross weight (66,000lb), design limit-g is only +4.8g or -1.9g.

Due to the increased airframe and pylon loads that accompany high-g rolling manoeuvres, the aircraft also has a design limit-g for abrupt full-stick rolls (FSR). Abrupt FSRs are defined as full lateral stick in less than 1 second. The positive design FSR limit is +6.0g below 42,097lb GW and 80% of the symmetric design limit-g above 42,097lb. The negative design FSR limit is -1.0g at all gross weights. At 66,000lb GW, the positive design FSR limit is only +3.8g. Roll rate limiting is enabled in R CAS when external wing tanks or A/G stores are mounted on wing pylons.

The g-limiter limits the amount of positive and negative g that can be commanded by the pilot at a particular gross weight in order to prevent an aircraft overstress. Once the pilot reaches the stick displacement required to attain the g-limit, further stick inputs do not increase g. During abrupt longitudinal stick inputs, g-limiter overshoots are not uncommon. G-limiter overshoots of up to +0.5g or -0.2g are allowed and do not constitute an over-g.

Due to the aerodynamic phenomenon known as transonic pitch-up, the g-limiter incorporates a g-bucket designed to prevent an aircraft positive over-g during transonic deceleration. In the g-bucket, the g-limiter reduces the positive command g-limit.

A g-limiter override feature can be enabled to allow a 33% increase in the command g-limit for emergency use (allows a 10g command). G-limiter override is selected by momentarily pressing the paddle switch when the stick is near the full aft limit. Override is disengaged when the stick is returned to near the neutral position.

Flight controls

A traditional centre-mounted control stick is used to provide pitch-and-roll inputs to the FCS. Since there is no mechanical linkage between the stick and the FCCs or the flight

THIS PAGE Designed with **HOTAS** – hand on throttle and stick – from the outset, the Hornet boasted one of the best pilot–vehicle interfaces of any contemporary fighter. The Super Hornet continued the tradition, delivering an exceptional man–machine interface for both the pilot and the WSO. In the front seat, the pilot interacts with the F/A-18's weapons systems and sensors using throttle- and stick-mounted switches. In the back seat, the WSO uses side-mounted hand controllers (these are fixed, so do not move), the design of which has evolved over the course of the Super Hornet's development. *(US Navy)*

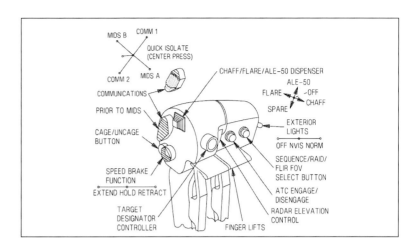

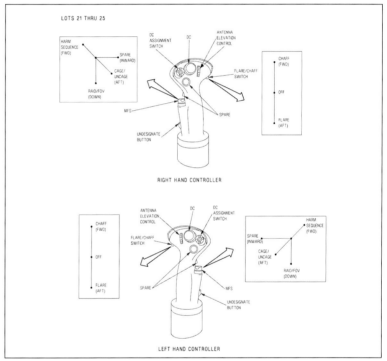

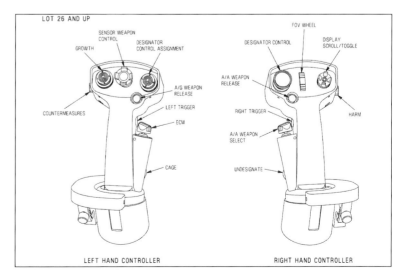

control surfaces, stick feel is provided by two feel-spring assemblies and two eddy current dampers. The feel spring assemblies provide a linear stick force versus stick displacement gradient in each axis. Two four-channel position sensors, one in each axis, measure stick displacement and send longitudinal and lateral stick commands to the FCCs proportional to stick displacement. The eddy current dampers provide stick motion damping in each axis. Additionally, the control stick is mass balanced to minimise longitudinal stick movement resulting from accelerations normally experienced during catapult launch.

In the F/A-18F (trainer configuration), a control stick is also fitted in the rear cockpit and is mechanically linked to the one in the front cockpit.

Two rudder pedals (left and right) are used to provide directional inputs to the FCS for yaw/roll control inflight or NWS control with WOW. Since there is no mechanical linkage between the rudder pedals and the FCCs or the flight control surfaces, rudder pedal feel is provided by two feel-spring assemblies. The feel-spring assemblies provide a linear pedal force versus displacement gradient. Two four-channel position sensors, one on each pedal, measure pedal displacement and send directional commands to the FCCs proportional to pedal displacement. The rudder pedals are also used to provide NWS commands and to actuate toe-operated wheel brakes.

In the F/A-18F (trainer configuration), two rudder pedals are also fitted in the rear cockpit but are not mechanically linked to the rudder pedals in the front cockpit. Pedal inputs from either cockpit are summed together and transmitted to the FCCs. A half pedal input from the front cockpit and a half pedal input from the rear cockpit results in a full rudder pedal command to the FCCs. Similarly, opposing rudder pedal inputs in each cockpit cancel each other out.

Spin recovery system

The Super Hornet incorporates an automatic spin detection and recovery system. A spin is declared when both of the following conditions are met: 1) airspeed is below approximately 120 ±15 KCAS and 2) the yaw rate threshold is exceeded. The yaw rate threshold is exceeded, for example, if a 15–20 degrees per second yaw

rate persists for approximately 15 seconds or a 50–60 degrees per second yaw rate persists for approximately 2 seconds. In cases where the pilot is intentionally commanding a high AOA roll (e.g. performing a pirouette) the yaw rate threshold persistence is increased from 15 seconds to 25 seconds.

Immediately following a low-speed manoeuvre less than 77 KCAS (a tail slide, for example), airspeed limits for SPIN logic are opened to 180 KCAS or 12 seconds, whichever comes first. During this time, the normal acceleration feedback gain is removed to avoid excess coupling, and spin mode arrows will be displayed to aid recovery if yaw rate exceeds the threshold.

Once a spin has been detected, the spin recovery system places the SPIN MODE recovery displays on both DDIs (digital display indicators), illuminates the amber FLAPS light and drives the LEFs to 34 degrees LED and the TEFs to 4 degrees TED. The displayed spin recovery arrow always indicates the proper direction for anti-spin lateral stick inputs whether the spin is upright or inverted. Anti-spin lateral stick inputs are aileron-into for upright spins and aileron-opposite for inverted spins. When lateral stick is placed with the arrow, automatic spin recovery mode (ASRM) is engaged. With ASRM engaged, all CAS feedback and control surface interconnects are removed, providing full aileron, rudder and stabilator authority for spin recovery. If the stick is neutral or is moved in the wrong direction, the SPIN MODE formats remain displayed and the LEFs and TEFs remain deflected, but the FCS remains in CAS, and ASRM is not engaged.

Automatic flight control system

The AFCS or autopilot provides three basic functions: pilot relief, coupled steering and data link control.

Different pilot relief modes are provided for the pitch-and-roll axes. Pitch-axis pilot relief modes include barometric altitude hold (BALT), radar altitude hold (RALT) and flight path attitude hold (FPAH). Roll-axis pilot relief modes include roll attitude hold (ROLL), ground track hold (GTRK), ground track select (GSEL), heading hold (HDG) and heading select (HSEL).

Coupled steering modes allow the roll-axis to be coupled to a TACAN station (CPL TCN), to a waypoint (CPL WYPT), to the azimuth steering line (CPL ASL) or to bank angle (CPL BNK).

Data link control modes include automatic carrier landing (ACL) and vector (VEC).

Weapon system controls

All of the primary controls for the aircraft's weapon systems (weapons, sensors and displays) are located on the front cockpit throttles and stick, the rear cockpit throttles and stick (trainer configured F/A-18F) or the rear cockpit hand controllers (missionised F/A-18F).

Hands on throttles and stick (HOTAS), allows the aircrew to manipulate the weapon systems without removing the hands from the aircraft's primary flight controls. Additionally, switch(es) on the canopy sill and on the rear cockpit grab handle provide secondary controls for dispensing expendables from the ALE-47 chaff and flare dispensers.

Missionised F/A-18Fs feature two hand controllers installed in front of the inboard section of each console. With the exception of weapons release, the hand controllers are used to provide the same weapon systems control as stick and throttle switches/controls do in the front cockpit. The right-hand controller is a mirror image of the left-hand controller. Each contains a multi-function switch (MFS), a designator controller (DC) assignment switch, a designator controller (DC), a radar elevation control, a chaff/flare dispense switch and an undesignate button. Except for the chaff/flare dispense switches, the functions of the left- and right-hand controllers are identical.

Environment control system

The environment control system (ECS) utilises engine bleed air to provide pressurisation, heating and cooling air to various aircraft systems. Warm air is provided for internal fuel tank pressurisation (Lot 23 and below), external fuel tank pressurisation, canopy seal inflation, g-suit operation, radar waveguide pressurisation, windscreen anti-ice and rain removal, gun gas purge, RECCE bay heating and onboard

ABOVE Aviation Electronics Technicians disassemble the APG-73 radar mount from an F/A-18 Hornet. The mount allows the radar to be mechanically gimballed left, right, up and down. The APG-79 AESA radar does away with this hydraulically powered system. *(US Navy)*

oxygen generating system (OBOGS) operation. Cold, dry conditioned air is provided for avionics cooling. Warm and cold air are mixed to provide temperature-controlled air for cabin heating, cooling and pressurisation and windscreen defog.

A liquid cooling system (LCS) is used to cool the radar transmitter. A digital ECS controller is used to schedule ECS output, regulate system temperatures, monitor system health and detect and isolate faults.

Oxygen systems

The OBOGS provides oxygen-rich breathing gas to the aircrew while either engine is operating.

Engine bleed air is cooled and routed through the OBOGS inlet air shut-off valve to the OBOGS concentrator. The breathing gas is routed from the concentrator to a cockpit plenum, where the temperature is stabilised and a limited supply is stored for peak flow demands. From the plenum, the breathing gas flows through the pilot services panel oxygen disconnect, through the seat survival kit, to the aircrew regulators and masks.

Fire detection and extinguishing, and bleed air leak detection systems

A fire detection system contains dual-loop fire detectors and three fire warning lights. The fire extinguishing system contains a READY/DISCH light and a fire extinguisher bottle. Together, the two systems provide

BELOW A flush-mounted boarding ladder is installed in the port (left) LERX, allowing the Super Hornet crew entry and exit without being dependent on specialist equipment. On the confined deck of an aircraft carrier, and when forward-deploying, this is a necessity. (US Navy)

engine bay, AMAD bay and APU bay fire warning, engine and APU emergency shutdown and selective fire extinguishing capability. The fire extinguisher bottle is located in the aft fuselage between the engines. The bottle contains a non-toxic gaseous agent which provides a one-shot extinguishing capability.

Electrical power from the 28V DC essential bus is required to operate the fire detection and extinguishing systems, although the systems can operate on battery power alone.

A separate dry bay fire suppression (DBFS) system is incorporated to automatically detect and extinguish a fire or explosion in the dry bays below fuel tanks 2, 3 and 4.

Canopy system

The cockpit is enclosed by a clamshell-type canopy. The main components of the canopy system are an electromechanical actuator, which provides powered and manual operation of the canopy, and a cartridge-actuated thruster with associated rocket motors, which provides emergency jettison. When closed, the canopy is latched in place by three hooks on the bottom of each side of the canopy frame and two forward indexer pins on the lower leading edge of the canopy frame. When the canopy is closed, the latch hooks and indexer pins engage fittings along the canopy sill, and the canopy actuator rotates the canopy actuation link over-centre, locking the canopy. A mechanical brake in the canopy actuator motor provides a redundant lock. An inflatable seal, installed around the edge of the canopy frame, retains cockpit pressure when the canopy is locked. A rain seal is installed outboard of the pressure seal to divert rainwater away from the cockpit.

Ejection seat

The SJU-17 (V)1/A, 2/A, 9/A, and SJU-17A (V)1/A, 2/A and 9/A NACES (Navy Aircrew Common Ejection Seat) are ballistic catapult/rocket systems that provide the aircrew member with a quick and safe means of escape from the aircraft. A leg-restraint system secures the occupant's legs to the seat during

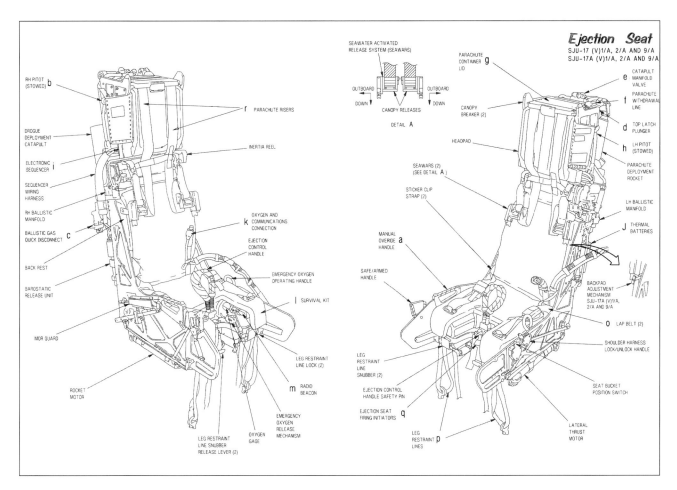

Ejection Seat
SJU-17 (V)1/A, 2/A AND 9/A
SJU-17A (V)1/A, 2/A AND 9/A

RH PITOT (STOWED) b

PARACHUTE RISERS r

DROGUE DEPLOYMENT CATAPULT

INERTIA REEL

ELECTRONIC SEQUENCER i

SEQUENCER WIRING HARNESS

RH BALLISTIC MANIFOLD

BALLISTIC GAS QUICK DISCONNECT c

BACK REST

BAROSTATIC RELEASE UNIT

MOR GUARD

ROCKET MOTOR

LEG RESTRAINT LINE SNUBBER RELEASE LEVER (2)

OXYGEN GAGE

EMERGENCY OXYGEN RELEASE MECHANISM

RADIO BEACON m

LEG RESTRAINT LINE LOCK (2)

SURVIVAL KIT

EMERGENCY OXYGEN OPERATING HANDLE

EJECTION CONTROL HANDLE

OXYGEN AND COMMUNICATIONS CONNECTION k

SEAWATER ACTIVATED RELEASE SYSTEM (SEAWARS)

OUTBOARD DOWN / CANOPY RELEASES / OUTBOARD DOWN

DETAIL A

PARACHUTE CONTAINER LID g

CANOPY BREAKER (2)

HEADPAD

SEAWARS (2) (SEE DETAIL A)

STICKER CLIP STRAP (2)

MANUAL OVERRIDE HANDLE a

SAFE/ARMED HANDLE

LEG RESTRAINT LINE SNUBBER (2)

EJECTION CONTROL HANDLE SAFETY PIN

EJECTION SEAT FIRING INITIATORS q

LEG RESTRAINT LINES p

CATAPULT MANIFOLD VALVE e

PARACHUTE WITHDRAWAL LINE f

TOP LATCH PLUNGER d

LH PITOT (STOWED) h

PARACHUTE DEPLOYMENT ROCKET

LH BALLISTIC MANIFOLD

THERMAL BATTERIES J

BACKPAD ADJUSTMENT MECHANISM SJU-17A (V)1/A, 2/A AND 9/A

LAP BELT (2) o

SHOULDER HARNESS LOCK/UNLOCK HANDLE

SEAT BUCKET POSITION SWITCH

LATERAL THRUST MOTOR

ABOVE AND RIGHT The Super Hornet features the SJU-17 series of ejection seat, designed and manufactured by the world-famous Martin Baker company. The seat is activated using the ejection handle located between the legs and attached to the base of the seat, and is fully automatic thereafter. *(US Navy)*

ejection. The system consists of two adjustable leg garters, a restraint line and a snubber box for each leg.

The seat system includes an initiation system which, after jettisoning the canopy and positioning the occupant for ejection, fires the telescopic seat catapult. Canopy breakers on the top of the seat give the capability of ejecting through the canopy. As the seat departs the aircraft and the catapult reaches the end of the stroke, a rocket motor on the bottom of the seat is fired. The thrust of the rocket motor sustains the thrust of the catapult to eject the seat to a height sufficient for parachute deployment, even

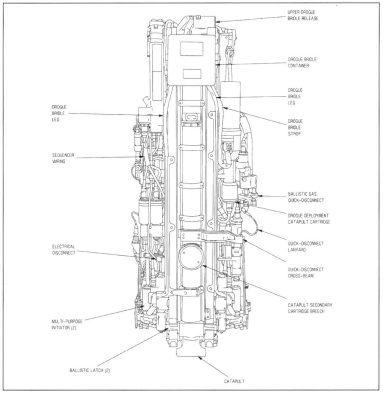

UPPER DROGUE BRIDLE RELEASE

DROGUE BRIDLE CONTAINER

DROGUE BRIDLE LEG

DROGUE BRIDLE STROP

DROGUE BRIDLE LEG

SEQUENCER WIRING

ELECTRICAL DISCONNECT

MULTI-PURPOSE INITIATOR (2)

BALLISTIC LATCH (2)

CATAPULT

BALLISTIC GAS QUICK-DISCONNECT

DROGUE DEPLOYMENT CATAPULT CARTRIDGE

QUICK-DISCONNECT LANYARD

QUICK-DISCONNECT CROSS-BEAM

CATAPULT SECONDARY CARTRIDGE BREECH

ABOVE A 'green-shirt', formally known as an Aviation Structural Mechanic, works on the SJU-17 ejection seat. The 'head-box' contains the tightly packed drogue and main parachutes. *(US Navy)*

BELOW The ejection sequence is broken down into four main phases. These start with ejection and aircrew extraction; then comes the deployment of the stabilising drogue parachute; then, if at low altitude or once the crewmember and seat have descended below 18,000ft MSL, opening of the main parachute and man/seat separation; followed by normal descent to the ground (or sea). *(US Navy)*

if ejection is initiated at zero speed, zero altitude in a substantially level attitude.

The ejection control handle, located between the crewman's legs on the front of the seat pan, is the only means by which ejection is initiated. The handle, moulded in the shape of a loop, can be grasped by one or two hands. To initiate ejection, a 20–40lb pull removes the handle from its housing, and a continued pull of 30–60lb is required to pull both sears from the dual initiators. Either of the initiators can fire the seat. After ejection, the handle remains attached to the seat. The ejection control handle safes the ejection seat safe/armed handle.

Timing of all events after rocket motor initiation is controlled by the electronic sequencer which utilises altitude, acceleration and airspeed information to automatically control drogue and parachute deployment and man/seat separation throughout the ejection seat's operational envelope. In the event of partial or total failure of the electronic sequencer, a 4-second mechanical delay initiates a barostatic release unit, which frees the occupant from the seat and deploys the parachute between 14,000 and 16,000ft MSL if the ejection occurred in or above this altitude range. The emergency barostatic release unit operates immediately after the 4-second delay if the ejection occurred below 14,000ft MSL. An emergency restraint release (manual override) system provides a backup in the event of failure of the barostatic release unit.

The seat is stabilised and the forward speed retarded by a drogue 'chute attached to the top and bottom of the seat. The parachute deployment rocket is automatically fired to withdraw the parachute from the deployment bag. Full canopy inflation is inhibited until the g forces are sufficiently reduced to minimise opening shock. There are five modes of operation.

At high altitude the drogue 'chute deploys to decelerate and stabilise the seat. The seat falls drogue-retarded to 18,000ft MSL where the drogue is released, the main parachute is deployed and man/seat separation occurs.

At medium altitude (between 18,000 and 8,000ft MSL), and at low altitude (below 8,000ft MSL), parachute deployment is automatically delayed from 0.45 to 2.90 seconds (depending upon airspeed and altitude) after first seat motion to allow the drogue 'chute to decelerate and stabilise the seat.

The main parachute is a 21ft aeroconical canopy type, stored in a head-box container on top of the ejection seat. The parachute is steerable and contains water deflation pockets, which aid in dumping air from the canopy after landing in water. The seat drogue 'chute is stored in a separate container on top of the drogue deployment catapult. The seat contains controls for adjusting seat height and for locking and unlocking the inertia reel shoulder restraint straps. A survival kit is installed in the seat pan.

Avionics

The avionics subsystem combines the integration and automation needed for operability with the redundancy required to ensure flight safety and mission success.

Key features of the system include highly integrated controls and displays, inertial navigation set with carrier alignment capability and extensive built-in test capability. The avionics subsystems operate under the control of two mission computers with primary data transfer between the mission computers and the other avionics equipment via the avionics multiplex (mux) buses.

The mission computer system consists of two digital computers (MC1 and MC2), which are high-speed, stored-program, programmable, general-purpose computers with core memory.

On Super Hornets with the AYK-14 mission computers, the two mission computers interconnect with the primary avionics equipment on the mux buses. MC1, referred to as the navigation computer, performs processing for navigation, control/display management, aircraft built-in test (BIT), status-monitoring operations and backup for MC2. MC2, referred to as the weapon delivery computer, performs processing for air-to-air combat, air-to-ground attack and tactical control/display. There are six avionics mux bus channels with redundant paths (X and Y) for each channel.

The mission computer:

1. Computes and controls the data sent to the cockpit displays
2. Computes missile launch and weapon release commands

3. Provides mode control and options for various avionics systems
4. Generates BIT initiate signals to and equipment operational status from various avionics systems.

On Super Hornets with the advanced mission computer and display configuration (AMCD, which replaces the AYK-14), the front and rear DDIs are driven directly by the MC over a high-speed interface bus, not by avionics mux bus commands. The HUD is driven directly by redundant connection to either MC. MC1 drives the front and rear LDDIs and HUD, while MC2 drives the front and rear RDDIs and HUD. When an MC is off or non-functional, the displays driven by that MC show a green square in the centre of the display. Each MC provides the same level of functionality in the single MC backup mode of operation.

AMCD II mission computers are used on aircraft with the aft cockpit 8×10 display installed. This display receives its primary signal through MC2, and is inoperative with computers prior to AMCD II. The AMCD II computer provides digital video colour capability to the 8×10 display via the Fiber Channel Network Switch (FCNS) and High-Speed Video Network (HSVN).

The computers receive inputs for navigational data and steering command computations from the inertial navigation system, electronic flight control system, multipurpose display group, TACAN and backup attitude and the navigation system. The computers control display symbology and information presented to the pilot by the multi-purpose display group.

BELOW A small HMD rotary switch in both cockpits allow the crew to moderate the brightness of the symbology appearing in the display.
(US Navy)

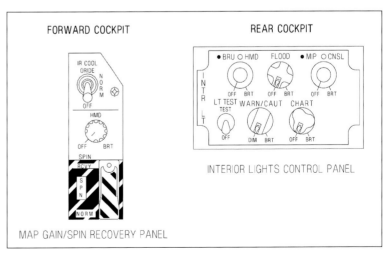

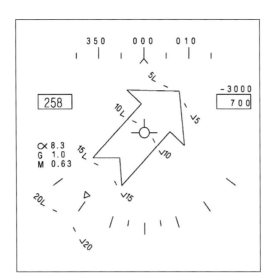

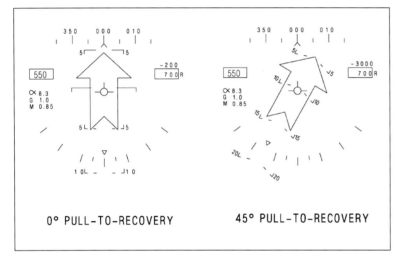

0° PULL-TO-RECOVERY

45° PULL-TO-RECOVERY

Terrain-awareness warning system (TAWS)

The terrain-awareness warning system alerts the aircrew of a controlled flight into terrain (CFIT) condition during all mission phases. TAWS operates any time that the navigation mission computer (MC1) and the digital mapping set (DMS) are functional. It has been designed to eliminate false warnings, minimise nuisance warnings and generate consistent aircrew response in all aircraft master modes.

Five possible voice warnings are provided to indicate the correct initial response to an impending CFIT condition, and a visual cue is provided to indicate the recovery direction of pull or, in some instances, to command an increase in turn rate. Aural warnings provide the aircrew with a wake-up call and correct initial response, while visual warnings provide the aircrew with correct follow-on recovery information.

All TAWS warnings should be treated as though an imminent flight into terrain condition exists. Pilot response to a TAWS warning should be instinctive and immediate. The aural warnings are: 'Roll Left . . . Roll Left', 'Roll Right . . . Roll Right', 'Pull Up . . . Pull Up', 'Power . . . Power' and 'Check Gear'. A visual recovery arrow is provided in the centre of the HUD and HUD format on the DDI to indicate the direction of recovery. TAWS visual recovery cues are designed to be used in conjunction with TAWS voice warnings. They are displayed when a CFIT condition is present and removed when the CFIT condition is cleared.

TAWS uses data from the following inputs: FCC, INS, RADALT, GPS and digital terrain elevation data (DTED). DTED resides in the DMS as part of the digital mapping set and is used to provide the forward-prediction capability that protects against flight into rising terrain. When a DMS is not installed in the aircraft or is not operational, protection from CFIT events is provided by the Ground Proximity Warning System (GPWS).

GPWS is designed to back up the pilot by providing an alert of impending controlled flight into terrain. GPWS provides warnings of potentially unsafe manoeuvring flight conditions, such as excessive bank angles, excessive sink rates, gear-up landings, floor altitude violations and altitude loss during recovery. The system is operational as long as MC1, the radar altimeter and air data systems are ON and functional.

Flight performance advisory system

The flight performance advisory system (FPAS) is provided to aid the pilot in making time, fuel and distance calculations. Readouts for maximum range and maximum endurance are provided for three flight conditions: current Mach and altitude, optimum Mach at the current altitude and optimum Mach and altitude. These three readouts can be used to adjust the aircraft flight profile to meet mission requirements. Additionally, FPAS provides fuel remaining at arrival and recommended distance to begin descent from the selected waypoint or TACAN station. Range, time, altitude, Mach and fuel are calculated by the FPAS algorithm and appear on the FPAS display.

Countermeasures system

The ALE-47 countermeasures dispensing set can be manually actuated or can use information from various electronic warfare (EW) systems to generate countermeasures dispensing programs.

The ALE-50 decoy dispensing set provides an expendable towed RF countermeasures capability. The system includes a multi-platform launch controller (MPLC) and a removable dispenser with three expendable decoys.

Joint helmet-mounted cueing system (JHMCS)

JHMCS allows the aircrew to target and employ existing short-range missiles (SRMs) and high off-boresight (HOBS) weapons, such as the AIM-9X, and cue the radar and other sensors. When using JHMCS to employ HOBS weapons, the aircrew can slave/acquire and shoot targets beyond the gimbal limits of the aircraft radar and designate ground targets. The main display provides a monocular 20-degree field of view that is visible in front of the crewman's right eye.

LEFT AND BELOW
A pair of VFA-211 'Fighting Checkmates' F/A-18Fs release flares for the camera. The F/A-18 launches flare and chaff bundles from ALE-47 or ALE-50 dispensers located flush with the underside of the fuselage. *(Steve Davies/ FJ Photography)*

BELOW The Joint Helmet-Mounted Cueing System bolts on to the standard fast-jet helmet used by the US Navy and US Air Force. *(Steve Davies/FJ Photography)*

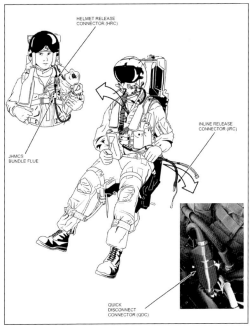

HELMET RELEASE CONNECTOR (HRC)

INLINE RELEASE CONNECTOR (IRC)

JHMCS BUNDLE FLUE

QUICK DISCONNECT CONNECTOR (QDC)

LEFT JHMCS features a bulky cable that connects to the aircraft and a corresponding inline release connector that is routed to the left side of the ejection seat. The cable must be securely positioned for flight. *(US Navy)*

Chapter Six

Power for the F/A-18E/F Super Hornet

With engines originally conceived of for the ill-fated A-12 Avenger program, the Super Hornet's F414 engines make it the beneficiary of around one third more thrust than the legacy Hornet. Not without its development issues, the GE engine is now viewed as a reliable engine – a particular must for carrier aviation.

OPPOSITE This EA-18G of VAQ-138 shows relatively clean exhaust nozzles, indicating either a recent engine change or perhaps even a new factory delivery. These nozzles open and close to maintain a steady pressure inside the exhaust and afterburner section. *(US Navy)*

F414
turbofan engines

22,000 lb thrust class

By 1988, the basic F404-GE-400 engine had accumulated 700,000 flight hours, and reliability and maintainability statistics were good. However, some problems surfaced at the million-hour mark. A number of fires broke out in these high-time engines, causing the loss of several aircraft.

The fires were eventually attributed to FOD (foreign object damage) eroding the coating on the compressor casing, which resulted in the titanium blades and any debris rubbing together and therefore causing a fire. New safety coatings were developed, but the installation of a new engine was inevitable. For the Legacy Hornet, that engine came in the form of the F404-GE-402 Enhanced Performance Engine (EPE).

The EPE was developed to meet the Swiss Air Force's requirements for its F/A-18C/D Hornets, but this engine would become the standard powerplant on US Hornets from 1992 onwards. Delivering 10% more static sea-level thrust than its predecessor, it also offers 18% more excess power at Mach 0.9 and 10,000ft (3,048m), as well as increased transonic acceleration. A typical runway-launched interception profile, from brake release to Mach 1.4 at 50,000ft (15,240m), takes 31% less time than before.

Navy technical documents give the uninstalled military thrust of the F404-GE-400 engine as approximately 10,700lb, with maximum afterburner thrust in the 16,000lb range. The uninstalled military thrust of each F404-GE-402 engine is approximately 10,900lb, with maximum afterburner thrust in the 18,000lb range.

RIGHT An F/A-18C assigned to the 'Vampires' of Fighter Attack Squadron VX-9 launches from the USS *Ronald Reagan* (CVN 76). The Legacy Hornet family is powered by the F404 series of engine – the predecessor to the F414 used in the Super Hornet and Growler.
(US Navy)

RIGHT Afterburner take-offs, like this one by an F/A-18A+ Hornet assigned to VMFA-115, the 'Silver Eagles', are essential where combat loads are carried in hot climates. *(US Navy)*

Super Hornet engines

The F/A-18E/F is powered by two General Electric F414-GE-400 engines. The engines are low bypass, axial-flow, twin-spool turbofans with afterburner. The three-stage fan (low-pressure compressor) and the seven-stage high-pressure compressor are each driven by a single-stage turbine. An inlet device is installed

LEFT, BELOW LEFT AND BELOW Sailors remove an F414 jet engine from an F/A-18E Super Hornet. Engine changes are a relatively uncomplicated affair, involving only a handful of disconnections from the 'mother ship' before the engine can be lowered on to the dolly and wheeled away. The modular nature of the F414 means that it can be serviced and repaired quickly. *(US Navy)*

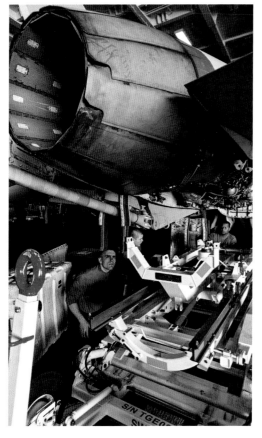

in each engine intake to reduce the aircraft radar signature and to improve survivability.

The basic functions are supported by the engine-driven accessory gearbox, which drives the engine fuel pump, variable exhaust nozzle (VEN/start) fuel pump, lubrication and oil scavenge pump, engine fuel control and alternator. Fuel flow from the VEN/start pump is used to drive the VEN actuator and to provide initial fuel pressure for main engine start.

The US Navy's technical manuals quote the uninstalled military thrust of each F414-GE-400 engine as approximately 13,900lb, with maximum afterburner thrust in the 20,700lb range.

FADEC

Engine operation is controlled by a full-authority digital engine control (FADEC), mounted on the engine casing. FADEC software implements engine control schedules by modulating fuel flow and engine geometry for the current flight conditions and the 'requested' throttle setting. With the throttles matched, engine parameters may vary significantly between the engines as control schedules are adjusted for optimum performance.

Each FADEC computer has two central processor units – channel A (CH A) and channel B (CH B) – and is integrated with the mission computers, flight control computers and throttles. Normally, both FADEC channels monitor engine and control system operation with one channel in control and the other in standby. In the event of a control system failure,

the FADEC automatically selects the channel with better capability.

Prior to first engine start, the battery is used to power CH A of both FADECs. When N2 reaches 10% rpm during start, the engine-driven alternator comes online and powers both channels of its corresponding FADEC. When an aircraft generator comes online (N2 greater than 60%), the aircraft's electrical system provides power to both channels of the other FADEC as well. With both engines operating, each engine-driven alternator is the primary source of FADEC power with the aircraft's 28V DC essential bus as backup. When both channels of a FADEC are powered after initial start, the FADEC automatically switches operation to the channel which was not in control during the previous flight/engine run.

Engine degrades are reported by the FADEC in one of two categories: minor failures that do not affect engine operability and significant failures that do. Due to a high level of FADEC redundancy, most minor control system failures do not cause any degradation in engine performance.

The FADEC provides simultaneous control of the main and afterburner igniters via the engine-driven alternator and ignition exciter.

The oil pressure sensing system utilises an oil pressure transducer and a separate oil pressure switch. The transducer provides an oil pressure value for display in the cockpit. The oil pressure switch provides an additional source to confirm the presence of oil pressure if the oil pressure transducer fails.

Engine features

A fan speed lockup system prevents inlet instability (buzz) at high Mach by holding engine speed and airflow at military power levels when the throttle(s) are retarded below MIL. Speed lockup is activated when the aircraft accelerates above Mach 1.23 and deactivated when the aircraft decelerates below Mach 1.18.

The Supersonic Engine Thrust Limiting (SETLIM) minimises the potential for an aircraft departure due to asymmetric thrust following an engine stall or flameout at certain supersonic (Mach greater than 1.8) or high-Q (energy) conditions equivalent to approximately 700

BELOW An Aviation Machinist's Mate uses a borescope to inspect the fan blades of a VFA-11 'Red Rippers' F/A-18E Super Hornet aboard the aircraft carrier USS *Theodore Roosevelt*. The F414 also drives an airframe-mounted accessory gearbox that provides hydraulic pressure. *(US Navy)*

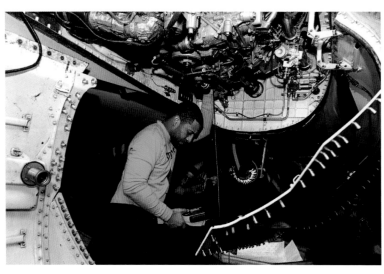

KCAS at sea level or 750 KCAS at 25,000ft. If the FADEC detects a stall or flameout condition, this function terminates afterburner operation in both engines. Normal afterburner operation is restored 12 seconds after engine recovery or immediately when airspeed drops below Mach 1.7 and q-conditions are equivalent to approximately 650 KCAS at sea level or 710 KCAS at 25,000ft.

A Reduced Authority Thrust System (RATS) reduces the wind-over-deck required for carrier landings by rapidly reducing thrust at the beginning of a successful arrestment, reducing the energy absorbed by the arresting gear. RATS logic, only resident in MC1, declares a successful arrestment if the landing gear and arresting hook are down and longitudinal deceleration is more than 1.0g (a typical arrestment is approximately 3g). MC1 sends a 'set RATS on' signal to the FADECs, which reduce thrust to approximately 70%

of MIL power. RATS logic also senses WOW, wheel speed (less than 20 knots) and THA (throttle handle angle) to prevent the engines from spooling back to MIL power at the end of cable pull-out. RATS operation is cancelled when the throttles are reduced to IDLE (THA less than 10 degrees), and is inhibited during single-engine operation.

An Armament Gas Ingestion protection (AGI) system provides pre-emptive engine ignition in case armament gas ingestion causes an engine flameout. AGI protection is a backup to the FADECs' inherent flameout detection and relight logic. The AGI signal is sent by the Stores Management Set (SMS) to the FADECs and is used to initiate engine ignition (both engines) for 5 seconds. The signal is sent when the gun is fired, or if any wing pylon-mounted A/A or forward-firing A/G weapon is launched. AGI is functional in the SIM mode as well as the tactical mode.

ABOVE LEFT AND ABOVE The afterburner section of the F414 features a spray ring (seen here looking aft and forward) that injects raw fuel into the hot exhaust as it flows out of the turbine section. This fuel ignites to create the afterburner flame, producing in the region of another 7,500lb of thrust. *(US Navy)*

LEFT Reliable engine response and AB ignition are important in carrier aviation. This is true not only when 'flying the ball' and landing the aircraft or waving off, but also when 'plugging in the burners' in case of a bolter, as this F/A-18C Hornet of VFA-94 'Mighty Shrikes' demonstrates. *(US Navy)*

An Afterburner Limiting (ABLIM) function limits engine power to half afterburner with the throttles at MAX to prevent engine stalls due to exhaust gas ingestion, but it is only used during carrier-based operations. With the function activated, only half afterburner power is available with the throttles at MAX. Indicated fuel flows are reduced from 35,000 to 45,000pph (pounds per hour) to about 25,000pph. The function is automatically deactivated with acceleration due to a catapult launch, or at 80 KCAS.

Engine anti-ice is provided to the engine inlet by bleed air controlled by the ENG ANTI ICE switch in the front cockpit. However, after engine start, the engine anti-ice system automatically turns on 45 seconds after the engine reaches idle power and remains on for 30 seconds, provided the throttle remains at idle.

When turned on, anti-ice air flows as long as the engine inlet temperature is between -40 and +15°C. Outside of these limits, anti-ice airflow is terminated immediately if airborne, or after 60 seconds with WOW. When anti-ice air is flowing, N2 rpm increases approximately 2% and EGT increases approximately 5°C.

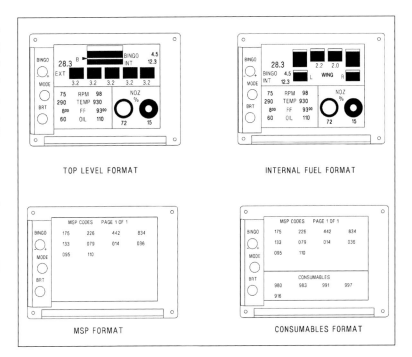

TOP LEVEL FORMAT

INTERNAL FUEL FORMAT

MSP FORMAT

CONSUMABLES FORMAT

Throttles

Two throttles, one for each engine, are located on the left console. Throttle movement is transmitted electrically to the corresponding FADEC for thrust modulation and to the FCCs for autothrottle operation. There is no mechanical linkage between the throttles and the engines.

During engine start, advancing the throttles from OFF to IDLE opens the engine fuel control shut-off valves and, when commanded by the FADEC, provides fuel flow to the engines.

Afterburner operation is initiated by advancing the throttles through the MIL detent into the afterburner range. During catapult launch or carrier touchdown (WOW and launch bar or arresting hook extended), an afterburner lockout mechanism extends to preclude inadvertent afterburner selection. In such cases, the throttles can be moved to the afterburner range by raising the finger lifts on the front of each throttle or by applying a force of approximately 30lb.

During engine shutdown, the finger lifts must be raised to move the throttles to OFF, closing the engine fuel control shut-off valves. The throttle grips contain switches that allow control of various systems without moving the hand from the throttles.

Displays

The engine fuel display (EFD), located on the main instrument panel below the left digital display indicator, is a night vision imaging system- (NVIS) compatible, monochromatic, liquid-crystal, grey/black display powered by the signal data computer (SDC).

The EFD normally displays critical engine parameters in the bottom half of the display and fuel quantities in the top half. Out-of-limit parameters are always highlighted by inverse video. Nozzle position is displayed both graphically and digitally in per cent open.

Automatic throttle control (ATC)

The ATC system has two operating modes: approach and cruise. The system automatically modulates engine thrust between flight IDLE and MIL power in order to maintain on-speed angle of attack (AOA) in the approach mode or calibrated airspeed (existing at the time of engagement) in the cruise mode.

During ATC operation, engine commands are sent to the FADEC directly from the FCCs instead of the throttles. FCC-generated engine

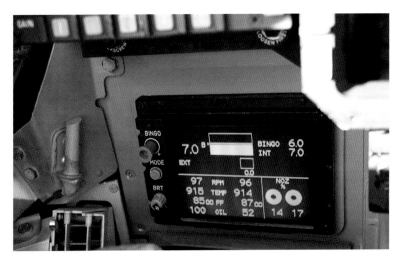

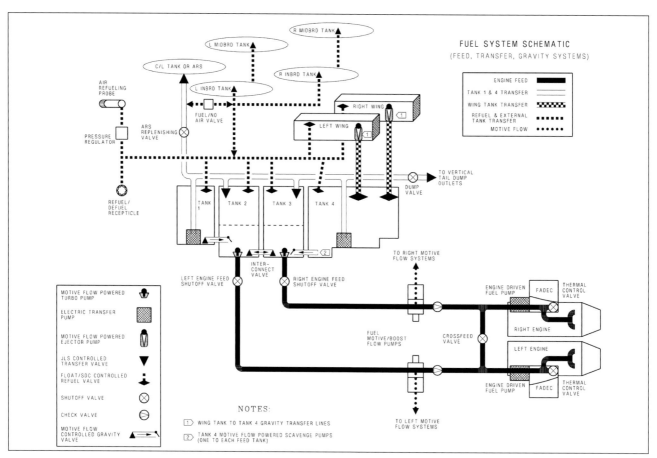

FUEL SYSTEM SCHEMATIC
(FEED, TRANSFER, GRAVITY SYSTEMS)

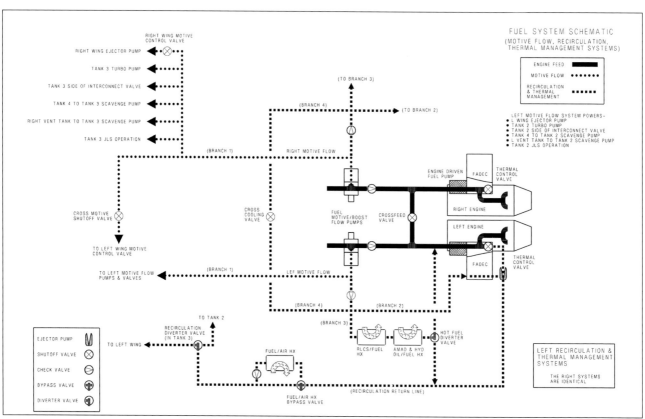

FUEL SYSTEM SCHEMATIC
(MOTIVE FLOW, RECIRCULATION,
THERMAL MANAGEMENT SYSTEMS)

commands are limited to a range slightly above idle to slightly below MIL. The throttles are continuously positioned by an FCC commanded backdrive unit to match the throttles with the current engine command and to provide feedback to the pilot.

Pressing and releasing the ATC button on the left throttle engages the approach mode with the FLAP switch in HALF or FULL and the cruise mode with the FLAP switch in AUTO. When either mode is engaged, an ATC advisory is displayed on the HUD. Because ATC mode engagement and ATC HUD advisories are not commanded until release of the ATC button, the pilot may need to deliberately pause after press and release to avoid inadvertent ATC disengagement/re-engagement. Automatic transition between the two modes or engagement during single-engine operation is not possible. Engaging ATC with the friction lever in the full aft position and with the throttles at mid-range power provides optimum pilot feedback with the smallest engagement power transients.

Normal disengagement is accomplished by reactuation of the ATC button or by applying a force of approximately 12lb (friction off) to either throttle for longer than 0.20 seconds. This force is sufficient to permit the pilot's hand to follow throttle movement without causing disengagement. Holding the throttles against the MIL or IDLE stop during ATC disengagement commands a rapid acceleration or deceleration to the commanded power setting instead of a smooth transition.

Fuel system

The aircraft is fitted with four internal fuselage tanks (Tanks 1–4), two internal wing tanks (left and right), two fuselage vent tanks and two vertical vent tanks. Tanks 2 and 3 are engine-feed tanks while 1, 4 and the wing tanks are transfer tanks. Total fuel can be increased by the carriage of up to four 480-gallon external fuel tanks on the centreline, inboard and mid-board pylons. All tanks, internal and external,

OPPOSITE PAGE The Super Hornet fuel system schematics provide information on fuel feed, transfer and gravity systems (top), and flow, recirculation and thermal management. *(US Navy)*

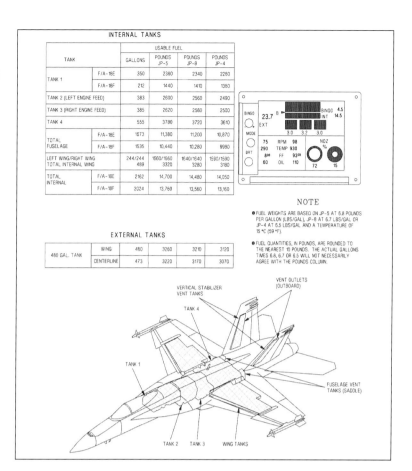

may be refuelled on the ground through a single-point refuelling receptacle or in flight through the inflight refuelling probe.

The aircraft's fuel system is composed of the following subsystems: engine feed, motive flow, fuel transfer, tank pressurisation and vent, thermal management, refuelling, fuel dump, fuel quantity indicating and fuel low-level indicating.

Each engine-feed system contains an AMAD-driven motive flow/boost pump, a feed tank with an internal motive flow powered turbo pump and an engine-feed shut-off valve. For survivability, the left and right feed systems are normally separated but can be interconnected by a normally closed cross-feed valve and a normally closed feed tank interconnect valve.

Each AMAD drives a two-stage motive flow/ boost pump. The first stage supplies low-pressure fuel to its respective engine-mounted fuel pump, while the second stage supplies high-pressure fuel to the motive flow system. Fuel from the motive flow system is used to cool accessories, power the feed tank turbo pumps and certain transfer/scavenge pumps and control certain transfer valves.

ABOVE The Super Hornet carries its internal fuel in four fuselage tanks and two wing tanks. The E-model can carry slightly more than the F-model because the two-seater's Tank 1 is smaller in order to make way for the second occupant. *(US Navy)*

ABOVE With the F414 at full power, overpressure in the fuel tanks can cause the fuel dump valve to open as a pressure-relief measure. This VFA-81 'Sunliners' F/A-18E Super Hornet demonstrates the phenomenon nicely. *(US Navy)*

BELOW Aviation Machinist's Mates run an F414 to maximum reheat on a test stand located at the rear of the aircraft carrier. *(US Navy)*

RIGHT Any of the Super Hornet's digital displays can be set to show the fuel 'page', which presents a top-down numerical summary of all the aircraft's internal and external fuel levels and provides a totaliser function. *(US Navy)*

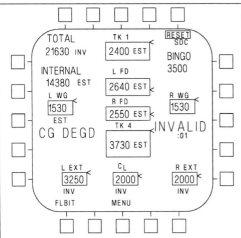

During normal operation, each engine receives fuel from separate fuel feed lines. Tank 2 supplies fuel to the left engine and Tank 3 supplies the right. A motive flow-powered turbo pump in each feed tank supplies fuel to its respective motive flow/boost pump.

Each feed tank has a horizontal baffle which traps fuel, providing a minimum of 10 seconds of negative g flight at MAX power. No sustained zero g capability is provided, and prolonged transitions through zero g (longer than 2 seconds) may produce a L and/or R BOOST LO caution.

If a feed tank turbo pump fails, fuel is suction-fed to the motive flow/boost pump. In this case, flight at high altitude with high feed tank fuel temperatures may not supply enough fuel for high-power settings.

In the event of a fire or fuselage fuel leak, engine-feed shut-off valves provide the capability to isolate a fuel feed system immediately downstream of the feed tank. Pressing the L or R FIRE warning light electrically closes the corresponding engine feed shut-off valve, isolating that fuel feed system.

The cross-feed valve, normally closed, allows a single motive flow/boost pump to feed both engines when boost pressure is lost on one side (e.g., single-engine shutdown, a leak, motive flow/boost pump failure or feed tank depletion). A loss of boost pressure downstream of the motive flow/boost pump sets the L or R BOOST LO caution and opens the cross-feed valve. An open cross-feed valve allows the output from the good motive flow/ boost pump to supply fuel to the opposite engine at rates sufficient for at least MIL power.

Pressing the L or R FIRE warning light electrically closes (inhibits opening) the cross-feed valve, isolating the two fuel feed systems.

A feed tank interconnect valve, installed between Tanks 2 and 3, is used to control gravity transfer/balancing between the two feed tanks. During normal operation, the dual flapper-type valve is held closed by motive flow pressure on either side (left motive flow on the Tank 2 side and right motive flow on the Tank 3 side), and no fuel gravity transfers.

If motive flow is lost on one side (e.g., single engine shutdown), the valve opens to ensure that feed tank fuel is available to the opposite engine. For instance, if motive flow is lost on the right side, the Tank 3 side of the valve opens, allowing fuel to gravity transfer to Tank 2.

The SDC (signal data computer) incorporates feed tank balancing logic, designed to keep Tanks 2 and 3 within 100lb of each other. With a normally operating fuel system, balancing begins after Tank 4 is effectively empty (less than about 300lb) and the feed tanks begin to deplete below full. If a feed tank imbalance reaches 100lb, the SDC shuts off the corresponding Tank 4 scavenge pump until the imbalance is 50lb in the opposite direction. With WoffW (weight off wheels), feed tank balancing continues until either feed tank reaches FUEL LO level (approximately 1,125lb). Feed tank balancing stops at FUEL LO to make sure Tank 4 fuel is transferred to both feed tanks in case one of these is damaged and is leaking. After transitioning to WonW (weight on wheels), balancing is reinitiated and continues until either feed tank is below 300lb.

In the event of a fuel transfer failure (e.g., a feed tank begins to deplete with fuel in Tank 4), feed tank balancing begins when either feed tank drops below approximately 2,100lb for 1 minute. This mechanisation attempts to minimise the effect of the fuel transfer failure by reducing the resulting feed tank split.

The fuel transfer system, controlled by the SDC, is designed to keep the feed tanks full or near full during normal engine operation. Fuel is routed from Tanks 1 and 4, the internal wing tanks, and external fuel tanks, if installed, through three independent sets of transfer lines. Additionally, the SDC schedules Tank 1 and 4 transfer to control fuel centre of gravity (CG).

Limitations		N_2 (%)	N_1 (%)	EGT (°C)	Nozzle (%)	Oil Press (psi)
Transient (MIL/MAX)		102	103	976	–	–
Steady state	MAX	100	100	952	50 to 100	80 to 150 (warm oil)
	MIL			932	0 to 45	
Ground IDLE		≥ 61	≥ 32	250 to 590	77 to 83	35 to 90 (warm oil)
Start		≥ 10	–	871	–	• Min 10 within 30 sec • 180 max after 2.5 min

ABOVE The F414 engine limitations include a steady state exhaust gas temperature of almost 1,000°C, such is the progress that has been made in the materials that are used in its construction. *(US Navy)*

BELOW This VX-9 F/A-18C hurtles down the deck of the carrier USS *Ronald Reagan* during squadron carrier qualifications. Note the toe-in angle of the rudders. *(US Navy)*

LEFT An F/A-18C Hornet assigned to VMFA-312 'Checkerboards' experiences an afterburner blowout on one engine during a cat shot. *(US Navy)*

Chapter Seven

F/A-18 firepower

The Super Hornet's phenomenal sensors and data fusion capabilities exist to better engage the threat, but it's the jet's ability to carry and employ a myriad of weapons – both air-to-air and air-to-ground – that harness that sensor capability and turn it into an enforcer of foreign policy so valued by combat theatre commanders.

OPPOSITE Loaded with two captive-carry AGM-88E Advanced HARM missiles, an F/A-18F Super Hornet assigned to the 'Salty Dogs' of Air Test and Evaluation Squadron VX-23 conducts a sortie out of NAS Patuxent River. *(US Navy)*

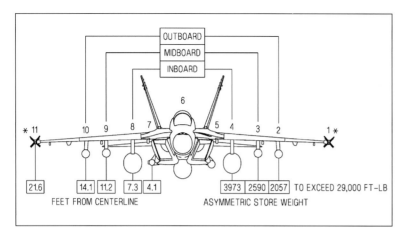

OUTBOARD			
MIDBOARD			
INBOARD			

6

* 11   10   9   8   7   5   4   3   2   1 *

21.6		14.1	11.2	7.3	4.1		3973	2590	2057	TO EXCEED 29,000 FT–LB
FEET FROM CENTERLINE							ASYMMETRIC STORE WEIGHT			

This chapter focuses on the firepower available to the F/A-18 family in US Navy and Marine Corps service.

While the Super Hornet's improvements over the Legacy Hornet include reduction in radar cross-section, superior avionics and an increased mission radius (520nm vs. 369nm), the F/A-18E/F also boasts an improved weapons carriage capability and compatibility with all of the US Navy's smart weapons.

The E/F model can carry a greater number of weapons than the A to D models, thanks to the addition of two extra wing stations. Its MIL-STD-1760 data bus allows communications

between the aircraft's computers and targeting systems, and a plethora of the world's most sophisticated air-launched weapons.

The variety and depth of the F/A-18E/F's weapons loadout options allow battlespace commanders to take full advantage of the aircraft's diverse capabilities. For interdiction and deep-strike roles, stand-off weapons such as the AGM-84 SLAM and AGM-154 JSOW allow the Super Hornet crew to engage targets even when the strength and sophistication of the enemy's defences are overwhelming. And, as has been explained in previous chapters, the E/F model is perfectly suited for more traditional battlefield interdiction, close air support, forward air control, time-critical targeting, offensive counter air and precision strike missions. These air-to-ground mission sets also call upon the F/A-18's ability to self-escort, which is itself an extension of its intercept and air superiority missions.

Air-to-air and air-to-ground ordnance are carried on 9 (F/A-18A/B/C/D) or 11 (F/A-18E/F) external stations, numbered from the right wingtip (STA1), to the left wingtip (STA9 for the Hornet, STA11 for the Super Hornet). The stations comprise two wingtip missile launch rails, four under-wing pylons for the Hornet and six for the Super Hornet, two semi-recessed fuselage stations (one usually occupied by a target pod) and a centreline station.

In all, 13,700lb (6,215kg) of external fuel and ordnance can be carried. The types of weapons that are compatible span the full range of conventional stores (guided and unguided) rockets and freefall nuclear weapons.

With the exception of the dedicated recce F/A-18D and F/A-18D(RC) Hornets in use by the US Marine Corps, and the Navy's EA-18G Growler, all F/A-18s feature an internal M61 20mm 'Vulcan' Gatling gun. Early Hornets carry the A1 version of the Vulcan, while the lighter A2 equips later Hornets and all Super Hornets. An ammunition drum provides storage for 578 rounds of M56 or M242 high-explosive incendiary (HEI); PGU-27, PGU-30, M55 or M220 target practice tracer; or PGU-28 HEI. The M61 is suitable for employment against both air and ground targets.

A range of launcher adaptors (LAU), bomb rack units (BRU), suspension pylons (SUU),

PYLONS AND RACKS

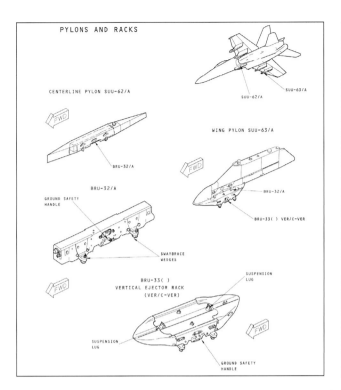

CENTERLINE PYLON SUU-62/A

SUU-62/A

SUU-63/A

WING PYLON SUU-63/A

BRU-32/A

BRU-32/A

BRU-32/A

GROUND SAFETY
HANDLE

BRU-33( ) VER/C-VER

SWAYBRACE
WEDGES

BRU-33( )
VERTICAL EJECTOR RACK
(VER/C-VER)

SUSPENSION
LUG

SUSPENSION
LUG

GROUND SAFETY
HANDLE

RACKS

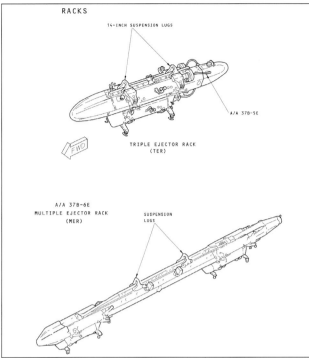

14-INCH SUSPENSION LUGS

A/A 37B-5E

TRIPLE EJECTOR RACK
(TER)

A/A 37B-6E
MULTIPLE EJECTOR RACK
(MER)

SUSPENSION
LUGS

THIS PAGE Various suspension pylons, adaptors and launch rails are installed on the F/A-18 family (F/A-18A shown here) in order to allow the aircraft to employ a wide range of both air-to-air and air-to-ground weaponry.
(US Navy)

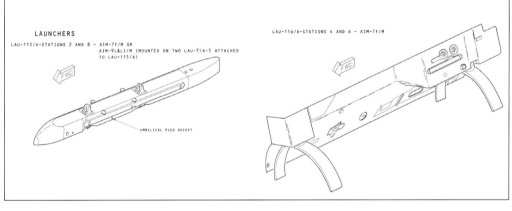

LAUNCHERS

LAU-115/A-STATIONS 2 AND 8 - AIM-7F/M OR
AIM-9L&LI/M (MOUNTED ON TWO LAU-7/A-5 ATTACHED
TO LAU-115/A)

LAU-116/A-STATIONS 4 AND 6 - AIM-7F/M

UMBILICAL PLUG SOCKET

LAUNCHERS

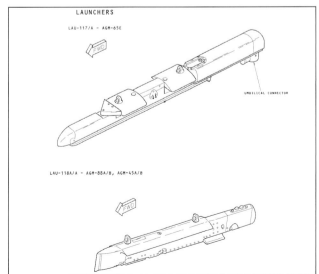

LAU-117/A - AGM-65E

UMBILICAL CONNECTOR

LAU-118A/A - AGM-88A/B, AGM-45A/B

LAUNCHERS

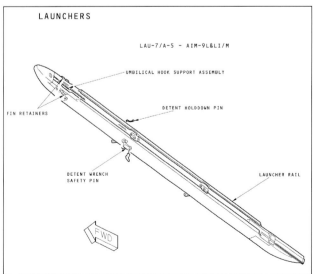

LAU-7/A-5 - AIM-9L&LI/M

UMBILICAL HOOK SUPPORT ASSEMBLY

DETENT HOLDDOWN PIN

FIN RETAINERS

DETENT WRENCH
SAFETY PIN

LAUNCHER RAIL

ABOVE The AN/ASQ-228 Advanced Targeting Forward-Looking Infrared (ATFLIR) pod, seen here being loaded on an F/A-18F Super Hornet, allows the aircraft to employ precision-strike weapons and freefall bombs; provide forward air control (airborne) and close air support services; fly at low altitude and at night; and bring back its own battle damage assessment. *(US Navy)*

SHEET 10
A

SHEET 12
C

18

14

26

IR WINDOW

SHEET 11 **B**

VIS WINDOW

FORWARD
SECTION
28

REAR
SECTION
29

ENVIRONMENTAL
CONTROL UNIT

multiple ejection racks (MERs) and triple ejection racks (TERs) provide a physical interface between munitions and the F/A-18's weapons stations, and support the necessary flow of data from aircraft to weapon and vice versa as required.

For example, the LAU-7 is a single wingtip adaptor for the AIM-9 or air combat manoeuvring pod, while the LAU-127 enables an AIM-120 to be carried on the wingtip. A LAU-115 adaptor can be used to carry two LAU-7s (AIM-9) or two LAU-127s (AIM-120 pylons) on STAs 2, 3, 7 or 8. The LAU-116 is a missile ejector installed on the fuselage stations for the AIM-7 and AIM-120, while the AGM-88 HARM requires the LAU-118 launcher.

In all, there are more than 11 different types of LAU, but the range of BRUs and MERs is smaller, limited primarily to BRU-32 ER, BRU-33A vertical and canted ERs, BRU-41 improved MER and BRU-42 improved TER. Mk 58 marine location smoke markers can be carried on the BRU-41 improved MER.

Fuel load can be increased with the carriage of up to five external FPU-6 (2,448lb JP5 jet fuel capacity) or FPU-8 (2,530lb capacity) tanks, or four 480-gallon (3,645lb) fuel tanks. The CNU-188 baggage pod – converted from an AERO 1D fuel tank – can be carried to ferry aircrew equipment, spares or contraband!

The aircraft can be configured as an airborne tanker by carrying a centreline-mounted air refuelling store, the A/A 42R-1 pod. It can also fly banner-towing missions when equipped with the TDU-32/B on the centreline station. The ALQ-167 electronic warfare pod may be carried if required, as can the ADM-141 towed air-launched decoy (TALD) and ALE-50 towed decoy.

It is usual to see the aircraft equipped with a target pod – typically the AAS-38 Nite HAWK for the Legacy Hornet, AAQ-28 Litening pod (USMC and Finnish Air Force) and the ASQ-228 ATFLIR for the Super Hornet, but sometimes the ASQ-173 Laser Detector Tracker/Strike Camera pod (LDT/CAM) is carried. Since 2003, the Fast Tactical

LEFT The AAQ-28 Litening pod can also be carried by the Hornet – and is often seen on US Marine Corps and European Hornets – and is installed as per this technical illustration. *(US Navy)*

Imagery (FTI-II) photoreconnaissance pod has also been available, allowing the aircraft to transmit and receive data to and from battlefield commanders within line of sight and in real time.

During training, captive carry missiles (CATMs) are combined with some form of air combat instrumentation pod carried on a wing pylon, typically an ASQ T-16, T-17 or T-31 TACTS (tactical aircrew combat training system) pod.

Air-to-ground

For peacetime continuation training, the aircraft can employ Mk 76, BDU-33, BDU-45, BDU-48 and BDU-57 practice bombs. In addition, LUU-2 parachute flares can be carried for night operations.

The AWW-9B data link pod and AWW-13 advanced data link pod, required for Walleye and SLAM operations respectively, are carried on the centreline station.

Unguided munitions

The F/A-18 can employ the full range of unguided air-to-ground weapons in the US Navy arsenal.

Rockets:

- LAU-61 and LAU-68 2.75in, and LAU-10 5in Zuni rocket pods

500lb class:

- Mk 82 LDGP, BLU-110, BLU-111 and the BLU-126/B Low Collateral Damage Bomb. The BLU-126 is externally identical to the BLU-111, but features a smaller explosive charge
- Sea mines include Mk36 Destructor, and Quickstrike mine Mk 62
- CBU-78 Gator, Mk 20 Rockeye II, CBU-79 and CBU-99 Rockeye II and CBU-100 cluster weapons
- Mk 77 fire bomb, more infamously known as 'napalm'

1,000lb class:

- Mk 83 LDGP, Mk 40 Destructor, Mk 52 bottom mine, Mk 63 Quickstrike mine
- CBU-97 Sensor-Fuzed Weapon

2,000lb class:

- Mk 84 LDGP, Mk 55 bottom mine and Mk 56 moored mine, Mk 60 CAPTOR moored mine and Mk 65 Quickstrike mine

Nuclear weapons:

- The Hornet and Super Hornet are cleared to employ the B61 and B83 nuclear freefall bombs.

Guided munitions

The Hornet and Super Hornet are both well equipped to deliver guided and precision-guided weapons.

Both boast targeting systems that are good enough to generate GPS-quality target coordinates – principally by finding the target visually or on radar, and then curing the target pod to generate the required target coordinates – but precise target locations can be preloaded into the mission computers before take-off, or passed inflight by voice or datalink transmission from other platforms.

500lb class:

- GBU-12 Paveway laser-guided bomb (LGB) and GBU-38 Joint Direct Attack Munition (JDAM)
- AGM-65 Maverick in EO, IR- and laser-guided variants

1,000lb class:

- AGM-88 HARM (high-speed anti-radiation missile)
GBU-16 Paveway LGB and GBU-32 JDAM Walleye I electro optically guided bomb
- AGM-154 Joint Stand-Off Attack Weapon (JSOW)

2,000lb class:

- GBU-10 Paveway LGB, GBU-24 Paveway LLLGB (low-level LGB), GBU-31 JDAM
- Walleye II EO-guided bomb

ABOVE A GBU-38 is prepped for launch by a red-shirt. The weapon is part of the JDAM series, offering precision capability regardless of weather conditions. *(US Navy)*

■ AGM-84D Harpoon, AGM-84E Stand-Off Land-Attack Missile (SLAM) and AGM-84H SLAM-ER.

Air-to-air

The Hornet and Super Hornet have taken over the mantle of Fleet Defender from the F-14, but they were designed from the outset to fight their way into the target area, then fight their way back out.

To enable them to operate in defence of the fleet, and as swing-role fighters, the F/A-18 family in US Navy service carry the AIM-7 Sparrow, AIM-9 Sidewinder and AIM-120 AMRAAM air-to-air missiles.

Super Hornet weapons, sensors and missions spotlight

ASD-12 SHARP

Armed and unarmed reconnaissance can be undertaken by Super Hornets equipped with the ASD-12 (XN-1) SHAred Reconnaissance Pod, a state-of-the-art tactical digital reconnaissance system. SHARP provides dual-band visible and infrared (IR) imagery collection, and downlinks the images in real time via a common data link (CDL) to the NAVy Input Station (NAVIS) ground station. This allows NAVIS analysts to perform real-time image screening and exploitation seconds after the Super Hornet crew overfly the target. SHARP is mounted on the centreline station and has two cameras for stand-off oblique imagery: one for medium range (approximately 5 to 15nm) and one for long range (approximately 15 to 50nm).

ASQ-228 ATFLIR

The Advanced Targeting Forward-Looking Infrared (ATFLIR) is the Super Hornet's primary passive cueing sensor. It integrates advanced EO and IR sensors with a laser rangefinder and designator, and has automatic identification algorithms built in, allowing the location, identification and designation of targets by day or night.

The pod, which is attached to one of the flush-mounted fuselage pylons, also features a laser spot tracker function, meaning that it can automatically spot the laser designation of other ground and airborne platforms.

APG-79 AESA

The Super Hornet's APG-79 AESA radar represents the very latest in active electronic scanned array radar technology. While it has been hampered by poor long-range search performance (this should be fixed by software updates), its multi-target track capabilities and resistance to conventional electronic jamming techniques, combined with the ability to near-simultaneously operate in air and ground modes, make it a 'game-changer'.

Tying the radar, weapons and sensors together is a very fast digital computer that uses fibre optic cables to receive huge volumes of data from each system, and which processes vast quantities of raw data before displaying it as digestible information to the pilot and WSO.

Suppression of Enemy Air Defences (SEAD): JSOW, Maverick, HARM and TIALD

The F/A-18 employs the AGM-154 Joint Stand-Off Weapon (JSOW) against distant or heavily protected targets. The first ever combat use of the JSOW was by an F/A-18C during an Operation Southern Watch in January 1999, and the community has since gone on to employ it in OEF and OIF, too. JSOW contains 145 BLU-97/B Combined Effects Bomb (CEB) submunitions, making it a devastating tool with which to incapacitate or destroy enemy air defence sites.

The Hornet and Super Hornet also employ the AGM-88C HARM in the suppression and destruction roles. The HARM has a sensitive seeker that detects radar emissions. It offers pre-briefed (PB), pre-emptive (PE), self-protection (SP) and target of opportunity (TOO) modes, and is a fire-and-forget missile.

In PB mode, the Super Hornet crew program it with the known locations and frequencies of threat emitters in the target area. If the threat emitters are transmitting as the Super Hornet approaches the planned shot time, the missile can refine its targeting solution before it leaves the aircraft pylon. If not, it will be fired regardless, but will keep 'looking' for a radar source to

guide on until it impacts the pre-programmed coordinates. PE mode offers a similar capability, but the missile is fired towards only a very general set of target coordinates. This mode leaves it with a slightly shorter range, as it must fly a less energy-efficient route to the target.

SP mode gives the Super Hornet a short- to medium-range defensive capability that allows it to engage targets within 360 degrees. The HARM is slaved to the radar-warning receiver and given a prioritised list of threats. The pilot or WSO can either select the most pressing threat or allow the missile to decide which to engage immediately after launch. SP mode is similar to TOO mode, but TOO mode has a smaller search pattern that is limited to the field of view of the HARM's seeker and is better suited to the Super Hornet's self-escort missions.

The flexibility of the HARM means that Super Hornet crews on SEAD missions can fire pre-emptive and pre-briefed HARM shots that are timed to coincide with the arrival over the target of the main strike force. Similarly, the TOO and SP modes allow the crew the flexibility to very quickly react to a 'pop-up' threat emitter.

For close-in work, the F/A-18 relies on the AGM-65 Maverick fire-and-forget series of

BELOW The laser-guided AGM-65E Maverick provides the Hornet pilot or crew with the option of either self-designating a target using the Nite HAWK or ATFLIR (or any other laser designator), or allowing a ground-based designator to lase the target. *(US Navy)*

missiles. It provides the Super Hornet crew with an excellent capability for taking out pop-up radar-guided AAA, and for finishing off surface-to-air missile sites following a successful HARM attack. It is also excellent for neutralising battlefield threats such as armoured vehicles, and is well suited to CAS and battlefield air interdiction (BAI) missions.

The EO and IR Maverick seekers present the WSO and pilot with an image of what the sensor sees, and the missile can be cued by the ATFLIR, radar, pilot's heads-up display (HUD) or the crew's JHMCS. Once launched, the missile becomes a fire-and-forget weapon that cannot be retargeted or updated. The laser-guided variant can be programmed to detect the laser designations of other 'players' in the battlespace, allowing other aircraft or even ground-based designators to guide the missile to target. It must be continuously guided to target by the laser.

When deception or confusion of enemy air defences is called for, the ADM-141 Tactical Air-Launched Decoy (TALD) comes into its own. This little decoy, which appears on radar as a much larger target than it actually is, was used to great effect during Desert Storm and OIF. Droves of them were fired ahead of attacking Coalition aircraft, forcing enemy search-and-tracking radars to activate, thus making them easy targets for the follow-on HARM shooters. The Hornet can carry up to six of the 400lb decoys.

AGM-84 series: Harpoon and SLAM

Of the Super Hornet's vast array of air-to-ground weapons, the AGM-84E Harpoon anti-ship missile and AGM-84H/K Stand-Off Land Attack Missile-Expanded Response (SLAM-ER), form the cornerstone of its stand-off, powered precision strike capability.

The Block II AGM-84L Harpoon uses the software, mission computer, integrated Global Positioning System and Inertial Navigation System and the GPS antenna and receiver from the SLAM-ER. Block III adds a data link to allow the missile to be updated in flight via the Super Hornet's AN/AWW-14 data link pod. Whether the target is a structure on land or a ship at sea, the weapon is devastating. It can be fired at a pre-planned target, using

GPS to hit a designated target aim point that is pre-programmed before flight, or targeted in TOO mode via the Super Hornet's radar or ATFLIR.

With the Block III missile in the terminal phase of flight, the AWW-14 can be used to send it the latest coordinates of the target. Thus, if the pilot continues to monitor the target on radar or on the ATFLIR, he can update the missile up until the moment of impact.

Out of the very successful Block I Harpoon came the interim AGM-84E Stand-Off Land-Attack Missile. SLAM used the seeker head from the AGM-65 Maverick missile and the data link from the AGM-62 Walleye missile, and the resulting weapon has been a great success.

SLAM spawned the AGM-84H SLAM-Enhanced Response, which can strike targets more than 150 miles distant and is therefore an 'over-the-horizon' precision-strike weapon. It, too, can be employed against sea and land targets, and it even has the ability to strike moving ground targets. It offers both pre-planned and TOO modes of attack, and can be used either as a fire-and-forget mode or in the tactically flexible 'man-in-the-loop' mode. GPS guides SLAM-ER into the target area (aided by mid-course updates generated by the Super Hornet's radar, if available) and ensures that its imaging IR seeker is pointed directly at the target. The missile then automatically computes target velocity and keeps the target within the missile-seeker field of view. The pilot or WSO can now refine its aim point or leave the missile as it is.

SLAM-ER was the first missile ever to permit retargeting after launch. For the Super Hornet crew this means that they can assess the state of the primary target through the missile imaging IR video display in the cockpit (transmitted to them via the AWW-14). If the primary target has already been destroyed or if the crew receive information while the missile is airborne that makes them want to assign a new target to the weapon, they can use the data link to re-aim it at a secondary objective.

This man-in-the-loop mode uses a software technique known as 'Stop-Motion Aimpoint Update', which allows the Super Hornet crew to freeze the target scene video in on the cockpit display, and then use their 'acquisition' cursors to designate a precise aim point.

Chapter Eight

Flying the Super Hornet

Pilot, Cdr Jason 'Tike' Gustin, US Navy

The Super Hornet is the world's premier strike fighter. Cdr Jason 'Tike' Gustin, US Navy, had the exciting opportunity to fly both the F/A-18E and the F for more than ten years. During that time he flew over 2,500 hours, dozens of combat missions and made 575 carrier-arrested landings in all types of weather, both day and night. In this chapter he shares a little of what that experience has been like.

OPPOSITE The Super Hornet is the ultimate incarnation of the F/A-18. The F/A-18F, seen here, carries a crew of two and is thoroughly adept at switching from air-to-air to air-to-ground combat at will. *(Steve Davies/FJ Photography)*

I'm going to talk you through what a typical air wing strike mission looks like during the pre-deployment evaluation that we call the Composite Unit Training Exercise (COMPTUEX).

Mission planning

Each mission begins with strike-lead planning. The strike is assigned to a Strike Lead to study the mission requirements, determine the strike composition, ordnance required, tactics to be employed and will be the overall lead for the planning, brief, execution and debrief. These flights are often part of a training syllabus to earn the qualification of Air Interdiction Mission Commander (AIMC), or CVW Strike Lead. This mission is to destroy simulated targets on a training range in central Florida, and is led by my squadron executive officer. He is a weapons system officer (WSO) who I am regularly crewed to fly with, and he formerly served as a squadron tactics instructor.

The combined mission-planning factors lead us to plan for eight Super Hornets, two Growlers and the Hawkeye. Four Rhinos will be a pre-strike sweep, clearing the path of any airborne threats for the division of Rhino strikers, who will each be carrying a single GBU-16 – a 1,000lb Paveway II series laser-guided bomb.

BELOW Swiss Air Force Hornet pilots brief in the relative comfort of a spacious, air-conditioned room. Navy pilots and WSOs must conduct their briefings in more cramped environs. *(Steve Davies/FJ Photography)*

The brief

Everyone gathers into the Strike Lead's squadron-ready room. The clanging of heavy steel swinging table tops and the grinding of the slide bearings of the sheet metal drawers increases as aircrew gather their kneeboards and place their coffee down in anticipation for the Carrier Intelligence Center, or CVIC brief.

Prior to every launch, CVIC provides an operational brief over the ship's closed-circuit television. It starts precisely on time, and includes information as basic as the current and forecast weather; the direction and distance to the nearest airfields (referred to as 'pigeons'); navigational information such as the expected latitude and longitude of the ship at launch; and any nearby restricted airspace or commercial air routes; as well as a summary of all the flights that are taking off and landing as a part of this event. Today's brief is pretty uneventful, except for a solid overcast layer from 8,000–10,000ft over water, but the target area is totally clear.

When the CVIC brief is complete, the overall Strike Lead takes the floor. He is responsible for the success of the mission and commands the attention of all players for the brief. There are far too many details for him to drill down into every element for each component of the flight. He needs to communicate the most important items, keep the plan simple, easy to understand and trust that the steely-eyed killers in the room will rise to the occasion. Any brief that starts to drag on upwards of an hour is tantamount to fratricide – friendlies will be lost to stagnant hypoxia before you even get near the jet.

The slides are succinct, few in number and get right to the point. The overall mission objective is reinforced, the primary and secondary targets and threat laydown are discussed and the friendly composition reviewed. It focuses on items that keep everyone on the same page: comm flow, formation flow, go/no-go and abort criteria, time-on-target (TOT), the suppression of enemy air defense (SEAD) gameplan and each element's overall responsibilities. The remaining details will be covered by the strikers, fighters and SEAD package in their individual element briefs.

From here, the individual element leads brief their components individually. Each lead is a senior flight leader, or a junior officer under instruction who is working on gaining his next qualification. Here the brief drills down a little more on the fundamentals – the 'blocking and tackling' if you will. They will discuss in detail the planned formation, radar mechanics, the specific fighter tactics gameplan, target area mechanics, target acquisition and area study, weapon pre-flight and fusing, checklist adherence, basic admin procedures (such as the carrier launch and recovery, how emergencies will be handled), airborne tanking and even a little on-ball flying. This portion of the brief is most important for our junior crews, because this is where we take the time to emphasise the basics.

Walk

The first stop is the duty desk, where the aircrew sign out all classified materials. A good duty officer has pre-staged a small stack of materials for each jet's aircrew to take custody of before heading to the aircraft. The 'mission card' is a small, rugged, high-capacity PCMCIA data card. It is loaded with a variety of mission data, including GPS almanac data, navigational waypoints, Link-16 tactical data link system files, channelisation of frequencies for the two UHF/VHF radios, smart weapons initialisation files and other information that will ultimately be initialised to the aircraft's onboard computers. Preloading this information in advance on to the card allows rapid transfer of the required information into the jet during start-up checks. The mission cards for today have been loaded by the junior members of the flight after the mission planning was completed the previous night. They also prepared the Removable Memory Modules (RMMs), which are highly rugged solid-state digital recording drives that permit the recording of various cockpit displays during flight – a critical tool for post-flight debrief and analysis.

During actual combat missions, each aircrew would remove all velcroed patches and nametags and sign for controlled items. These include the mission card with the classified data for the flight, an M11 sidearm (Navy variant of the Sig Sauer P228), two loaded magazines and a blood chit.

The next stop is Maintenance Control, the central nervous system for the squadron's maintenance department. The 'A-sheet' is signed by the pilot-in-command, essentially taking legal custody for the aircraft for the upcoming flight. There is also a Form-F, or a weight-and-balance sheet, that provides us with the overall gross weight and centre-of-gravity data required to calculate our trim setting for catapult launch.

After all the paperwork is done, it's off to the paraloft, or 'PR shop'. Here the Parachute Riggers, or PRs, maintain all the flight gear and survival equipment. Ashore, the PR shop looks and feels like a locker room. During cyclic operations embarked, the tiny PR shop can be downright crowded, with aircrew coming and going from flights all throughout the day. We don the g-suit, parachute harness and survival vest. We cautiously unpack and put on our helmets, all fitted with the Joint Helmet-Mounted Cueing System (JHMCS) – a bulbous visor and helmet attachment that always made me think of John Merrick. It repeats HUD information, such as target data and aircraft speed and altitude to the inside of the visor, while simultaneously allowing the pilot to cue his radar, targeting pod or AIM-9 to anything he can point his head towards. There is a long pigtail that attaches to the aircraft by way of a rugged adapter plug that we weave through our webbing and attach to the parachute harness.

ABOVE On deck, flight helmets are mandatory for all aircrew. Here, VFA-102 'Diamondback' aircrew prepare for an early morning launch. *(US Navy)*

LEFT A green-shirt carries the weight board that the catapult officers and the Super Hornet crew check prior to the cat shot. This board shows a weight of 51,000lb with zero asymmetry. *(US Navy)*

at the conclusion of the catapult stroke. The Shooter and the catapult crew must account for the current local temperature, pressure and humidity, the relative wind over the deck and the required aircraft endspeed, in addition to the aircraft weight and ordnance configuration. Too much steam energy can cause the catapult to do severe damage to the aircraft at the beginning of the stroke, while not enough energy will result in insufficient speed to generate the aerodynamic lift required to sustain flight. Providing the weight chit in advance will make sure we have no problems during the launch.

The flight deck

It is very difficult to explain the feeling I get when I get to the flight deck – it is a strange dichotomy of emotions. On the one hand, there is excitement and energy that is so difficult to describe to someone who has never experienced it. There are scores of sailors – some of America's most vibrant youth – all frenetically working at their assigned tasks in what can only be thought of as 'organised chaos'. Every member of the flight deck crew wears a colour-coded jersey and float coat, which helps to rapidly identify their job on the flight deck. The purpled-shirted 'grapes' refuel aircraft and reposition fuel hoses that are the diameter of a fire hose; red-shirted ordnancemen – 'ordies' – push around dollys loaded with thousands of pounds of bombs in preparation to upload them to the aircraft *by hand*; brown-shirted plane captains (PCs) scramble to complete turnaround inspections and last-minute preparations for the upcoming launch; blue-shirted tractor drivers manoeuvre aircraft with a low-profile tow tractor, packing them as close together as possible in order to make use of every square inch of the flight deck. Flight quarters often run for 16 or 18 hours a day for six – sometimes seven – days a week in some of the most austere environments on earth. I gaze in awe at the pride, effort and passion that these

The junior pilot heads to Flight Deck Control, where he will deliver the 'weight chit' to the Catapult Officers, or 'Shooters'. The weight chit will have the event number, launch time, aircraft side number, gross weight at launch and category of asymmetry. Armed with this information, the Shooter and his team will calculate the required steam pressure required to propel the aircraft down the catapult with enough energy to achieve the necessary 'endspeed'

BELOW Pre-flighting a live GBU-12 LGB prior to a combat sortie, this WSO checks the seeker head to ensure that the correct laser pulse code has been dialled in. *(US Navy)*

FAR LEFT With deck space at a premium, external boarding ladders are rendered unnecessary thanks to the F/A-18's fold-down ladder, stored in the bottom of the port (left) LERX. The ladder is seen extended on this Swiss F/A-18C. *(Steve Davies/FJ Photography)*

LEFT Even the ALQ-99 jammer pods of the Growler must be pre-flighted – here an electronic warfare officer (EWO) checks that the nose-mounted propeller that powers the pod's electrical generator spins freely. *(US Navy)*

young men and women put into their work. Their professionalism and dedication to the mission is amazing – it is truly the source of our military's strength.

But on the other hand, there is serenity and calmness that comes with the sea; the steady winds mute the bustling activity and the unbroken horizon is devoid of distinction in all directions. Despite being 100 or so miles from the Florida coast, it feels like it could be thousands of miles away, and the magnificence of this business can be overwhelming. It is here that one really first realises – really *feels* – the truly unique capability that comes with strike-fighter aircraft launched from an aircraft carrier at sea.

Standing beside the aircraft boarding ladder to the plane is a young, sweaty, grimy airman – his face and hands covered in almost as much grease and grime as his brown jersey and float coat. But the long days and hard work of lugging heavy tie-down chains and doing pre-flight maintenance have no effect on his beaming smile. I give him a firm handshake and point to the GBU-16 hanging ominously under the wing and tell him a little about the upcoming mission. 'We are going to join up with about a dozen or so jets, head about hundred miles to the east, kill a whole bunch of bad guys, drop

this big monster on their toys and then kill some more on the way home.' His face lights up with excitement. These young sailors work their tails off seeing aeroplanes launch and seeing them

BELOW Red-shirts are the armourers, responsible for preparing, building, loading, hanging and fusing the Super Hornet's weapons. Here, a group of red-shirts install an AIM-9X Sidewinder on a Super Hornet wingtip pylon. *(US Navy)*

land, never knowing what happens over the horizon. It means the world to them knowing that the care and hard work they put into their job really makes a difference – even more so on the seventh or eighth month of deployment in 120+°F weather in the North Arabian Gulf.

My WSO and I quickly perform a pre-flight inspection, as we have literally thousands of times before – 'kick the tires and light the fires'. We spend a little extra focus on the fusing and wiring of the GBU-16. After climbing the ladder and conducting a cockpit sweep of all switches and knobs, I begin to strap in. There are 11 connections between the aircrew and the jet. The ejection seat has 8 – shoulders, hips, thighs and calves; the combined oxygen/comm cord; the g-suit; and the JHMCS, which can be particularly challenging to connect and fasten correctly to the quick-disconnect rigging on the hip of the parachute harness – it is definitely an acquired skill.

I quickly verify the position of all the switches. I run through fire detection circuit A. 'Bitchin Betty' speaks to me: '*Engine Fire Left, Engine Fire Left, Engine Fire Right, Engine Fire Right, APU Fire, APU Fire, Bleed Air Left, Bleed Air*

Left, Bleed Air Right, Bleed Air Right.' I cycle the battery to reset the test logic before testing circuit B – I could wait the 30 seconds for it to time out, but pilots have a strange sense of urgency and each little time-saving step becomes hardwired into us all.

Start-up and deck checks

As it does almost a dozen times a day on every carrier at sea, the ritual begins exactly 30 minutes prior to the scheduled launch. The booming voice of the Air Officer – the Air Boss, or simply 'Boss' – fills the flight deck from the flight deck announcement system (5MC) as if it were the voice of God: '*Onnnnn the flight deck, aircrew are now manning up for the event one launch. Clear the flight deck and catwalks of all unnecessary personnel. Ensure helmets are on and securely fastened, goggles down, gloves on and sleeves rolled down. Check all shot lines and foul lines. Check for loose gear about the deck. Ensure all engine exhaust and APU exhaust are clear of fuel lines and ordnance. Start the event one aircraft, START 'EM UP!*'

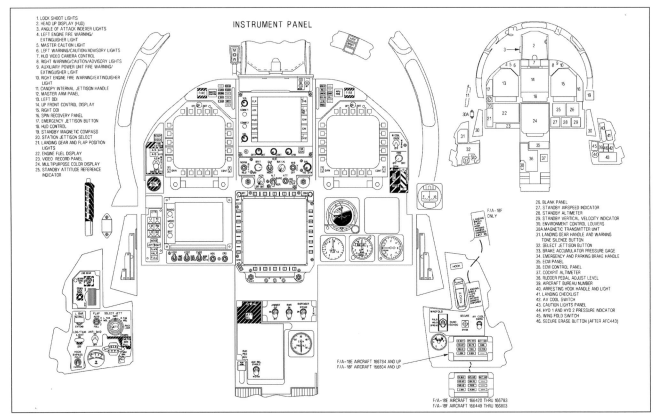

INSTRUMENT PANEL

1. LOCK SHOOT LIGHTS
2. HEAD UP DISPLAY (HUD)
3. ANGLE OF ATTACK INDEXER LIGHTS
4. LEFT ENGINE FIRE WARNING/ EXTINGUISHER LIGHT
5. MASTER CAUTION LIGHT
6. LEFT WARNING/CAUTION/ADVISORY LIGHTS
7. HUD VIDEO CAMERA CONTROL
8. RIGHT WARNING/CAUTION/ADVISORY LIGHTS
9. AUXILIARY POWER UNIT FIRE WARNING/ EXTINGUISHER LIGHT
10. RIGHT ENGINE FIRE WARNING/EXTINGUISHER LIGHT
11. CANOPY INTERNAL JETTISON HANDLE
12. MASTER ARM PANEL
13. LEFT DDI
14. UP FRONT CONTROL DISPLAY
15. RIGHT DDI
16. SPIN RECOVERY PANEL
17. EMERGENCY JETTISON BUTTON
18. HUD CONTROL
19. STANDBY MAGNETIC COMPASS
20. STATION JETTISON SELECT
21. LANDING GEAR AND FLAP POSITION LIGHTS
22. ENGINE FUEL DISPLAY
23. VIDEO RECORD PANEL
24. MULTIPURPOSE COLOR DISPLAY
25. STANDBY ATTITUDE REFERENCE INDICATOR

26. BLANK PANEL
27. STANDBY AIRSPEED INDICATOR
28. STANDBY ALTIMETER
29. STANDBY VERTICAL VELOCITY INDICATOR
30. ENVIRONMENT CONTROL LOUVERS
30A. MAGNETIC TRANSMITTER UNIT
31. LANDING GEAR HANDLE AND WARNING TONE SILENCE BUTTON
32. SELECT JETTISON BUTTON
33. BRAKE ACCUMULATOR PRESSURE GAGE
34. EMERGENCY AND PARKING BRAKE HANDLE
35. ECM PANEL
36. ECM CONTROL PANEL
37. COCKPIT ALTIMETER
38. RUDDER PEDAL ADJUST LEVEL
39. AIRCRAFT BUREAU NUMBER
40. ARRESTING HOOK HANDLE AND LIGHT
41. LANDING CHECKLIST
42. AV COOL SWITCH
43. CAUTION LIGHTS PANEL
44. HYD 1 AND HYD 2 PRESSURE INDICATOR
45. WING FOLD SWITCH
46. SECURE ERASE BUTTON (AFTER AFC443)

F/A-18F ONLY

F/A-18E AIRCRAFT 166784 AND UP
F/A-18F AIRCRAFT 166804 AND UP

F/A-18E AIRCRAFT 166420 THRU 166783
F/A-18F AIRCRAFT 166449 THRU 166803

(US Navy)

Like a dozen other pilots across the flight deck, I wag a three-fingered OK to my PC, who confirms the area surrounding the Auxiliary Power Unit (APU) exhaust is clear. The APU hums into life in preparation to port its high-pressure exhaust air into the turbine-starting units of the powerful General Electric engine. Once the APU is stabilised, I wag two fingers at the PC, who confirms we are ready to crank the starboard engine. As its rpm begins to rise, I advance the throttle to idle and it quickly starts to stir, with rising exhaust temperature, rpm and oil pressure all signs of the engine springing out of its quiet slumber. The generator kicks on and the whirr of countless cockpit systems energising fills the cockpit. What was only moments ago a quiet flight deck at sea is now

(Steve Davies/FJ Photography)

RIGHT, OPPOSITE BOTTOM AND BELOW
The pilot's office of the F/A-18E/F is spacious. The three displays dominate and the stick is noteworthy for its selection of buttons and switches – each shaped differently to allow the pilot to distinguish between them all by feel and position alone.

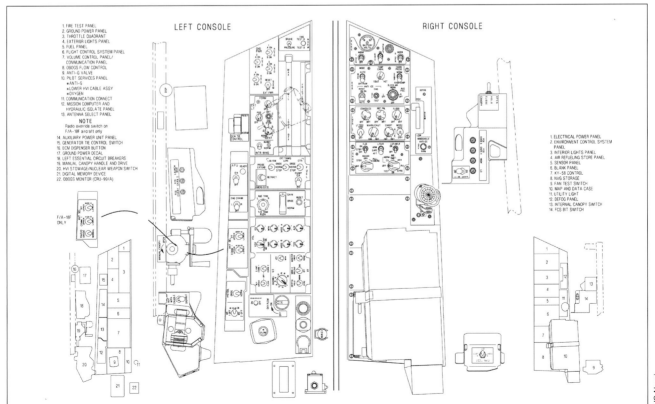

(US Navy)

roaring with the deafening sounds of combat aircraft preparing to launch.

At the pre-briefed time, we conduct a series of comm checks with the members of the Hammer division. They are highly scripted, and are used to verify the proper channelisation and set-up of the various radios and tactical communications nets. These are critical, because if you can't pass the comm checks, you can't communicate in the fight.

> *'Hammer check in pri, Hammer 21.'*
> *'Hammer 22.'*
> *'Hammer 23.'*
> *'Hammer 24.'*

Hammer 21 leads the element through a half-dozen or so checks without a hitch. This is a good sign. Shortly thereafter, the overall check-in is commenced by 'X-ray Papa' – XP is the callsign for the strike element watch officer on board the carrier – a member of the embarked CVW staff, and an experienced carrier bubba himself. He will maintain a link to the Strike Lead via the controllers in the E-2 Hawkeye. Just prior to launch, he verifies the status of the strike package and passes any late breaking intel, or 'words'. *'Tarbox check in. X-ray Papa.'* (Tarbox is the callsign for the air wing).

Each element lead responds in order: *'Sweep 11.' 'Hammer 21.' 'Tron 31.' 'Screwtop.' 'Shield 91.'* (Shield flight is the combat air patrol – CAP – scheduled to launch and support air defence of the ship during our event. The Shield lead is also our alternate lead for the fighter element in the event of a late-breaking change, such as an aircraft malfunction.) No one has checked in with any 'alibis' (system issues that may affect our go/no-go decision), which is a good start. XP then passes words, *'Tarbox, Harley reported active, Utah, three-six-zero, twelve. No other words to pass. TOT as planned.'* Harley was the code word for one of the simulated surface-to-air threats. There was intel that the system is up and operating, just north of our bullseye – this is important information to have.

I pass a thumbs-up to my plane captain, who then stands at the nose of the aircraft with his thumbs-up signal on the tip of the radome, signalling to all that we are ready to taxi for launch. A yellow-shirt trots over to my aircraft, makes eye contact and verifies that I am up and ready. He then gives the signal to break

BELOW An Aviation Boatswain's Mate (Handling) – better known as a yellow-shirt – directs a VFA-115 F/A-18E over the shuttle on the flight deck of the USS *George Washington* (CVN 73). *(US Navy)*

down and unwrap the jet, removing all chocks and tie-down chains. Once this is complete, the PC stands abeam the cockpit laden with six heavy chains and gives me the signal for the numeral six (an index finger pointing horizontally), indicating that all six chains have indeed been removed from the aircraft prior to commencing taxi. I dutifully report to my WSO over the cockpit intercom system, or ICS, *'Breaking us down, ready to arm up?'* He replies, *'Armed in the back, aft initiate.'* I respond, *'Armed up front.'* Because the flight deck is an extremely unforgiving environment, there are *almost zero* circumstances where one would want to taxi an aircraft on the flight deck without having your ejection seats armed and ready to egress in the event it was needed. This verbal verification between crewmembers is also critical in order to ensure both are properly strapped in with the seat armed and ready to go prior to commencing taxi. It also begins the take-off checklist, which is conducted in the reverse order from shore-based operations. We complete the checklist, using challenge-and-reply, and wrap up with, *'wings, trim, and controls to go'* – indicating that these items will be completed after we cross the jet blast deflector immediately prior to launch.

No aircraft moves on the flight deck except under the direction of a yellow-shirt. The close tolerances and high premium for real estate on the flight deck makes it impossible for the pilot at the controls to see all he needs to see. In many cases, portions of the aircraft jut out over the water during taxi. In fact, the nosewheel assembly is actually slightly behind the pilot's seat, which can often lead you to feel like you are out over the water! As you have probably concluded, there is an inherent bond of trust between the pilot and the director during taxi. It is much different than a lineman on an airfield ramp, who may signal that the aircraft is clear of obstacles, or give the 'line up on me' signal – one which will *never* be used on the flight deck. Yellow-shirts wave both arms when the aircraft should taxi straight ahead – even if this is not straight at the director. A steady hand pointed to a mainwheel indicates to the pilot that a turn is required in that direction. A clenched fist indicates to perform a locked wheel turn. A tilt of the head urges a small, gentle steer. Pilots learn to judge the speed and magnitude of the

signals from the yellow-shirts, and by the end of an at-sea period, a tremendous amount of trust has been developed, leading to smoother, more efficient taxi operations. This trust is paramount, as every pilot learns when being taxied within inches of the edge of the flight deck . . . in some places where nothing is there to stop the aircraft from going over the side . . . *at night*.

Several yellow-shirts work together to taxi the aircraft to align in sequence for the launch. The Strike Lead will have provided a 'launch sequence plan' to facilitate the rendezvous and tanking order for the mission. This is another excellent example of the ship and airwing team working together. An organised launch plan provided to the Handler the previous night permits him to 'spot the deck' in order to make the taxi sequence as efficient as possible.

As we cross over the jet-blast deflector (JBD) the taxi director gives the wingspread signal, and after checking left and right my WSO confirms 'wings clear' to ensure we don't crunch anything as the wings lower from their folded position. I wrap up the final portion of the take-off checklist, *'Wings down and locked, lights out, beer cans are down, switch is lever-locked, trim 15, 40, 40, 40 and eleven-delta-three, right wing down,'* reading these numbers directly from the aircraft's flight control system status display in order to verify the flaps, ailerons and horizontal stabilator trim is correctly set for launch (the stabilator is set for a baseline of 11, but requires a 3-degree differential based on the lateral asymmetry generated by the GBU-16 on the left wing).

Carrier launch

Approaching the catapult shuttle, a green-shirt holds up a large black box, which displays white digits reminiscent of a 1970s-era alarm clock. The digits displayed match those we sent forward on the weight chit – 53200. My trusty WSO passes the green-shirt a thumbs-up and informs me 'Rogered fifty-three-two.' In this case, we are 53,000lb with a level-2 asymmetry, with an afterburner take-off. In the spirit of a country auctioneer, I verbally rattle through my emergency procedure for 'Emergency Catapult Flyaway': *'Throttles max rudder full against yaw roll emergency jettison push maintain 10 to 12 degrees pitch attitude with the waterline symbol do not exceed 14 degrees AOA (AOA tone) if unable to arrest yaw roll or stop settle eject.'*

My WSO and I subconsciously both reach forward and brush our left thumbs across the face of the emergency jettison button in our respective cockpits, reinforcing both the procedural knowledge and the muscle memory that would be required to find the button that would slick our jet of all external stores in just under 500 milliseconds. With the high gross weight and level-2 asymmetry, we know that we will be expecting 170 knots at the end of the catapult stroke, which by design gives us a 15-knot 'excess', or margin of error to ensure adequate flyaway performance. If the misfortune of an engine or catapult malfunction were to occur, we may likely have less airspeed than

necessary – so the rapid jettison of 7,000+lb of external stores may be enough keep the aircraft out of the water.

All around the aircraft, squadron maintenance personnel are conducting 'final checks' while on the roll, so that very few remaining checks occur while the aircraft is at full power in tension on the catapult. We are spotted on Cat-1, the rightmost catapult on the bow. I peek at my watch and note that we are approximately 2 minutes from launch.

My taxi director holds up both hands and makes a shooting gesture. In front of the jet stands the lead of the ordnance arming team. My WSO and I raise our hands above our heads to visually confirm that we are not touching anything in the cockpit. He signals to an 'ordie' to arm the CATM-9X mounted on the wingtip launcher. A second ordie electrically arms the ALE-47 countermeasure dispenser. Once arming is complete, the taxi director again has control of the aircraft and directs me to increase power and drive the launch bar up and over the catapult shuttle. A gentle click can be felt as the director clenches his fists, signalling me to hold the brakes. We stop momentarily for the catapult crew to verify we are settled into the spreader before running up the power to take some of the slack out of the system.

At approximately 45 seconds prior to launch, the director looks aft along the shot line, then forward towards the bow, and passes the 'take tension' signal. I release the brakes and

BELOW **Two catapult officers ('shooters') signal for launch aboard the USS *George Washington* (CVN 73). The VFA-102 F/A-18F Super Hornet strains-to against the holdback and all that remains is for the cat to shoot them down the deck.** *(US Navy)*

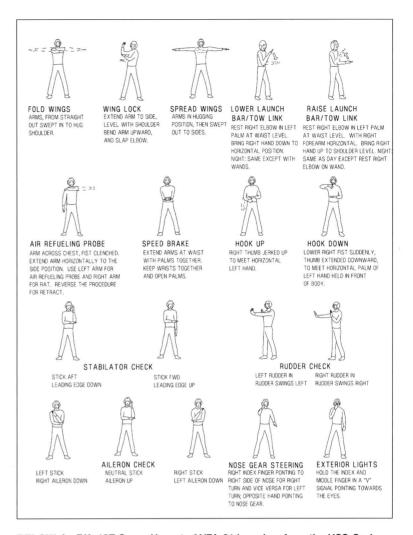

FOLD WINGS ARMS, FROM STRAIGHT OUT SWEPT IN TO HUG SHOULDER.

WING LOCK EXTEND ARM TO SIDE, LEVEL WITH SHOULDER BEND ARM UPWARD, AND SLAP ELBOW.

SPREAD WINGS ARMS IN HUGGING POSITION, THEN SWEPT OUT TO SIDES.

LOWER LAUNCH BAR/TOW LINK REST RIGHT ELBOW IN LEFT PALM AT WAIST LEVEL. BRING RIGHT HAND DOWN TO HORIZONTAL POSITION. NIGHT: SAME EXCEPT WITH WANDS.

RAISE LAUNCH BAR/TOW LINK REST RIGHT ELBOW IN LEFT PALM AT WAIST LEVEL. WITH RIGHT FOREARM HORIZONTAL. BRING RIGHT HAND UP TO SHOULDER LEVEL. NIGHT: SAME AS DAY EXCEPT REST RIGHT ELBOW ON WAND.

AIR REFUELING PROBE ARM ACROSS CHEST, FIST CLENCHED. EXTEND ARM HORIZONTALLY TO THE SIDE POSITION. USE LEFT ARM FOR AIR REFUELING PROBE AND RIGHT ARM FOR RAT. REVERSE THE PROCEDURE FOR RETRACT.

SPEED BRAKE EXTEND ARMS AT WAIST WITH PALMS TOGETHER. KEEP WRISTS TOGETHER AND OPEN PALMS.

HOOK UP RIGHT THUMB JERKED UP TO MEET HORIZONTAL LEFT HAND.

HOOK DOWN LOWER RIGHT FIST SUDDENLY, THUMB EXTENDED DOWNWARD, TO MEET HORIZONTAL PALM OF LEFT HAND HELD IN FRONT OF BODY.

STABILATOR CHECK STICK AFT LEADING EDGE DOWN — STICK FWD LEADING EDGE UP

RUDDER CHECK LEFT RUDDER IN RUDDER SWINGS LEFT — RIGHT RUDDER IN RUDDER SWINGS RIGHT

LEFT STICK RIGHT AILERON DOWN

AILERON CHECK NEUTRAL STICK AILERON UP

RIGHT STICK LEFT AILERON DOWN

NOSE GEAR STEERING RIGHT INDEX FINGER PONTING TO RIGHT SIDE OF NOSE FOR RIGHT TURN AND VICE VERSA FOR LEFT TURN; OPPOSITE HAND POINTING TO NOSE GEAR.

EXTERIOR LIGHTS HOLD THE INDEX AND MIDDLE FINGER IN A "V" SIGNAL POINTING TOWARDS THE EYES.

feel what can be described as a heavy mallet hitting the underside of the jet as the catapult shuttle tugs forward to remove the remaining slack. The yellow-shirt is pointing at a catapult crewman who is under the aircraft verifying that tension is properly set. Once the green-shirt is safely out of the way, I am handed off to the Shooter, who is staring directly at me passing the 'run-up' signal.

My attention shifts inward as I smoothly advance the throttle to full military power. The aircraft squats in the shuttle as the nozzles open and almost 28,000lb of thrust comes alive. I flick the launch bar switch to the retract position and start my litany of pre-launch checks: *'That's a good squat, launch bar's up, lights out, no nosewheel steering, motors good, no overspeed, no overtemps, good hyds, good volts, I like it.'* My WSO dutifully replies *'I like it.'* I wipe out the controls, moving the stick and rudder throughout their full range of motion, testing the health of the hydraulics under load. I look to the Shooter who has now begun the 'raise the roof' signal – an open palm pressed up to the sky like a table waiter carrying a tray – the indication to select afterburner. I advance the throttle to full-AB and listen to the engines roar as they spew out over 40,000lb of combined thrust. I smartly salute the Shooter, indicating that we are ready for launch. My left hand continues to press the throttles forward, as they are prone to drift backwards during the cat stroke. My right hand reaches up and holds on to the grab handle on the canopy bow; the Rhino, and Hornet before it, requires zero pilot input during the catapult launch. The trim setting that was entered commands the flight control computers to capture the optimum pitch rate at the end of the catapult stroke. All that is required of the pilot is to monitor the endspeed, final pitch attitude and verify a positive rate of climb.

The Shooter returns the salute and commences the final round of checks. For

BELOW An F/A-18E Super Hornet of VFA-81 launches from the USS *Carl Vinson* (CVN 70). Waiting time on the deck is kept to a minimum and launches of pairs of aircraft further expedites the launch cycle. *(US Navy)*

While local area missions may not require air refuelling, most combat missions make full use of it. Here, a VFA-102 F/A-18F extends its fuel probe in preparation for a trip to the tanker. *(US Navy)*

what seems like an eternity, he points at all members of the launch team to verify their required elements are still a 'thumbs-up'. He checks the wind, the weight board, the aircraft final checkers, clear shot lines, takes one last look at his watch and leans forward in a lunging crouch, touches the flight deck and points to the bow.

A young petty officer has been standing in the starboard catwalk with his hands over his head in what can only be described as a 'stick 'em up' pose. He looks aft, looks forward, then reaches down and presses the button that starts the launch sequence, releasing the steam pressure to the catapult. The force of the shuttle on the launch bar overcomes the holdback, and the 26 tons of fuel, fire and steel jolts forward, pinning us backwards in our seats. Approximately 2 seconds and 300ft later, we are flying away at 175 knots, at *exactly* 16:00:00Z.

Rendezvous

Pre-launch on the flight deck went well, as evidenced by the fact that our wingman was positioned for launch and was catapulted at *exactly* the same time on Cat-3 as part of a 'covey launch' – simultaneous launches are possible with one on the bow and one on the waist. This procedure helps expedite the launch and rendezvous, makes for a more efficient mission profile and ultimately saves fuel. The Assistant Air Officer, or Mini-Boss, is heard on the primary frequency, *'201, 205, cleared to join.' I reply, '201.'* My wingman gently snuggles into cruise position as we level off at 500ft and accelerate to 300 knots on the departure profile.

Pairs of aircraft continue to launch together at approximately 40- to 45-second intervals, until the entire cycle's jets are airborne.

Immediately, we both begin to conduct our in-flight tacadmin checks. The ATFLIR is powered up, moving from its stowed position. The video modes are checked and the laser designator checked for proper operation and valid target ranging. Lead and wing alternate dispensing a test salvo of chaff and flare to verify proper operation. We cycle through our air-to-ground master mode to verify the proper operation of the uplock mechanism which secures the GBU-16 to the aircraft pylon – if it doesn't test correctly, we may have a bomb that won't release when commanded. During this time, we have checked in with two air-defence controllers who have verified our transponder systems are working properly – in addition to Mode-3, military IFF systems have Modes-2 and -4 that are used to indicate friendly forces. At 7 miles from the ship, we start a military-power climb to our en-route altitude. My wingman drifts into cruise formation as I watch the tactical data link display other elements of the strike package doing the same. As we approach the rendezvous stack, Hammers 23 and 24 have joined in position. Finishing up the tactical checklist, I 'fence' the flight in (FENCE being an acronym from ages ago, standing for Fire control, Emitters, Navigation, Communication, Expendables, but has since grown to include numerous other items on a tactical checklist). *'Hammer 21, fenced in, 14.9'* – 14.9 being my fuel state. My wingmen reply crisply in order and we slow to conserve gas as we await the strike package to join.

All friendly aircraft check in with Screwtop on the primary strike frequency. As our air-intercept controller (AIC), the E-2 must verify our Link-16 track information and friendly IFF. He will pass a quick 'alpha check' to each element, where we confirm our direction and distance from a pre-briefed geo-reference point, or 'bullseye' – in this case called 'Utah'. The Strike Lead also checks in with the Range Training Officer (RTO), an experienced aviator who is monitoring the frequency and a bandit frequency for safety of flight, proper kill removal of fighters and bandits and airspace compliance. The type of fight, weather and any restrictions are agreed upon.

'Hammer 21, RTO, bandits recommend all

altitudes, decks and blocks as briefed, 180 degrees of turn for strikers, target area is clear, altimeter 29.98, your bandits are set.'

'RTO, Hammer 21, all altitudes, decks and blocks as briefed, 29.98. Tapes on, fights on.'

'RTO echos, tapes on, fights on.'

Sweep push

Within moments, and approximately 45 seconds before the briefed time, the Sweeps push out. The fighters can be seen increasing their separation into the planned formation as they accelerate downrange. Screwtop provides the 'picture' – or the location of all the known enemy and suspected enemy aircraft. *'Screwtop, four groups, group Utah. …'* Four groups?! A little more than we expected, but each fighter has three AIM-120 AMRAAM, and each striker has one as well. Provided everyone employs proper tactics, four groups should be no problem – however, it sounds like intel needs to tighten up a little. Sweep 11 assigns targeting and his wingmen get down to work.

The strike element continues to hold patiently at the rendezvous point as we watch the fight unfold on our tactical displays. The data link allows us to see all information that the friendly fighters' radars are sharing. Today, it shows things are going well. Nothing but clean, concise, comm is heard, indicating everyone is really on their game:

'Sweep 23, Fox-3.'

'Screwtop, south lead group faded.'

'Sweep 22, timeout 2-ship, south trail group.'

I manage my turn to account for the winds and try to arrive at the push point exactly 5 minutes prior to our push, which will allow me one more lap to get set up for our ingress.

Tarbox push

The strike package pushes on time, drifting into our tactical formation. The Sweeps have started out well – we've heard three of the groups removed from the problem, but things are starting to break down.

'Screwtop, north trail group, Utah, 050, 55, leaning on Sweep 23, recommend Sweep 24 target north trail group.'

'Sweep 24.'

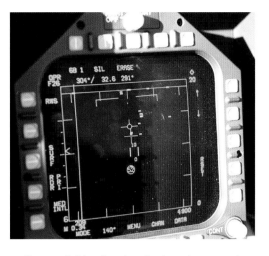

Dang – fighter flow has broken down, and it is time for the strikers to push. Based on the data link, it looks like Sweep 24 has drifted too far north in prosecuting his previous group to make the intercept geometry work and will not get a shot off.

AIC confirms the worst, the bandit isn't headed to Sweep 23, but towards the strike package: *'Hammer 21, Screwtop, north trail group Utah, 060, 60, hot, hostile, recommend target.'* This is where the Rhino, like the Hornet before it, stands out – as a true multi-mission platform. Laden with ordnance and planned as a dedicated strike asset, we can quickly transition to the air-to-air mission: my WSO calmly replies, *'Hammer, target north*

trail group.' All four of our radars have been sanitising the airspace in front of us, and we have pretty solid situational awareness (SA). On our employment timeline, we 'meld' into the north trail group – which is to say, shrink down the radar scan volume and focus its processing solely into the small chunk of airspace around the bandits, stepping through HOTAS 'finger-fire' required to properly reconfigure the radar modes. We are looking for 'breakout' – pre-meld we may not know how many bandits are in the group, but we will know soon. In fact, there are three – too bad the Sweeps didn't get at least one of them. On my aux radio I pipe up, letting my flight know what I see:

'Hammer 21, sorted three ship.'
'Hammer 22, sorted.'
'Hammer 23, sorted.'

Excellent – we all see the same radar breakout, and are set to engage our pre-briefed contacts within the group. Approaching our planned shot range, we get some good news from AIC: *'Screwtop, north trail group, Yugo.'* Nice! 'Yugo' was today's code word for a low-capability bandit – one without a radar, nor the ability to shoot us at range. *'Hammer, nose on.'* We hold our shots until we can reduce the range, giving our AMRAAMs more energy in the endgame of their flyout.

Four Rhinos with AMRAAM and AIM-9X against three 'Yugos' – it will be like taking candy from a baby. Each striker squeezes the trigger and reports the shot:

'Hammer 21, Fox-3.'
'Hammer 22, Fox-3.'
'Hammer 23, Fox-3.'

I immediately get tally of three tiny specks, the JHMCS aiding in the quick pick-up. I rock my weapons selector to AIM-9X and immediately hear the tone pick up in my headset. For training, I will employ an additional shot – in combat, I would try to conserve it until I knew how the AMRAAM fared. *'Hammer 21, Fox-2'* – my wingmen follow suit. *'Hammer 21, kill three-ship, north trail group.'* Moments later, I see flares pop out of the two F-5 Tiger IIs that are closing towards the striker division at a combined 900 knots or so. The south bandit looks like an A-4 and is rocking his wings, indicating he is confirmed dead.

I point the flight back towards the route and begin to sanitise the airspace ahead of us to ensure there are no threats that we may have missed. The picture is clear, and we continue on.

'Tron, Harley active, Utah, 360, 10' – the Growlers tell us the surface-to-air threat is rearing its head. This is not a problem, as our suppression plan accounted for this. It just goes to show how much a good intelligence shop can pay off.

We are only a few miles from our decision point, and I glance across the formation – everyone is more or less in the proper position. Due to the offset taken earlier, we are roughly 30 seconds behind timeline. I elect to turn the division and establish our attack formation early – cutting the corner 4 miles early will make up that timing perfectly. I broadcast, *'Screwtop, Hammer 21, picture.'* We need one last picture call from Screwtop before we take off our air-to-air hat and put on our air-to-ground hat. From

BELOW Visual cues are used to ensure that proper formation is maintained – lining up a wingtip with the pilot's head, or making sure that the sight picture of the exhaust nozzles looks just right are two examples.
(US Navy)

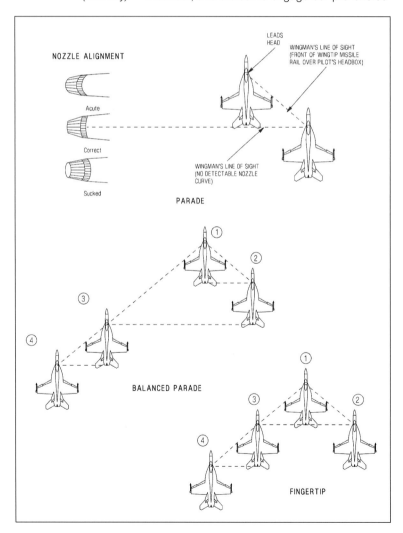

the brief, we formulated a 'bubble' around the target, which we want to be free from airborne threats while we prosecute the ground target. The size and shape of this bubble is based on complexity of the attack profile, types and locations of threat airfields and their fighters, as well as other factors. *'Screwtop, single group at Memphis, drag north, no factor.'* Immediately following and exactly on time, I hear the EA-18G Growler open the SEAD window with his first simulated HARM launch that opens the suppression window, *'Tron, magnum.'* The strike package is firing on all cylinders.

Hammer attack

With the target area clear of threats, the Hammers are now dedicated strike platforms. On primary, I command the flight, *'Hammer, attack',* and I start our pre-briefed turn into the attack formation.

My WSO toggles the aircraft to the A/G Master Mode, and we begin to execute our attack checklist. The waypoint steering to the target shows us about 10 seconds behind our desired TOT, but as we accelerate to our release airspeed, we will almost exactly make up the time. Weapon fusing and delay settings are verified, laser codes confirmed and video recording enabled as we watch the target

ABOVE Flying in close formation into combat is not very 'tactical', but it can help mask the true number of aircraft in the raiding party until the last minute. These F/A-18E Super Hornets from the 'Royal Maces' (VFA-27) form part of a fly-by, but they provide some idea of what such a deception might look like. *(US Navy)*

BELOW While the sweepers and strikers are out throwing missiles and iron at the enemy, the Growler attacks with a mix of HARM missiles and 'trons, ensuring that the threat is first suppressed and (if all goes to plan) then destroyed. *(US Navy)*

HARM launch, the enemy site is destroyed and he continues on to the target. He will be slightly behind but is able to make up ground and strike his desired point of impact (DPI).

As TREL counts down, my WSO surveys the target area on the ATFLIR, verifying the target area features we covered in the brief. Our DPI is an earthen bunker – simulating an IED factory – the second from the north in an array of six bunkers. With the target acquired, he reports on ICS, *'Captured.'* The ATFLIR laser fires to verify range to target and sweeten the delivery computation. With 10 seconds TREL, I centre the aircraft on the azimuth steering line, verify my attack checklist complete and press and hold the pickle button, essentially giving the jet permission to release the bomb at the calculated ballistic release point. At TREL of zero, I feel a gentle thump reverberate through the jet as the left wing pops up gently as the GBU-16 falls away at 510 knots. The TREL indication is replaced with a TTI (time-to-impact) readout, and we ensure the laser is firing on the proper code during the critical portion of the weapon flight. When TTI ticks from one to zero, a white trail zips across the ATFLIR display like a tiny comet before being saturated with infrared energy.

Within approximately 2 seconds, all four 1,000lb laser-guided bombs from the Hammers hit exactly on their intended DPIs, filling the strikers' ATFLIR displays with a rapidly blooming ball of fire, smoke and debris. My WSO zooms out the display and captures the area surrounding the target, which will help the targeting team determine the effects of the

ABOVE When the air is humid, no other aircraft can create vapour and condensation like the Super Hornet. The cloud of compressed gas that burbles off the back of the aircraft indicates that it is pulling a good number of gs. *(US Navy)*

area come into focus on the ATFLIR display. The Rhino's mission computer is continuously calculating the effects of wind, aircraft attitude and g, true airspeed and the ballistic profile of the GBU-16 to determine the proper release point. With this system, a skilled pilot can deliver even an unguided Mk 83 to within a few feet of his desired target – plenty close enough for 1,000lb of high explosive. The system calculates a time-to-release (TREL) of 35 seconds. I verify we are at minimum altitude and airspeed for the weapon release when I hear my wingman – *'Hammer 22, defending South . . . [something garbled]'* – he has been targeted by the 'Harley', the simulated surface-to-air threat. However, due to the timely and well-planned

RIGHT A Royal Canadian Air Force drops a 500lb GBU-12 LGB. Just like the bigger GBU-16 LGB in the narrative, the Paveway's rear fins are spring-loaded to open following release. *(US Air Force)*

strike. He dutifully steps through each of the other Hammers' DPIs and cues the ATFLIR on each momentarily, pausing to collect bomb hit assessment (BHA) there as well – redundancy pays off, in the event of a recorder failure in another jet, we will have video confirmation of the bombs hitting their assigned targets.

Egress

As we leave the target area, we see two sections of Sweeps on the data link, who have set up 'sponge CAPs' to cover the Hammer egress. Unfortunately, Sweep 11 has run himself to a low fuel state, so he and his wingman have to leave the problem: *'Sweep 11, Sweep 12 terminate, bingo.'* Not ideal, but this is exactly how it may be in combat: without adequate fuel, a fighter cannot commit and engage adversary fighters due to risk of loss due to fuel starvation.

Just when we thought things were going well, Hammers 23 and 24 are engaged by the surface-to-air threats surrounding the target area now that the HARM window is closed. I look out and see two of my three wingmen execute a nose-low descending turn away, afterburners lit and expendables popping out in an attempt to defeat the simulated threat. Good execution, I think to myself, and they will be mutually supportive. Hammer 22 and I will continue to flow east.

Then it happens: *'Screwtop, picture, two groups; first additional group Utah 110, 15, track east, bogey spades; second additional group, Utah 260 15, track east, bogey spades.'* Two groups of unknown identity have entered the problem during our egress, and our south sponge CAP, Sweeps 11 and 12, are no longer available to defend the Hammers as we flow back to the ship. Is this where it all comes unravelled?

The AIC controller has changed his tone and inflection, passing a sense of urgency and importance to his next transmission, *'Hammer 21 Screwtop, first additional group, hot, very fast, bogey spades, leaning on Hammer 21.'* I immediately think, 'Did we miss something?' It may be a 'training-ism' to have bogeys mysteriously appear behind us after we just kicked the door down and broke a bunch of their toys – but it could also really happen in

the real world, a 'strip alert' or low-altitude CAP that managed to go unnoticed by friendly radars until now.

In any case, I have someone on my tail that I cannot identify, pointed at me, going really fast, and I shot my one and only radar missile on the ingress. *'Hammer 21, 22, target second additional group. VID, VID.'* I remind everyone that we cannot shoot this guy until we have positive visual identification. Just another day at the office.

Hammer 22 and I execute a pre-briefed manoeuvre to separate the flight and isolate the bogey by forcing him to choose one of us to pick on. He chose poorly, for he is still leaning on me. A couple of brief comm calls later, and Hammer 22 is pitching back in to scrape this guy off my tail. As Hammer 22's radar picks up track, I see the bogey pop up on my data link display. The bogey is closer than we thought, and Hammer 22's nose is too far in trail: he doesn't have the geometry to make the intercept! Because I am on my own, highly defensive, tail-on to a supersonic bandit that will very soon have me within his missile range, and I am at risk to get shot in the burner cans right now, I do the only thing that offers me a shot at survival – time to bare my fangs and pitch back in.

Being close to 500 knots, I have the full nose and pitch authority that the Rhino has to offer. I roll on to a knife's edge, smoothly pull full aft-stick right to the g-limiter and settle into a 7.5g, slightly

ABOVE Entering slow-speed flight following aggressive manoeuvring, wingtip streamers will continue to trail even after the voluminous clouds of vapour have gone. This F/A-18F demonstrates the effect during the relatively benign phase of flight that is take-off. *(US Navy)*

nose-high break turn to try to meet the bogey coming down from above me. The jet performs like a race car, no longer burdened by the 1,000lb weapon we recently deposited on the enemy. As my g-suit inflates, my body automatically responds to the increased g with a 'hic' manoeuvre – designed to keep the blood in the upper body during high g-forces. I momentarily back the throttles off to ensure I am not in afterburner and am not needlessly arcing in a big sloppy circle – which would be a fundamental error. The wing of the aircraft erupts into a milky white cloud and thin strands of 'vapes' trail off the wingtip pylons as the low pressure atop the wing forms instant condensate. My hands, head and shoulders slouch down under the increased forces, weighing me down as if I were a 1,300lb man. I 'hic' again to keep the lights on; it will ease up as the airspeed bleeds down and less g is available . . . just a little bit longer!

I know the bogey can see me, so if it hasn't shot yet he will soon – I instinctively pulse out chaff and flare to protect myself against any missile he may be employing. My wingman may be out of position and out of radar missiles, but his radar gets a lock and the tactical data link gives me a high-quality trackfile to designate as my primary target. I get range, a target designation box, and most comfortingly, my AIM-9X slaves to the bogey. For the shortest of moments, we hear a low-pitched growl; but almost immediately it establishes a track, when it then shifts to the steady purr indicating it is ready to fire. I get sight of the bandit, a little less than 2 miles – good, I can keep my turn in and hopefully meet him high-aspect! I will be slow, but at least he will be in front of me. As I continue to track the nose around, I note that we are decelerating through 200 knots – *much* slower than I want to be. Flares continue to come out, and as the merge happens, I plug the blowers back in and squint to recognise an F-21 Kfir – an Israeli-made fighter flown by the contract adversary firm that supplements our training. *'Shoot shoot, Kfir!'* I hear my wingman reply sheepishly, *'Hammer 22, no shot.'* Looking over my shoulder, I see the Kfir has turned across my tail to his left. Due to his speed and turn performance, I know that I must reverse and take advantage of my smaller turn circle. In full afterburner, I reverse, plant the stick in my

lap, and pull to the lift limit. The Rhino's nose quickly tracks to the right as the jet squats beneath me. My fingers rapidly running through the HOTAS to select my AIM-9X and enable my 'uplooks' – cueing pointers that point out of the helmet as if they were deer antlers, which allow the pilot to slave the missile at very high angles off the nose. I successfully get a seeker track as the Kfir is through about 90 degrees of his turn and just over a mile away – he arrived at the merge with far too much airspeed to manage his turn and is arcing in a big left-hand turn across the horizon. I crane my neck around to verify the AIM-9X seeker indicator in my JHMCS is tracking him, and squeeze, *'Hammer 21, Fox-2.'* After doing some mental maths for the missile time-of-flight, I proudly report, *'Hammer 21, kill single Kfir, left-hand turn, fourteen thousand.'*

We flew east again, sanitise the area around us with a short-range radar profile and use our data link to assess where the closest friendlies are – Hammer 22 is approximately 3 miles in trail. We head towards the ship and get a picture from the Hawkeye's controller. All airborne threats are destroyed, and we have a clear path to Mom. I wrap things up with a standard knock-it-off cadence, which is echoed by all the flight leads and the RTO. The fight is over.

Each flight lead gets confirmation of the knock-it-off from each fighter on the tac frequency and start the RTB profile. With 40 miles or so to the ship, we have a lot of admin to do in a short period of time, and our recovery window is only 15 minutes away. The overall Strike Lead contacts XP with the real-time intel and reports our tally: at least ten splashed bandits, and four primary targets destroyed.

Carrier recovery

My division of Hammers is back together, and we are back on the throttle in a fuel-conservation profile. The ship will not be ready for us to land until the next launch is complete – those aeroplanes are all started up and have taxied to queue up for launch, leaving no room on the deck for landing aircraft until the launch is completed. I get a quick fuel check, and find that Hammer 22 is 300lb below ladder. A fuel ladder is a rough fuel plan that covers each 15-minute interval from your expected ramp time and runs backwards until your launch time. Each rung of the ladder shows the amount of fuel required to simply stay airborne on a max endurance profile. Depending on aircraft configuration and drag, this is roughly 1,300–1,600lb per 15 minutes. Because we have a little time and are on a descent profile, we will burn less than required, and should show up with enough fuel for at least two landing attempts before needing to get gas from the tanker.

We switch the flight through the strike controller and marshal controller, who passes the basic ship's weather and expected recovery course. With my right hand, I lower my hook, signalling to the flight to verify their feet-wet checks are complete. Silent confirmation is received when all three of their hooks are also down. When we get eyes on the ship, we report, *'Marshal, 201 see you at 12, low state five point eight.'* As we descend, we switch the tower frequency and enter the holding stack.

The overhead holding pattern at the ship is a comm-out, pilot-controlled stack. If things go well, not a single word will be said on the radio – 'Ziplip' we call it. It is only used in relatively good weather in the daytime, and is highly reliant

ABOVE Post-mission refuelling can be used to allow supporting players like the Growler – or this F/A-18A armed with AGM-88 HARMs – to remain on station longer and to cover the egress of other strikers. *(US Air Force)*

BELOW Approaching the carrier, the pilot has yet to complete what some consider to be the most difficult part of the mission – landing aboard the boat. This F/A-18A Hornet assigned to the 'War Party', VFA-87, approaches the USS *Theodore Roosevelt* (CVN 71) with hook lowered. *(US Navy)*

on strict procedural compliance and a vigilant visual lookout. Overhead holding is used to expeditiously recover aircraft as soon as possible after the launch is complete. As we descend to our standard holding altitude, we see the tanker launch exactly 10 minutes before the main launch. He will climb overhead and get another jet to check the operation of his refuelling store. After that, he will quietly watch the recovery, and be ready to 'hawk' any low fuel-state aircraft that has trouble getting aboard – which is usually far more likely at night than in the day.

As the on-time launch commences, I manoeuvre my formation gracefully around the 5-mile holding pattern, setting up 180

degrees out from the Sweep division. We are both at 2,000ft overhead, which is a non-verbal challenge to each other, for there is tremendous pride in being the first to enter the pattern, or 'break the deck'. It is a game of cat-and-mouse, as aircraft can only commence for the initial from 'point three' – which is opposite the circle from the ship, 5 miles across and headed opposite the recovery course. It must be expertly timed so that you arrive overhead the ship at 350KIAS (minimum, of course), 800ft AGL, at exactly the time that the last aircraft is being shot from the waist catapult. Any earlier, and you may arrive to find a foul-deck and get waved off. Any later and there is open-deck time, which we strive to avoid. Aircraft carriers have to steam into the wind in order to launch and recover aircraft, which may not be in the most desirable direction – it may slow transit, drag the carrier further away from the target, or closer to threats, maritime traffic or someone's territorial waters. If you are responsible for excessive open-deck time, you will likely get the attention of at least the Air Boss, if not the ship's captain – and it won't be the kind of attention you want to get.

As we jockey for position across the circle, we watch the coveys of jets launch. When there are two to go at the waist, I make my play. At point three, I momentarily put my fuel dumps on – not because I am above my maximum landing weight, but as a signal to all those in the stack that I am 'going for it'. My wingmen tighten up the formation as we accelerate in the arc at 5nm, gently descending to 800ft, and then rolling wings-level approximately 3 miles behind the ship. I update my system's TACAN steering course line to align with the ship's wake, make my best mental guess at the windspeed based on the white caps, verify my

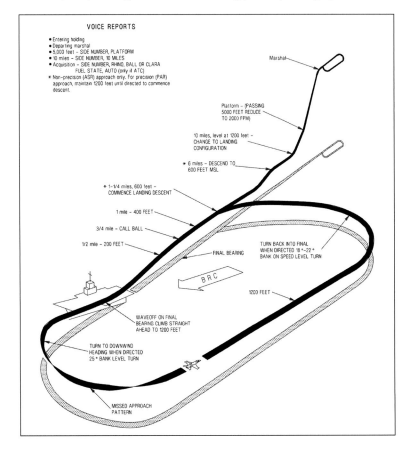

VOICE REPORTS
- Entering holding
- Departing marshal
- 5,000 feet – SIDE NUMBER, PLATFORM
- 10 miles – SIDE NUMBER, 10 MILES
- Acquisition – SIDE NUMBER, RHINO, BALL OR CLARA
  FUEL STATE, AUTO (only if ATC)
* Non-precision (ASR) approach only. For precision (PAR) approach, maintain 1200 feet until directed to commence descent.

Marshal

Platform – (PASSING 5000 FEET REDUCE TO 2000 FPM)

10 miles, level at 1200 feet – CHANGE TO LANDING CONFIGURATION

* 6 miles – DESCEND TO 600 FEET MSL

* 1-1/4 miles, 600 feet – COMMENCE LANDING DESCENT

1 mile – 400 FEET

3/4 mile – CALL BALL

1/2 mile – 200 FEET

FINAL BEARING

TURN BACK INTO FINAL WHEN DIRECTED 18°–22° BANK ON SPEED LEVEL TURN

BRC

1200 FEET

WAVEOFF ON FINAL BEARING CLIMB STRAIGHT AHEAD TO 1200 FEET

TURN TO DOWNWIND HEADING WHEN DIRECTED 25° BANK LEVEL TURN

MISSED APPROACH PATTERN

radar altimeter is set at 450ft and peek back at my three wingmen, who are perfectly positioned in starboard echelon. As we approach the wake from behind the ship at 450 knots, the final jet breaks tension on Cat-4. I can't help but smile when my WSO simply says, *'Nailed it.'*

Arriving with 100 extra knots and immediately snapping the jet into the break overhead the ship is pretty challenging, which is how and why fighter pilots tend to try to one-up each other in this regard. The 's**t hot break' as it is called, is fully acceptable at most ships, provided it is done safely and does not delay the recovery. The sight and sound of a division of strike fighters breaking overhead the ship the moment the launch is complete is indescribable, so it becomes almost a mortal sin to be first into the pattern and commence the break upwind of the ship – especially with a four-plane.

So I kiss off my flight and aggressively bank into an 85–90-degree angle-of-bank turn right over the landing area – I can see the fighter on Cat-4 just getting airborne under my wing. I smoothly pull to 7.5g to bleed the airspeed and in the mirrors I can see the rapid

decompression of the warm moist air form a cloud that crawls up the leading edge of the wing and blossom into a flickering cotton ball. I ease the pull in order to float the turn and arrive at the abeam position at 600ft and just over 1 mile from the ship. By this point in 'standard' shipboard approach, the gear and flaps would be down and airspeed stabilised at 136KIAS – but where's the fun in that?

I continue the turn and modulate the g until I reach 250KIAS, at which point I lower the gear and flaps. I ease into a descent to make my checkpoint at the '90' position – approximately 500ft with roughly 200fpm descent. The jet decelerates and yaws gently as the landing gear gently thumps into the down position. I rattle through the landing checklist:

'One two three down and locked lights out flaps full showing full hooks down no light skids off no light harness as you like dispensers off FLIRs standby on speed one thirty five.'

On the ICS, the WSO replies *'Three down aft initiate.'* During this time, countless personnel are scurrying about readying the deck for

BELOW LEFT AND BELOW The F/A-18E/F pilot is presented with a range of instrumentation and displays - from the HUD and EAD (below), to the angle of attack indexer lights (below left) to ensure that his approach to landing and progress down the 'groove' is as it should be. *(US Navy)*

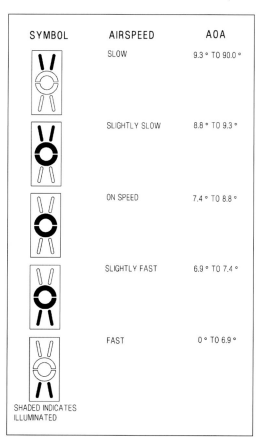

SYMBOL	AIRSPEED	AOA
	SLOW	9.3 ° TO 90.0 °
	SLIGHTLY SLOW	8.8 ° TO 9.3 °
	ON SPEED	7.4 ° TO 8.8 °
	SLIGHTLY FAST	6.9 ° TO 7.4 °
	FAST	0 ° TO 6.9 °

SHADED INDICATES ILLUMINATED

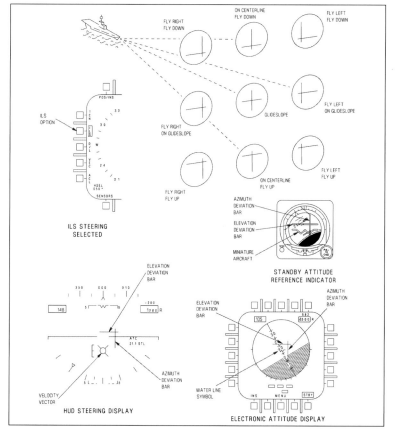

RIGHT The LSO is a squadron pilot who provides landing talk-down and grades every landing. He (or she) usually remains silent other than to direct corrections to power, line-up and glideslope. If the deck is fouled or the approach is dangerous, he holds a switch that allows him to show the wave-off signal on the 'meatball'. *(US Navy)*

recovery. Most importantly, they must clear the landing area (LA), which includes 'wrapping the waist', as Cats-3 and -4 sit squarely in the LA. They are motivated by my presence and the encouragement of the Air Boss on the 5MC to hustle and make a ready deck.

With the gear and flaps down, the jet rapidly decelerates, but I am still 40 knots fast. With approximately 45 degrees of turn to go, I take the throttles off the idle stop to ensure I have adequate spool-up when power is required. I ease the angle of bank as I cross the wake. I peek out at the Improved Fresnel Lens Optical Landing System (IFLOLS) – or the 'meatball' – and see the wave-off lights briefly flash, followed by the cut lights – this is the final operational check required before landings are permitted. We hear the radio check between the Landing Signals Officers (LSOs) and the Air Boss:

'Tower, Paddles, radio check.'
'Have you loud and clear.'
'Loud and clear on the backup, sir.'
'28 knots right dowwwn the angle.'

I am just reaching centreline and roll level to get my wings underneath me as I arrive at my landing speed – a true 8.1-degree angle-of-attack. I see cut lights – a non-verbal clearance to land – with the 'meatball' indicating a very slightly high approach.

To assist in the approach, I engage autothrottles with the tap of my ring finger and gently tug backwards on the stick to ensure they are working correctly. Over the course of the next 15 seconds, I nudge the stick gently forward and aft, inducing slight speed deviations that the autothrottles compensate for with power adjustments. Two very small, very rapid applications of back stick forces the ball slightly high as I wobble through 'the burble' – a region of rough air behind the ship

CENTRE An F/A-18F Super Hornet comes in to trap aboard the USS *Abraham Lincoln* (CVN 72). This VFA-2 'Bounty Hunters' pilot is trying to snag the 'three wire'. *(US Navy)*

LEFT The Fresnel Lens system – better known as the 'meatball' – is the primary glideslope reference for the pilot once he's in the groove. He'll correct line-up visually, but will rely on the meatball to correct for height. *(US Navy)*

that tends to pull jets down towards the ramp like the lava-hand from the old console game *Joust*. Being underpowered there can be pretty scary, so it is best to 'energise the ball' just a little bit. The ball settles back down to glideslope just as I touch down.

At touchdown, I slam the throttles forward – a mandatory action for all landings, so that in case a wire is missed, the aircraft can still fly away. In the blink of an eye, I feel the jet rapidly decelerate beneath me, forcing me forward in the straps. I pause a moment and bring throttles to idle. A yellow-shirt is waiting just to my right giving the 'brakes release' signal. I feel the wire gently tug the jet backwards, and the director signals me to raise the hook. In rapid succession, up come the flaps, I unlock the wings to enable full-time high nosewheel steering and quickly taxi out of the landing area – I must be clear within about 30 seconds, as successive planes will be landing in roughly 50- to 55-second intervals behind me.

Immediately clearing the LA, we have all of our ordnance de-armed, and we are taxied for shutdown. Climbing out of the jet, our PC looks to us with excitement in his eyes, noting that the GBU-16 we launched with didn't come back with us.

'How'd it go, sir?'

'It was AWESOME – I think we killed ten enemy jets, and we shacked the targets!'

I give him a high-five and shake his hand one more time. The sense of pride he feels is palpable, as we all know the amount of teamwork required to accomplish the mission. We go below, strip out of our flight gear and get ready for our mission debrief.

Summary

There comes a time in every pilot's career where he will fly his final flight. With every change in a duty assignment, we wonder if we will make it back to the cockpit. I can clearly recall my last flight in the Rhino, manning-up that beautiful October morning in Fallon, Nevada, with the uncertainty of ever flying again after my upcoming duty in the Pentagon. My path has returned me to flying in the Training Command, where I now have the privilege of training and developing the next generation of

LEFT Two VFA-211 F/A-18Fs cross the beach as they return to NAS Oceana, Virginia. Shore-based landings are flown on to runways painted to represent the carrier deck, ensuring that the pilot does not completely lose perspective during spells spent not at sea. *(US Navy)*

Navy and Marine Corps tailhook aviators. I will forever be grateful that I served my country as a Navy fighter pilot, and I will fondly look back at the awesome leaders, peers, wingmen and sailors who shared this journey with me.

I will leave you with one more thought, a sentiment cherished by many of my peers and predecessors that flew 'the Big Fighter'. It gracefully captures the spirit that lives in us all, and will forever be fitting:

A man has only one virginity to lose in fighters, and if it is a lovely plane he loses it to, there is where his heart will forever be.
Ernest Hemingway

BELOW Leaving their F/A-18A+ Hornets behind, pilots of the 'River Rattlers', VFA-204, conduct an informal debrief on their performance. The real debrief will begin once they have signed back their jets, deposited their flight gear and returned to the squadron-ready room. *(US Navy)*

Chapter Nine

Flying the Super Hornet

Weapons System Officer 'ShWRECK'

'Flying as a Weapon System Officer (WSO) in the F-18F is easily the most challenging and rewarding thing I have ever done. I can think of no more fruitful a career to have chosen, than to count myself among the small cadre of "zipper-suited sun Gods" who have made a life in the Navy strike fighter community.'

OPPOSITE The US Navy operates mixed squadrons of E- and F-model Super Hornets, but some squadrons are exclusively equipped with one type or the other. Here, two F/A-18Fs of the 'Checkmates' return to NAS Oceana following a training sortie. *(Steve Davies/FJ Photography)*

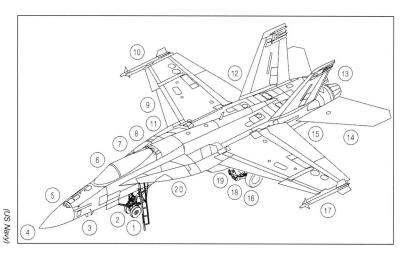

(US Navy)

The present-day F-18F is the culmination of 100 years of naval aviation. On the exterior it simply looks like a Hornet on steroids. Inside its skin, however, is housed the most sophisticated avionics suite and tactical displays the US Navy has ever fielded.

Though the F-18 series aircraft was initially designed as a single-seat multi-role fighter, it has become so advanced in its capabilities that it requires a second crewmember in the jet to truly take advantage of everything this aircraft has to offer.

Though Hollywood has usually depicted the Naval Flight Officer (NFO) as the Sancho Panza of military aviation, the truth is, an F-18F WSO is very likely quarterbacking a large force strike.

Selection and training

An aspiring WSO starts his career in the 'Cradle of Naval Aviation' at NAS Pensacola, Florida. Prior to earning wings of gold upon graduating from the VT-86 Sabre Hawks, a student NFO may be selected for Super Hornets. If so, he will soon be headed for training in the FRS (fleet replenishment squadron, still affectionately known by its former name, 'RAG', or replacement air group). The Super Hornet RAGs are the VFA-106 'Gladiators' at NAS Oceana, Virginia, and the VFA-122 'Flying Eagles' at NAS Lemoore, California.

During their time at the RAG, CAT One (category 1) WSOs hone their skills both in mission planning and in the cockpit. All phases of training include arduous academics, mission planning, simulators and flights.

Training for RWSOs (replacement WSOs)

places great emphasis on the crew concept, stressing that the success or failure of a crew is wholly reliant on how well the pilot and WSO adhere to Crew Coordination Standards (CCS) and Tactical Crew Coordination (TCC). A crew that works well together can achieve resounding success and near omniscient situational awareness that a single-seat crew simply may not be able to achieve, though a crew who does not mesh well can have a flight end in complete disaster.

Flight leadership is also greatly stressed during training with RWSOs performing the majority of syllabus events as 'Lead' in a section (a flight of two aircraft) or division (a flight of four aircraft), while their pilot counterparts are focusing on their responsibilities as a wingman. Crew solos – flights where RPs (replacement pilots) and RWSOs fly together in the same jet – are interspersed throughout the syllabus to build a sense of trust and crew self-reliance. With no instructor in the jet to save them from bad decision-making, these crews are forced to work together for success, almost right from the outset of their F-18F careers.

During the Familiarisation Phase, RWSOs learn about the navigation and communications capabilities of the Rhino. Simulators focus on emergency procedures, crew resource management as well as system familiarisation. Flights include aerobatics, VFR (visual flight rules) and IFR (instrument flight rules) navigation as well as day and night formation flying.

Once a student has mastered the basics, it's time to move on to the Strike Phase. Students will begin with low-level navigation, learning to use the jet's navigation system to pick through mountain ranges at 500ft and 480 knots to arrive on time and on target.

Next, the replacement aircrews will learn how to avoid and defeat various surface-to-air threats. As the students progress, they will learn how to first employ unguided bombs, culminating in 'Live Day', where a Replacement Pilot and Replacement WSO will be entrusted to deliver two live 500lb bombs on target, and perform strafing runs with live 20mm rounds.

After the basics have been mastered, the later portion of the strike will focus on the delivery of Precision-Guided Munitions (PGMs). Academics will be extensive,

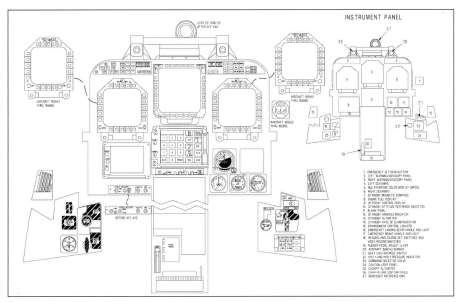

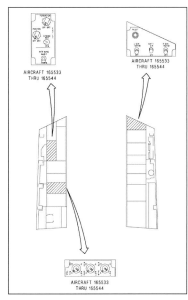

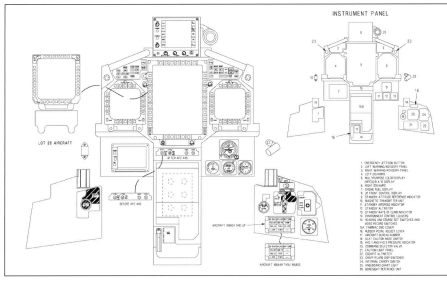

THIS PAGE Lots 21 to 25 F/A-18Fs featured rear cockpits in the training configuration (above left and above), effectively replicating most of the systems from the front cockpit. From Lot 26 onwards, F-model Super Hornets were delivered with the 'missionised cockpit' (left and below), featuring the removal of dual controls, the addition to twin hand controllers and the installation of an 8×10in LCD display in place of the aft multi-purpose colour display (MPCD). *(US Navy)*

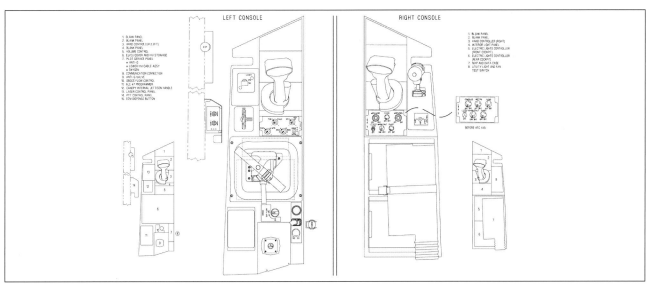

focusing on air-to-ground radar and FLIR target acquisition as well as mission planning for both GPS-guided JDAMs as well as laser-guided bombs (LGBs).

The intricate sequence of events that must occur to ensure these PGMs guide to their intended target is where the WSO really begins to shine. If the WSO does his job, all the pilot has to worry about is to 'put the thing on the thing and push the thing', meaning manoeuvre the jet to line up symbology and push the 'pickle' button to release the weapons.

The Strike Phase reaches its zenith in the Close Air Support and Urban Close Air Support flights. The dynamic nature of these missions truly highlights the importance of having a well-trained crew to maintain SA (situational awareness) and deliver deadly munitions in close proximity to friendly forces.

When students have completed Strike, they move on to Fighter Phase. Once again, RWSOs focus on becoming brilliant with the basics. The early stages of this phase consist of 1v1 intercepts. RWSOs first learn the basics of using the air-to-air radar, but then focus on their primary tactical displays. From these displays, the WSO can run the fight with a bird's eye view of the battlespace.

Once RWSOs are comfortable with a 1v1 fight, the challenge increases as they move on to section tactics. As the aircrew become more proficient, they rely on all previously applied building blocks and RWSOs will find themselves leading a Division Offensive Counter Air or Defensive Counter Air mission, requiring incredible

amounts of SA to manage the fight effectively, 'kill' all the bandits and return with no blue losses. In the final fighter event, a new RWSO will be leading the communication, managing formation, keeping SA to wingmen and making tactical decisions for a flight of four F-18s.

In conjunction with the Fighter Phase, students also go through a BFM (basic fighter manoeuvres) syllabus where new F-18 crews learn the basics of dogfighting. While it's true that BFM is a very pilot-centric skillset, a sharp WSO can save the day. RWSOs learn the basics of lookout, pursuit curves, offensive, defensive and high-aspect BFM. With proper training the pilot and WSO can fight as crew sharing lookout responsibilities.

In an offensive fight, the WSO can back up his or her pilot with airspeed and altitude awareness while recommending appropriate weapons and radar modes if the pilot's bucket is getting full. In a defensive fight, the WSO's primary objective is to maintain sight of the bandit and deck awareness while the pilot fights the jet, putting out defensive countermeasures at appropriate times. Where a two-seat crew really comes in handy is in a 2v1 fight where the crew must maintain SA to more than one aircraft.

After successfully completing the above-mentioned phases, the WSO may or may not go to Carrier Qualification. It is not a required part of the WSO syllabus at this time, but is highly beneficial and most RWSOs do go to 'the boat' in the RAG. During this phase of training (or in their first fleet squadron), WSOs learn the differences between operating shore-based and around the boat. Once they have completed the syllabus, newly qualified WSOs are 'patched'. A member of the fleet squadron they will be transferring to, tears off their old patches and places the new squadron's patches on the new WSO's flight suit, welcoming him or her to the fleet.

The fleet

WSOs are integral members of the squadron, the same as pilots. As far as 'ground jobs' go they have every opportunity as their pilot brethren. In an F-18F squadron it is not uncommon at all to have the skipper be a WSO, and the XO be a pilot (or vice versa), with the

department heads and division officers at a roughly even split between the two designators.

F-18F crews conduct all missions handed to the Strike Fighter community to include strike, CAS, armed reconnaissance, defensive and offensive counter air, and – yes – even the venerable tanker mission. The last mission uniquely reserved for F-18F crews is that of Forward Air Control (Airborne) or FAC(A). During FAC(A) missions, a qualified F-18F crew will direct CAS fire from various platforms, often in very close proximity to friendly ground troops. Instead of delivering ordnance from their aircraft, this crew will manage 'the stack', which could be comprised of F-18s, F-15s, B-1s or any number of Coalition aircraft. They will be in direct communication with ground forces, directing attacks on targets from the various aircraft in their stack. While all this is going on they are also de-conflicting artillery fire so that the strikers don't unexpectedly run into something nasty. Most importantly the FAC(A) crew is always maintaining SA to friendly positions to prevent fratricide.

From mission planning to the debrief, WSOs play an essential role in the mission's success. WSOs are responsible for making targeting products and using mission-planning software for both navigation and weapons delivery, as well as making the administrative kneeboard card and prepping recording devices. The WSO can be a crewmember in attendance of a brief, or he can be the mission lead giving the brief.

All briefs typically have the following flow: Objective Risk Management, Admin, TAC Admin and Execution, followed by any parting comments and keys to success. A brief can be as simple as a 'circle the wagons' bombing mission which doesn't take very much time at all, or it can be a multi-element large-force strike, and a WSO can be the lead of any F-18 element all the way up to and including the overall Mission Commander.

If the WSO is the mission lead, he will give the mass brief, which will then break down into individual elements. If the WSO is an element lead, that element will be in attendance at the mass brief, going over the major admin points, and the element lead will brief mission specifics to that group of Strike Fighters. After the brief there is usually a little bit of 'cowboy time' for

LEFT **The US Navy has never fielded so much computational power in a tactical fighter. Unsurprisingly, the missionised cockpit of the F/A-18F requires the full processing power of the Advanced Mission Computer and Display (AMCD) II to function.** *(Steve Davies/FJ Photography)*

the crews to decompress a little, grab a cup of coffee and get their mind right before a mission. At 'walk time' the crews dress in their flight gear; if on a combat mission they will check out their blood chit, M-11 sidearm and mission-essential products. The crew will then check the maintenance logs, the pilot will sign for the jet and they will pre-flight the aircraft before 'manning-up' the jet.

For the actual execution of the mission, let's take this from the perspective of a WSO fighter lead launching off the boat during a large force exercise, or LFE. After manning-up, the crew will divide responsibilities in preparing to go flying. At APU [auxiliary power unit] time, the pilot starts the jet (all the jets on the carrier start at the same time, to the second), with the WSO backing up any safety-related items.

While the pilot is getting his/her systems online, the WSO is checking the weapons, the targeting pod and ensuring the navigation and communications systems are set appropriately. The WSO conducts the flight check-in to ensure everyone in the strike and in his element is up and ready.

During taxi to the catapult, both crew members have their head on a swivel, making sure that the jet clears the many obstacles on

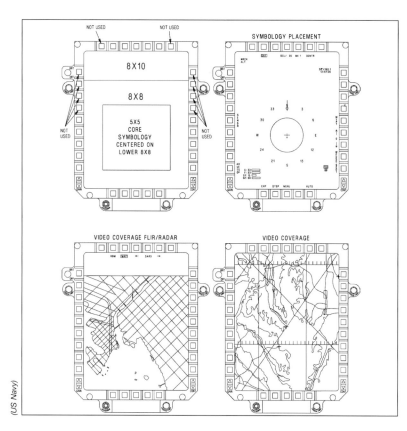

SYMBOLOGY PLACEMENT

8 X 10

8 X 8

5X5
CORE
SYMBOLOGY
CENTERED ON
LOWER 8X8

NOT USED

VIDEO COVERAGE FLIR/RADAR

VIDEO COVERAGE

(US Navy)

THIS PAGE The 8×10 display dominates the rear cockpit in terms of physical space and in terms of the focus that the WSO gives it. As shown in the schematic (above) and the two images (below and right), the display is highly configurable and can be used in a number of range scales. With its high resolution and massive 'real estate', it is easy to read and helps the WSO build a top-down picture of the battlespace. These images were shot on the ground, post-flight and once the Super Hornet's classified systems were inactive, but operationally the WSO would expect to see the display populated with symbology generated from data supplied by the radar, RWR, ATFLIR, HARM and off-board sensors on other Link 16-equipped assets.

(Steve Davies/FJ Photography)

the flight deck. During a Case 1 launch there is no communication over the radio. The flight deck crew hooks the launch bar to the catapult, the aircraft is put under tension, the engines are run up, final checks are completed, the pilot salutes, the Shooter touches the deck and off you go . . . there's nothing quite like the satisfying thump in the chest of a good cat shot.

After climbing away and performing a g-awareness manoeuvre, or 'G-Warm', the WSO checks out with Strike and Red Crown [command networks] making sure their IFF is sweet – functioning properly – before continuing on mission. The fighter element will then 'fence in' (check fuel, then configure emitters, navigation, communications and electronic countermeasures equipment for combat) and proceed to their CAP awaiting the COMEX (start of the exercise) and their 'push time'.

At the push time, the fighters will assume their briefed formation and proceed down-range toward the bandits' territory. From this point on it is the lead WSO's responsibility to manage the engagement. He or she will take the information broadcast by the E-2 Hawkeye and use that to create a picture of the airspace. It is the lead WSO's task to make tactical decisions for the flight that are best suited to the presentation at hand. He must also keep SA to his wingmen's

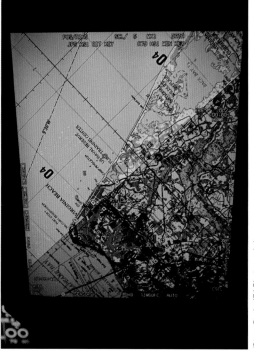

(Steve Davies/FJ Photography)

weapons status, fuel states and positions throughout the fight.

During a 4vX (four versus many) engagement with both fighters and bandits executing advanced tactics, there could be a lot to keep track of. An effective crew which fights in accordance with TCC and maintains a high level of SA can lay waste to even the most advanced adversaries that could currently threaten a strike package. With two people in the cockpit, the pilot only has to worry about fighting the jet, manoeuvring it into the best position to kill the enemy and staying alive. The WSO is making the big-picture tactical decisions for the fight. If the WSO is on top of his/her game (which should always be the case), they will be continuously feeding the pilot and flight the necessary SA from the initial call, to the merge, to engaged manoeuvring.

Simply put, the pilot is concerned with the *next* thing trying to kill them; the WSO is concerned with *everything* trying to kill them. A crew that works well together in the lead, with competent wingmen, have a much greater chance of success.

When the fight is over, and 'knock it off' is called, ending the engagement for all players,

ABOVE An F/A-18F of the 'Diamondbacks', VFA-102, launches from the USS *John C. Stennis*. The WSO monitors safety-critical items during this portion of the sortie. *(US Navy)*

BELOW Two VFA-2 'Bounty Hunters' F/A-18Fs prepare to launch from the USS *Abraham Lincoln* (CVN 72). While the pilot calls out his verbal cockpit checks, the WSO responds as appropriate. The nearest Super Hornet carries an unusual load of AIM-7 Sparrows on the outboard pylons and AGM-88 on the mid-board pylons. *(US Navy)*

and the pilot manages the push time. When it's time to execute the approach, the aircraft leaves the stack, the WSO transmits 'commencing' and dials in the final bearing. Passing 5,000ft, the WSO calls 'platform', cueing the pilot to slow the descent rate. The WSO is continuously monitoring airspeed altitude and course line, simultaneously keeping track of fuel state and possible diverts while the pilot flies the jet perilously low over the water at night.

At ¾ of a mile the WSO will transmit the Ball Call, '203, RHINO, BALL, 5.8'. There is a lot of information in this brief transmission. '203' lets the ship know which aircraft from what squadron is approaching. 'Rhino' and '5.8' let the ship know that the approaching aircraft is a Super Hornet (as opposed to a Legacy Hornet) with 5,800lb of fuel, so the arresting gear can be properly set. 'Ball' lets the Landing Signal Officer (LSO) know the crew sees the Fresnel lens or 'meatball' to serve as the primary visual aid when landing.

After the Ball Call the jet is now in the 'groove'. The WSO at this point is closely monitoring altitude, airspeed, descent rate and angle of attack, giving the pilot any information he requests (such as vertical airspeed) or that has fallen out of the pilot's scan. The WSO must be very careful not to use phraseology that could be confused with a directive call from 'Paddles', the LSO. After a successful trap (preferably an OK 3 wire), the WSO gives a hand signal to the flight deck chief regarding the jet's status and the crew taxis to wherever they are being parked.

Post-flight, the crew divvies up responsibilities once again after navigating the dangerous flight deck back to the relative safety of the 'island' (the carrier's superstructure). The pilot will head to maintenance to fill out the paperwork and let the maintainers know of any gripes. The WSO heads to CVIC (intelligence centre) to give the intel debrief and spin the recorders if need be. Following the maintenance and CVIC debriefs, the crew will meet back up with their element to do a 'scrub' so that everyone has the proper SA of what occurred during the fight before they go to the mass debrief.

Once again the order of the debrief follows: Safety of Flight/Training Rule Violations, Admin, TAC Admin, Execution, Mission Objectives, Training Objectives and parting shots.

After the debrief, it's time for the crews to

TOP While the E-2 Hawkeye provides the strike group with expanded radar coverage and C3 services, the overall mission commander is likely to be an F/A-18F WSO. *(US Navy)*

ABOVE A VFA-41 F/A-18F equipped with a SHARP pod on the centreline station. The presence of the WSO enables the SHARP pod to be fully utilised during the mission. *(US Navy)*

the element will 'fence out' and proceed back to the carrier. Once again, the WSO is primarily responsible for all communication and navigation flying to and from the carrier. The WSO checks in with Red Crown and Strike while giving the aircraft's position in relation to 'Mother' (the carrier), and then dials in the TACAN radial for the marshal stack. It is the WSO's duty to ensure all the systems from the TACAN, ILS and ACLS (automatic carrier landing system) to the Radar Altimeter (RADALT) are properly set. Failure to do so can lead to deadly consequences.

During Case 1 recoveries, everything is done with radio silence. There is no need for communication and the pilot and WSO divide lookout responsibilities, coordinate inside the cockpit and with the flight (normally by using hand signals) and execute the landing checklist to trap successfully on board the carrier.

Case 3 recoveries (at night or in bad weather) are a different matter. The crew enters holding on the directed radial and distance from the carrier decompress over a roll 'em (a movie played by the Squadron Duty Officer in the Ready Room), Mid Rats (late evening meal) and perhaps even cigars on the Flag Bridge (at the discretion of the squadron's skipper, of course).

F-18F crews are unique in the Hornet community, because a single pilot *is* capable of performing nearly every mission a Rhino can be called upon to do, with the exception of FAC(A). What makes an F-18F crew more lethal and survivable is that there are now two people in the cockpit dividing tasks appropriately to most efficiently and effectively utilise all of the capabilities the Super Hornet has to offer. There are simply too many functionalities for one crew member to be able to do it all on every flight.

The crew concept is bred early in F-model pilots and WSOs. Being in an F squadron is being in a family. There are no pilot problems or WSO problems; only challenges that both have to solve as a crew. Each crewmember trusts and depends upon the other. Each member of the Ready Room is looked upon as an equal. Whether you are sitting on the catapult on a moonless night with a low overcast, preparing to launch into the abyss for a strike, or on an

ABOVE An F/A-18F Super Hornet assigned to Air Test and Evaluation Squadron Nine (VX-9) conducts an operation test mission as a desert rainstorm dissipates over the Coso mountain range, California. The APG-79 AESA radar makes it possible for the WSO to focus on air-to-ground, while the pilot scans ahead for air-to-air threats. *(US Navy)*

instrument training flight returning from Grand Junction, Colorado, chasing the sunset over the mountains all the way back to Lemoore, California, it's the other guy in the jet you have to depend on when things go sideways. You don't want to let that person down.

BELOW Awaiting its next sortie, this VFA-211 Super Hornet soaks up the setting sun at NAS Oceana. *(Steve Davies/FJ Photography)*

Chapter Ten

Maintaining the Canadian Hornet

Crew Chief Sgt Daniel Paré, RCAF

A much-quoted saying by groundcrew maintainers asserts that an aircraft cannot fly without them, and those who work on the Canadian CF-18 are certainly no exception. In this chapter 433 Squadron Crew Chief Sgt Daniel Paré, a French-Canadian technician who has served for 33 years with Canadian Armed Forces (27 of those years on the CF-18), describes what it takes to keep the best multi-role jet fighter in the sky.

OPPOSITE Aircraft maintainers from the Canadian Air Task Force carry out a fuel inspection of a 425 Tactical Fighter Squadron CF-188 Hornet in Siauliai, Lithuania, on 11 December 2014 during Operation 'Reassurance' in support of NATO Baltic Air Policing. *(Air Task Force – OP Reassurance, DND)*

Beginning

After signing allegiance to Her Majesty the Queen, the Canadian Armed Forces send you to boot camp for basic military training to make a man (or woman) out of you. When you've completed recruit training your next move is to Canadian Forces Base (CFB) Borden in Ontario, Canada, where you receive apprentice-level training in the various technical trades at the Canadian Forces School of Aerospace

BELOW At the Canadian Forces School of Aerospace Technology and Engineering a student on the Air Weapons Systems (AWS) technician course checks serial numbers on a M61A1 gun system in a CF-18 during training. *(RCAF)*

Technology and Engineering (CFSATE). Later you commence your specialised technical aviation trade training (in one of three on-aircraft occupations – Aviation (Avn), Avionics (Avs) and Aircraft Structures (ACS)). Back in 1983 mine was known as an Integrated Systems Technician (IST), now it's called an Avionics Systems Technician (AVST), which includes all aircraft electronics systems ranging from the simple radio to complex electronic warfare systems (EWS) equipment.

After your basic trade training, and prior to work on any type of aircraft, you will go on your Aircraft course. For me this was the CF-18 school, located at 10 Field Technician Training Squadron (10 FTTS) in CFB Cold Lake, Alberta, Canada. On this course you will learn your trade with hands-on practice. No doubt you'll have a sleepless night before your first encounter with the CF-18, afraid of making a single mistake. For us the CF-18 is the state-of-the-art, and is in the Canadian Forces fighter group to this day.

Daily routine

Canadian Forces have four operational fighter squadrons and one pilot training squadron and the daily routine is quite similar in all five of them.

My squadron, 433 Squadron, can trace its origins to the Royal Canadian Air Force (RCAF) in the Second World War when it flew Halifax and Lancaster bombers from Skipton-on-Swale in Yorkshire. It disbanded when the war ended and re-formed in Canada in 1954 as an all-weather fighter unit at CFB Cold Lake, Alberta, in November 1954, and moved to CFB North Bay, Ontario, in October 1955. The squadron flew CF-100 Canuck aircraft on North American air defence until it was disbanded in August. Re-formed post-unification of the Canadian Armed Forces in 1964, 433 *Escadrille tactique de combat* (ETAC) was a French-language squadron of Mobile Command based at CFB Bagotville, Quebec. No 433 Escadrille flew the CF-5 Freedom Fighter in the tactical and reconnaissance role until conversion to the CF-18 Hornet in 1984.The squadron was stood down in 2005 and its assets and personnel were amalgamated into 425 Tactical Fighter Squadron. The squadron was reactivated on 9 June 2015.

Every workday is a happy day because everybody enjoys their work – you can tell from their smiles every morning. The way it works in 433 Squadron, we have three desks with three crew chiefs whom the day and evening shifts count on, so those positions are very, very important. One of them is the Servicing Desk crew chief, who decides which aircraft (A/C) will fly and in what order, based on the flight schedule requested by the ops the night before. He then transfers the list to the second position, which is the Manpower Desk, with a crew chief or the most senior technician with experience. His job is to take care of all the personnel for launch and recovery and all other servicing tasks required during the day. The third person is the Snag Desk crew chief, who plans and manages repairs of all broken (snag) aircraft from the day before or continues with longer repairs during his shift, which is eight hours. For the evening shift, the same thing happens, with three other crew chiefs taking up their positions after a debrief from the previous shift's crew. Afterwards, the Snag Desk crew chief has a 15-minute meeting with the aircraft maintenance officer and his deputy to wrap up the daily maintenance issues. From there the crew chief determines which technician will work on which aircraft depending on his experience/qualifications and the difficulty of the problem.

In the meantime, at the Servicing Desk, the crew chief will have designated the aircraft for the daily schedule, while the Manpower Desk will have already assigned a technician to an aircraft number to do the 'DI' (daily inspection) check and the 'B' (before flight) check prior to starting the procedure if the A/C is serviceable. In Canada, we don't have a specific aircraft with our name on it, thus all technicians work on all CF-18s in the same squadron. For whatever reason, when you have to work on another jet at the same time, you have to examine every step of the technical order in order to make sure you haven't missed anything. Typically, though, you'll stay on your own jet. Once you finish your B check inspection, you sign your inspection so that the crew chief can verify it and release the jet to ops and then the waiting game begins, depending on the slotted flight time. If you have time, you assist the other members of your flight in getting their jets prepped, or tinker around with whatever maintenance is going on.

Prior stepping

Fifteen minutes prior to flight time the tech goes to the A/C to remove all safety pins and have a last look at the A/C to make sure it's all good. At the same time, the pilot will glance at the forms from the electronic log book at the squadron Ops Desk and the Ops Desk officer will brief the pilot for the mission and on weather and activities around the airfield. The pilot walks to the jet and shakes hands or starts a conversation, as it is always good to have nice chemistry among the team. He then

ABOVE CFB Bagotville hosts 3 Wing with its two CF-18 units, 425 (Alouette) and 433 (Porcupine) Tactical Fighter Squadrons. Pictured is the Alouette's CF-18A (188787) taking off during Exercise 'Maple Flag 2013' (JOINTEX 13), at CFB Cold Lake, Alberta, on 27 May 2013. *(MCpl Marc-André Gaudreault, Canadian Forces Combat Camera)*

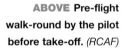

ABOVE Pre-flight walk-round by the pilot before take-off. *(RCAF)*

ABOVE RIGHT Groundcrew ready remove the nose-wheel chock on start-up. *(RCAF)*

performs his own walk-round of the jet, and might also ask a couple of questions. I never had a pilot find anything on their walk-round. I did, however, have a student pilot actually kick the tyres once like he was checking the pressure, which made me laugh quietly. Even if that tyre didn't have the 350psi that was required, the kick of your boot will reveal nothing more than that you just kicked a steel-belted super-tyre designed to help absorb the impact of a 28,000lb jet impacting a runway at 160kts – and, even if it was completely flat, it wouldn't flex. In Canada, with the new NACES ejection seat SJU-17B installed in the CF-18 A/B, we don't help the pilot strap in anymore because the harness is so easy to attach to the new seat and the pilot already has a routine established in the cockpit prior to starting.

Starting procedures

After settling himself in the cockpit, when the pilot is ready he gives a hand signal to the only groundcrew in front of the aircraft nose. In the Canadian Forces fighter group we only use one person to launch and park a CF-18 because of a shortage of personnel. Thus his hand signal is a closed fist waving in a circle above his head, used for a scrambles start. At this point the pilot turns on the auxiliary power unit (APU) and the technician looks for any fire or leaks between the engines where

the APU exhaust is located. When the pilot gets his green light, he turns on the number 2 engine crank switch and at the same time the technician positions himself on the right side to be able to see the engine start-up. After the number 2 engine start-up is complete, the technician repositions himself to be able to see the number 1 engine start-up procedure at the same time as the pilot cranks the number 1 engine. After each engine start-up, the technician gives the pilot the thumbs-up signal to confirm serviceability. After the start-up, the pilot begins a flight control system-initiated built-in test (FCS I-BIT) of the serviceability of the flight controls. When the pilot receives the 'go' from his computers, he verifies his flight controls' movement and limitations with its electronic display indicator. Afterward he gives a hand signal to the technician to confirm the hook is down, the IFR probe out and the speed break out. After verification of this equipment the technician signals those three components back in.

Prior to taxi, the pilot asks by hand signal for a last check of the aircraft. The technician checks one side at a time for loose panels, leaks, or any anomalies before the pilot takes off, then repositions himself in front of the aircraft, confirms the horizontal stabilisation position for take-off, and gives the pilot the last chance sign, which is a rolling down index finger pointing at the ground with the thumb up. In addition, sometimes when the pilot has an old maintenance code he asks us to reset it by resetting the nosewheel digital display indicator. The last sign is the chock-off call from the pilot; at this time the technician calls for him to apply the brakes before he removes the chock. At this point it is time to marshal the aircraft from its parking spot and give the pilot a sharp salute, which is of course returned. The pilot bumps the throttles up and, as the jet starts to move, checks the brake and wiggles his nosewheel steering to make sure everything is in good shape. Every time we do a flight check and finally see the jet prepare to take off, no matter how many times we have done it in our technician's life, it is always a pleasure, just like the first time. Adrenaline is always running through our veins and the sensation is double in real theatre operation sorties. Once your jet is airborne, it is time to grab something to eat or pitch in on other maintenance activities on the line or in the hangar, and then wait for your jet to return.

Recovery

After each mission the pilot calls the jet code 1, 2 or 3. Code 1 means the aircraft is serviceable, code 2 means there are some minor issues, and code 3 means the jet is broken and requires maintenance before it can fly again. At this point the technician marshals the aircraft to the parking spot and after it stops the pilot signals the technician to chock in the aircraft.

The shutdown procedures are quite easy. The technician asks the pilot to shut down one engine and after shutdown, the pilot moves all his flight controls to verify the functionality of the hydraulic switching valves. After this is all done, the pilot shuts down all of his electronic devices and secures his ejection seat. At this point you put the crew ladder on the jet and when the pilot comes down he will give you a small debrief of any problems that occurred. From there, you start to do your work, beginning with an after-flight check (A-check). At the same time, the pilot gives a longer debrief at the Operation Desk (Ops Desk) with a delegate crew chief. The line chief truck, in communication with the op desk, communicates whether the aircraft will be flying

again or will be going to bed, depending on the serviceability of the aircraft. For example, an aircraft might be flown two or three times a day for a personal purpose, in which case we would do an AB check, which is a quick-turnaround inspection to get the jet ready faster.

Shift change

In all the Canadian fighter squadrons there are only two work shifts: one in the day and one in the evening, lasting eight hours each, so the shift change is at 1500 whether the aircraft is flying or not. Usually the younger guys with less experience will work in servicing to familiarise themselves with the CF-18. The way it works is the crew chief and the senior technician get together to debrief progress on the snag, and when the servicing members arrive they go to Manpower to get a job assignment, or replace the other crew on the line. In this way no work will stop, servicing will fly and the snagging will carry on.

A typical squadron has about twelve jets, with approximately six to eight jets on the line daily. The evening shift works until 2300 to fix the jets and if repairs are not completed, the senior technician records in a debrief book the work still to do for the next day. There are a variety of issues that require different specialists' attention. A typical fighter squadron includes avionic, weapons, jet engine technician, structural

BELOW A technician replaces the bleed air door actuator, which can be seen to his right, with the 'no-step' sign. *(RCAF)*

ABOVE Alouette CF-18A (188766) taxying in a Canadian winter. *(RCAF)*

Engine run-up

The workload of a Canadian engine technician includes removing, installing and repairing engines, but they also take care of all ECS (Environmental Control Systems) belonging to the A/C, for example all the air conditioning and heat for the winter – everybody knows how cold a Canadian winter can be – but most often their job is the engine.

The removal and re-installation (R&R) process involves an exhaustive engine bay inspection that requires a team to evaluate every rivet, every surface, every rib and every wire in the entire bay. There is no room for error. After a POM technician (Performance Objective Maintainer – like a journeyman) completes the inspection, a more experienced level A technician (like a craftsman) double-checks the work as well, before finally Quality Assurance – another craftsman who has not worked on this job at all – does a tertiary inspection before the new engine is slid back in on rails, connected, and tested. Oddly enough there are only two mount bolts that hold the engine in, which are inspected by the crack checker NDT technician (Non Destructive Tech), then it's just a matter

repair, airframe technician, and of course crew chief. Each trade has responsibility for certain systems, while the crew chief is responsible for the entire operation of the jet. Most days involve the avionic specialist ('electron') doing some troubleshooting or box swapping on the jet. These folks are incredibly knowledgeable about the system and invaluable in keeping those critical systems up and running. A weapons crew consisting of three people will come round and address any issues with the weapons systems, such as removing/replacing missiles, pylons, explosives charges in the pylons or even working the gun systems from time to time. You never see them in groups of less than three, which has led to many suggestions as to why!

BELOW AND RIGHT Engine R&R – removal and re-installation is a labour intensive process. Here, technicians from Air Task Force Romania change one engine on a CF-18 Hornet in Constanta, Romania, during Exercise 'Resilient Resolve' on 17 March 2016. *(RCAF/MS Steve Picard, 3 Wing Bagotville)*

of connecting the PTO (power take-off) shaft, the fuel line, and a few wires. Most of the work done to the engines requires a live engine run-up by the qualified run-up technician, who sits in the cockpit and starts up the engines to verify all engine parameters. The runs are either accomplished right there on the ramp at a designated spot for run-up below 80% of engine power, or on the AB (afterburner) pad if an afterburner run is required.

The AB pad is located at the hammer head of runway 36, where the jet blast is angled up at about 45° into the woods far away. The jet's nose gear is connected to a massive hook with a huge chain and the tyres are double chocked to contain the nearly 32,000lb of thrust. There is no feeling quite like sitting on the throttles of a CF-18 in full afterburn, stationary on the ground. It's terrifying and exciting. It's also an incredible feeling to be standing just feet away from the afterburner on the ground, especially if there is an AB blowout. The power of the jet resonates through your body and damn near cleans out your sinuses as it rattles your insides relentlessly.

We also have an engine bay test cell. This is a state-of-the-art engine diagnostics facility where you connect the jet in the same way as at the AB pad, but inside a hangar that barely fits the aircraft and to a control room on the side of the hangar. There is a giant exhaust pipe that runs out the back of the test cell and directs the blast out and up. Due to the precise location requirements of the jet within the test cell – the exhaust must go directly down the pipe – the towing team has to park the jet perfectly in the facility. Putting a jet into the 'Hush House' accurately on the first try was one of many games we played on the flight line, and only the best tow drivers could accomplish this. When pushing a jet backwards, the tow truck faces the jet and is connected to the nose gear by a tow bar. You have to account for and manipulate all three pivot points, which is a skill that some people never really master while others are just naturals at it.

Each of these specialists is critical to keeping your jet flyable and ready to accomplish its mission. There is a lot of playful rivalry between the specialties on the flight line, but in the end the jet wouldn't be able to accomplish its mission without each of them. Saying all

this, the engine test cell is more often used by the second-line engine bay facility that repairs the engine. Again, they attach the engine to a special engine stand and the stand is attached properly to perform the tests.

Long night

Although no night is typical on a swing shift for an AFT (airframe technician), looking back on ageing aircraft it was most often the hydraulics that kept us there late.

The CF-18 utilises two hydraulic systems: system 1 from the left engine, and system 2 from the right engine. Each system is run by a pump mounted on each AMAD (Aircraft Mounted Accessory Drive) connected to each engine by the PTO shaft. The pump itself is simple, but one part of the installation is notoriously challenging: you have to line up the drive gear splines with the splines in the AMAD and wiggle the pump in. Sometimes

ABOVE With tow bar connected to its nose gear, this CF-18A receives attention from technicians during a deployment in Kuwait. *(RCAF)*

BELOW On the flight line at Bagotville, 433 Squadron's CF-18 pilots are helped to strap in. *(RCAF)*

it slides right in, but other times you have to push, shove, and curse for an eternity, only for another level A qualified tech to walk up and slam it in first try! These AMADs, hydraulic pumps, electric generators called CGUs, air starters, are all lumped together and are called the secondary power system and, in my opinion, account for most of our work.

Outside of these systems, typical issues involved the hydraulic reservoirs for each system, which could be finicky; flight control actuators, or random hydraulics lines that would leak or burst, each buried and tangled in its own special way deep inside the jet. Some may consider it odd, but I enjoyed the complex work that came with finding these problems and then fixing them.

AMSE – Aircraft Maintenance Support Equipment

Whether it was the AMAD, a hydraulic reservoir or servo, each repair required ground testing, which in turn required some sort

of electric and hydraulic power being applied to the airframe. For the CF-18 we have many AMSE but the most commonly used are the Stewart Stevenson (generally known as the power unit), which is about half the size of a small family car with a diesel engine that can supply 115V AC 400Hz three-phase electrical power to the jet; or we can also use a CSU (Combined Starting Unit), which contains a jet engine that supplies power to the jet via a giant electrical cord that plugs into the CF-18 near the nose gear, and air pressure that duplicates the bleed air system of the jet to start the engines if needed. The hydraulic test stand is similar in size but it is towed with a mule, and we have an electrical one for inside the hangar and a diesel engine version to work outside. This hydraulic test stand only has the capability to supply hydraulic pressure to one system at a time, so if you need it for two systems you will require two test stands. Other smaller pieces of AMSE that are used include the oil (PONs 6) and hydraulic carts (known as 'fill & bleed'), usually used for servicing purposes.

Phase (periodic)

There are other aspects of flight line maintenance besides launching, recovering, and repairing jets. Each jet will cycle through other stages that are carried out away from the squadron every 600 hours. For this the jet will go to a second-line facility, 3EMA (3e Escadron de maintenance d'aéronef) for CFB Bagotville, Quebec, and 1AMS (1 Aircraft Maintenance Squadron) for CFB Cold Lake, Alberta.

Phase maintenance is an extensive inspection of the entire jet that takes about a month. The phase team disassembles and inspects most of the aircraft, looking beyond the superficial leaks and drips. A large part of the phase inspection inevitably ends up being structural repairs due to hairline cracks resulting from the relentless effect of g-forces, take-offs and landings. The structural repair specialists do a lot of hard work during the phase inspection of jets, in addition to all the assistance provided on the line. The worst thing that can happen is for your jet to become the 'robbed' jet. Sometimes this is scheduled and sometimes it is out of necessity, as your jet is already broken, and if an operational jet needs a component and the supply chain does not have it immediately available, your jet will be used to donate the part. This robbing action is done when no parts are available from supply and usually lasts about a month and involves extensive work afterwards to make your jet mission-capable again, but it is a necessary evil in maintaining the health of the fleet.

Then there are short stops, like the paint shop, wash bay, and fuel barn. The entire fleet is a well-oiled machine on a constant cycle through all these different phases of maintenance so that, in the end, you can generate enough jets to meet the flying demand each and every day.

A sense of belonging to your squadron

As I look back on my time as a CF-18 technician, I value and appreciate the times out on that flight line. Through all kinds of weather we developed a bond of brotherhood while working on these amazing aircraft. You make some of the best friends you'll ever have for the rest of your career, and, of course, you encounter other people who just constantly get on your nerves – just like any family! You spend much of your time with these people, towing jets around, running ground tests, troubleshooting, and having family days or parties together. Looking back on these times, I remember duct taping a new guy to a chain and putting him under the emergency shower for his birthday, and all the TDs (Temporary Duty) in Mexico, Florida, and Europe in wintertime that gave us a break from the coldest days in Canada.

We have had the CF-18 for over 34 years and it remains one of the greatest multi-purpose fighter aircraft of all time. I think that with the new way of doing things in the era of social media, we are losing, year by year, a little bit of the brotherhood that used to bond the tech with the pilot and the rest of the squadron.

LEFT Hydraulic fluid is topped up with a 'fill & bleed' during the engine start procedure. *(RCAF)*

ABOVE The 2016 season Royal Canadian Air Force CF-18 Hornet demonstration jet was provided by 410 Squadron and unveiled on 5 April 2016 at 4 Wing, CFB Cold Lake, Alberta. From left to right: Chief Warrant Officer Alain Roy; Colonel Eric Kenny, commander of 4 Wing; Jim Belliveau, design and paint crew lead; and Captain Ryan Kean, the CF-18 Demonstration Hornet pilot. Sgt Daniel Paré (not in this picture) was the CF-18 East Team crew chief. *(RCAF/Cpl Bryan Carter)*

RIGHT Flown by Captain Ryan Kean, 410 Squadron's 2016 demonstration Hornet shows off its vivid colour scheme commemorating the wartime British Commonwealth Air Training Plan (BCATP). *(RCAF/Mike Reynolds)*

Appendix

Technical specifications – F/A-18E Super Hornet

Dimensions	
Length	60ft 3½in (18.38m)
Wingspan	44ft 8½in (13.62m)
Wingspan (folded)	30ft 7¼in (9.33m)
Wing area	500sq ft (46.45m²)
Height	16ft (4.88m)
Wheel track	17ft 9½in (5.42m)
Wheelbase	10ft 2in (3.11m)
Powerplant	
Two General Electric F414-GE-400 turbofans each with an *uninstalled* rating of 13.900lb thrust dry and 20,700lb with afterburning	
Weights	
Empty	31,500lb
Maximum take-off	66,000lb (29,938kg)
Maximum payload for catapult launch	34,000lb (15,422kg)
Maximum carrier landing	42,900lb (19,459kg)
Fuel and load	
Internal fuel	14,460lb (6,559kg)
External fuel	approximately 16,290lb (7,390kg)
Maximum ordnance	17,747lb (8,050kg)
Maximum bring-back capacity	9,900lb (4,491kg)
Performance	
Maximum speed at 36,089ft (10,999m)	Mach 1.6
Approach speed	144mph (231km/h)
Operational radius on a hi-lo-hi attack mission with four 1,000lb (454kg) bombs, two AIM-9, two external fuel tanks	390nm (448 miles, 722km)
Radius on a fighter escort mission with two AIM-120 AMRAAM and two AIM-9 Sidewinder AAMs	410nm (471 miles, 759km)
Combat air patrol (CAP) endurance at 150nm (173 miles, 278km) with six AIM-120 AMRAAM and three external tanks	2 hours 9 minutes
Service ceiling	c53,000ft
g-limit	+8

Index